Skyscrapers Hide the Heavens

Your buildings tall, alien,
Cover the land;
Unfeeling concrete smothers,
    windows glint
Like water to the sun.
No breezes blow
Through standing trees;
No scent of pine lightens my burden.

I see your buildings rising skyward,
    majestic,
Over the trails where once men walked,
Significant rulers of this land
Who still hold the aboriginal title
In their hearts
By traditions known
Through eons of time.

Relearning our culture is not difficult,
Because those trails I remember
And their meaning I understand.

While skyscrapers hide the heavens,
They can fall.

Rita Joe, *Poems of Rita Joe*
(Halifax: Abanaki Press 1978)
Reprinted by permission of the author

J.R. Miller

Skyscrapers Hide the Heavens

*A History of
Indian-White Relations
in Canada*

UNIVERSITY OF TORONTO PRESS

Toronto Buffalo London

© University of Toronto Press 1989
Toronto Buffalo London
Printed in Canada
ISBN 0-8020-5803-5

Printed on acid-free paper

Canadian Cataloguing in Publication Data

Miller, J.R. (James Rodger), 1943–
Skyscrapers hide the heavens

Bibliography: p.
Includes index.
ISBN 0-8020-5803-5

1. Indians of North America – Canada – History.
2. Indians of North America – Canada – First
contact with Occidental civilization.
3. Indians of North America – Canada – Commerce.
I. Title.

E78.C2M54 1989   971'.00497   c89-093316-2

This book has been published with the help of a grant from the Social Science
Federation of Canada, using funds provided by the Social Sciences and
Humanities Research Council of Canada. Publication has also been assisted
by the Canada Council and the Ontario Arts Council under their block grant
programs.

To my mother and the memory of my father

Contents

PART THREE: CONFRONTATION

MAPS

ILLUSTRATIONS

Preface

Two themes are meant to dominate the arguments that follow. The first is the simple proposition that the nature of a relationship between two peoples of different backgrounds is largely determined by the reasons they have for interacting. This notion is a variation on the theme popularized by Marshall McLuhan that 'the medium is the message.' But in my case I did not adopt this view directly from McLuhan. Rather, it was from the pioneering social scientist to whom McLuhan was himself indebted intellectually, Harold Adams Innis, that the idea came. The insights that Innis had about the first two Canadian industries of the historic period, the cod fishery and the fur trade, were the starting point for many of my own ideas about relations between natives and European newcomers. In some respects, the arguments in the pages that follow are merely the application to Indian-European relations of some of Innis's interpretations.

The other theme that this work emphasizes was suggested by a generation of Canadian scholars much younger than Harold Innis. From people such as B.G. Trigger, C.J. Jaenen, A.J. Ray, S.F. Wise, S. Van Kirk, R.A. Fisher, J.L. Tobias, T. Morantz, D. Francis, J. Gresko, and G. Friesen I learned that Indian peoples were not the passive victims that were found in so many older accounts of Canadian history. In the works of these scholars I discovered that the indigenous peoples had in fact been active agents of commercial, diplomatic, and military relations with the European new-comers and their Euro-Canadian descendants. Indians, and later the mixed-blood people called Métis, largely determined the terms of trade, the nature of military alliances, and the outcomes of most martial engagements down to the nineteenth century. Even after Indians became numerically inferior to, and economically depen-dent upon, Euro-Canadians, they continued to assert themselves in their relations with governments, churches, and the ordinary population. Readers will not find in this account a portrait of the Indians of Canada as people to whom others did things. If these pages succeed in persuading some people that the native peoples have always been active, assertive contributors to the unfolding of Canadian history, they will have achieved their primary objective.

In this work these themes are illustrated within the framework of a historical study of the evolution of relations between indigenous peoples and European newcomers to North America. What follows, then, is not a work of Indian history, but a study of the history of Indian-white relations in Canada.

In elaborating these two themes I have had to be selective. Any attempt to survey an evolving relationship over five centuries in five different geographical and economic zones is, besides being foolhardy perhaps, of necessity somewhat superficial. Specialists in Canadian history will not find all the topics that they would have liked dealt with here. To take only a couple of examples from a recent period, there is no attempt to portray the urban friendship centre movement and community development programs of the 1960s and 1970s. To keep this survey within manageable limits, the omission of some specific topics was necessary. It is hoped that those that are examined are both numerous and representative enough to give an accurate picture of the relations between indigenous peoples and other Canadians.

As has already been intimated, this study has been greatly stimulated by the work of others. It is also one that relies heavily on the research and publications of other students of the topic. Because the subject is so vast, it was impossible to do exhaustive primary research on all phases of it myself. Such a task would have taken a lifetime. On some topics, particularly where published studies are lacking, the evidence used is mainly from primary documents; in dealing with other issues that have been well studied I have relied on what I hope is an extensive and thoughtful reading of others' work. I am greatly indebted to all those whose publications are cited in the notes.

I am also obligated to many people whose names do not always appear in the references. I should like to express my thanks to the office of the dean of arts and science and the Office of Research Services of the University of Saskatchewan, which provided assistance in meeting the costs of photocopying and illustrations. A generous Canadian Writing Award from the Association for Canadian Studies was of great help in completing the final stages of research, preparing illustrations and maps, and photocopying the final draft. Revisions to the manuscript could be carried out expeditiously, thanks to a Research Time Stipend granted by the Social Sciences and Humanities Research Council of Canada. The students in History 301 at the University of Saskatchewan during the winter term of 1987 also provided me with a number of useful suggestions for improvement of an early draft of this study. One of them, Christine Fowke, allowed me to use a map she had drafted, and cartographer George Duff prepared that and the other maps that accompany the text. Professor A.J. Ray kindly permitted the use of one of his maps in the generation of the map in this work that depicts the location of the western Indians around 1820. My colleague Bill Waiser gave generously of his time to read an earlier version of the manuscript and to make valuable suggestions for its improvement. In addition to all the people mentioned so far I should like to acknowledge several who have given me helpful advice over the past few years: M. Davidson, J. Pollard, D.B. Smith, E.B. Titley, and J.D. Wilson. Gerald Hallowell, a friend of many years as well as an editor of great acuity, was efficient, helpful, and supportive in seeing the manuscript from first submission to publication. Anonymous readers for the University of Toronto Press and the Social Sciences Federation of Canada provided a number of useful suggestions for correction and improvement. Rosemary Shipton edited the manuscript with sensitivity and insight.

Finally – and most important – my wife Mary patiently read several drafts and offered valuable suggestions on structure, argument, and style.

Of course none of these long-suffering people is responsible for any errors of fact or interpretation that remain.

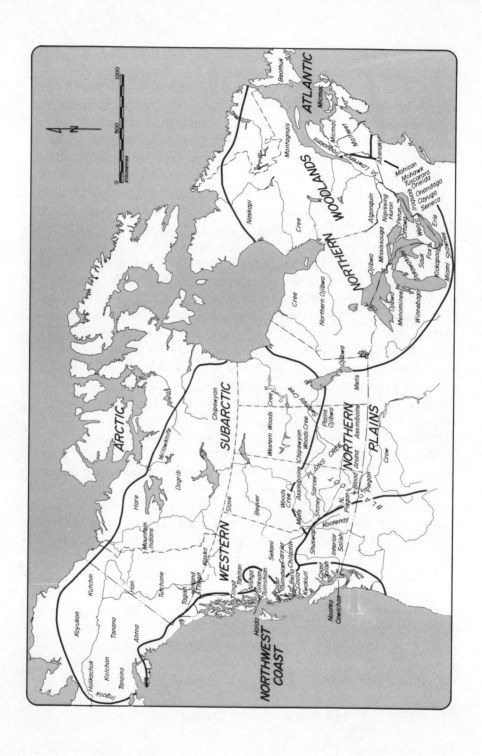

INTRODUCTION

1

Indians and Europeans at the time of contact

On 24 July after more than a week of observing and bartering with the native inhabitants, the newcomers set about erecting a landmark at the mouth of the harbour on the Bay of Chaleur. Jacques Cartier's men

had a cross made thirty feet high, which was put together in the presence of a number of the Indians on the point at the entrance to this harbour, under the cross-bar of which we fixed a shield with three *fleurs-de-lys* in relief, and above it a wooden board, engraved in large Gothic characters, where was written, LONG LIVE THE KING OF FRANCE. We erected this cross on the point in their presence and they watched it being put together and set up.

When we had returned to our ships, the chief, dressed in an old black bear-skin, arrived in a canoe with three of his sons and his brother; but they did not come so close to the ships as they had usually done. And pointing to the cross he [the chief] made us a long harangue, making the sign of the cross with two of his fingers; and then he pointed to the land all around about, as if he wished to say that all this region belonged to him, and that we ought not to have set up this cross without his permission.[1]

The encounter of Micmac and Frenchmen at Gaspé in July 1534 contained many of the elements of early relations between natives and intruders. The French explored, traded, and attempted to leave their permanent mark on the place. The Indians happily bartered but rejected the white men's presumption at erecting a signpost. This epitome of early relations was all the more remarkable because it brought together two dramatically different peoples, two contrasting societies that would nonetheless cooperate successfully for centuries before relations deteriorated into conflict and confrontation.

The aboriginal societies with whom Cartier and those who followed him came into contact were diverse and well established in their respective territories. Their ancestors had entered North America from Siberia by way of the Bering Strait in search of game perhaps as long as 40,000 years ago. Sometime in the subsequent millennia they had made their way southward, in part following a path in the lee of the continental spine formed by the Rockies and Sierras, and diffused throughout the continent. Evidence of what were undoubtedly the original human occupiers of the continent that was unearthed in the Yukon indicates that they were there as long as 27,000 years ago.[2]

These peoples began to diffuse into the northeastern part of the continent approximately 12,000 years ago. As the glaciers retreated northward at the end of the last ice age, humans migrated after them in search of fish, game, and arable land in which to cultivate a few crops that they had developed further south. Chief among these agricultural products was maize or corn, which was being grown and harvested a thousand years ago in the territory that at present is southern Ontario and Quebec. Other groups of aboriginal peoples who lived north of the arable land, in the Precambrian Shield or the colder regions to the north of that, were more dependent on hunting and fishing. Naturally, those peoples who migrated to the eastern seaboard developed an extensive fishery, which they supplemented with hunting and gathering of berries and nuts. In short, long before the European intruded in North America the indigenous peoples had entered and diffused into many parts of the continent, in the process showing an impressive ability to adapt to local climatic, topographical, and ecological conditions.

By the year 1000 the northeastern part of the continent was peopled by a myriad of bands, villages, and confederacies. Upon this complex and heterogeneous human community later scholars

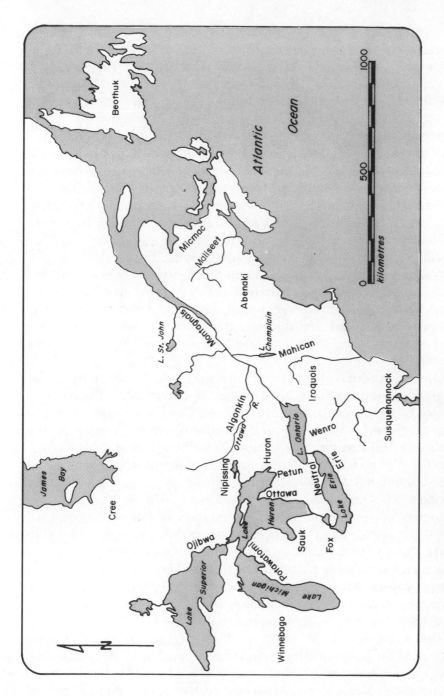

Indian nations of northeastern North America at contact

have imposed a system of classification that permits a clearer understanding of their nature. Anthropologists divide the indigenous peoples of northeastern North America into two principal linguistic groupings or language stocks: Algonkian and Iroquoian. Within each of these linguistic families there were many distinct collectivities. Generally speaking, what distinguished these groups were their languages and economies.

Algonkians consisted of a large number of nations or tribes. In present-day Newfoundland were found the Beothuk, who were distinctive for their habit of decorating themselves with ochre, a reddish substance that led newcomers to describe all the indigenous peoples of the continent as 'red Indians.' The Beothuk were primarily hunter-gatherers and fishing people. It was either Beothuk or Inuit who made contact with the first European immigrants who attempted settlement in northern Newfoundland and Labrador, the unfortunate Norse. Within three years the Norse had retreated to Greenland, repulsed by the indigenous people they called *skraelings*. Later contacts would be more successful for the Europeans and less happy for the indigenous populations.

On the landmass of North America itself dwelt many other Algonkian nations. In what is today northern New Brunswick, Prince Edward Island, and Nova Scotia lived the Micmac, and to the southwest in central and southern New Brunswick the Maliseet. Still further south, in what today is the state of Maine, was the Abenaki Confederacy, which contained such groups as the Passamaquoddy and Penobscot. All these nations were migratory peoples who relied on a combination of fishing, hunting, and gathering of berries and nuts. Their migrations followed a seasonal pattern in search of sustenance: in winter they generally moved in small bands, though in summer they would gather in larger groupings at suitable places for fishing and berrying. The unity of these peoples was largely one imposed retrospectively by anthropologists; aside from participation in a common language stock and similar economy, they were highly diverse.

The same could be said of other Algonkian peoples who inhabited the lands north of what they called 'the river of Canada,' the St Lawrence. East of what is now the St Maurice valley were the Montagnais; along the Ottawa River were found Algonkin; and near Lake Nipissing the nation that gave the lake its name. The other major Algonkian nations were the Ottawa, found on the east side of Lake Huron; the Ojibwa or Chippewa near Lake Superior; and the Cree in the more northerly lands that were drained by rivers flowing into James Bay. Indeed, various groups of Cree were to be found throughout northerly regions stretching to the western prairies and the woodlands north of the plains. As with the Micmac and Maliseet of the Atlantic region, what all these Algonkians of the interior had in common was language and economy. They were all principally hunter-gatherers, although some who occupied fertile lands cultivated some crops. Reliance on the wild rice that was found in some lakes was also common.

The other major linguistic grouping of eastern and central Canada was the Iroquoian. They, too, consisted of a number of different people. In the St Lawrence lowlands were people whose identity has baffled scholars. They occupied this region in the early sixteenth century when French explorers penetrated it, but vacated the district by the seventeenth, when the next wave of French exploration took place. (They are usually identified simply as the St Lawrence Iroquoians.) In what is today New York state was found a larger, more permanent concentration of Iroquoians, known usually as the Five Nations Confederacy. The five peoples that constituted this extraordinary League of the Iroquois were stretched in a band west of the Hudson River as far as the lands south of Lake Ontario. From east to west they were the Mohawk, Oneida, Onondaga, Cayuga, and Seneca. (In the early years of the eighteenth century they would be joined by a sixth people, the Tuscarora, who were fleeing agricultural settlement in the Thirteen Colonies, to become the Six Nations.) To the west of the Iroquois Confederacy were smaller groupings of Iroquoian peoples known as the Wenro and the Erie. Further south, in present-day Pennsylvania, lived the Susquehannock.

In that part of the Great Lakes–St Lawrence drainage basin that lay north of the lakes and river were numerous other important Iroquoian groups. Immediately north of Lake Erie lived the Neutral, and north of them the Petun or Tobacco nation. But the biggest Iroquoian grouping in what would later become Canada was the Huron Confederacy, which consisted of four nations who called themselves the Bear, Rock, Cord, and Deer. Huron was a term that would be applied to them by the French, who used the French word *hure* (literally boar's head, but also brute or ruffian) in reference to the hairstyle affected by Huron men.[3] These people called themselves *Wendat*, which literally meant 'islanders' or 'Dwellers in a Peninsula.' It is not clear whether the term referred to the fact that Huronia, the territory they inhabited near Georgian Bay, was surrounded on three sides by water or if it was a reference to their belief that the world was an island that rested on a turtle. The term was later to crop up as the name of an American tribe, the Wyandot, which was formed in part by Huron fleeing Huronia in the seventeenth century. Indeed, some scholars refer to the peoples of Huronia as the Wyandot Confederacy.[4]

The Huron, like all the Iroquoians, had a number of features in addition to their language that distinguished them from Algonkians. Their economy relied on crops as well as game and fish. For most of them the staple crop was corn or maize, but the Petun – as their alternate name illustrates – also grew tobacco that they both consumed and traded with others. Because the Iroquoians relied on crops, they were of necessity much more sedentary than the migratory Algonkians. Their usual practice was to reside in one place for ten or twelve years, until soil exhaustion forced them to move on. When the time for relocation approached, the men of the village would prepare the fields a year in advance of the time that the women would begin to plant, tend, and harvest the crops. When a new agricultural site was readied, the village would move. The Iroquoians' relatively secure food supply meant that theirs was a sedentary way of life and their concentrations of population were much greater than those of nomads. Some of the towns in Iroquoia numbered as many as 1500 people, and villages of several hundred were quite common for all the Iroquoians. This settlement pattern was responsible for one of the physical features that distinguished the Iroquoians: they lived in large multifamily dwellings called longhouses, and these distinctive buildings were found in fortified, palisaded villages. The members of the Iroquois Confederacy were sometimes called the people of the longhouse.

Other consequences flowed from the economy and settlement pattern of the Iroquoians. For one thing, the important economic role of the women, who were responsible for agricultural operations (the men having to carry out what might be termed the capital

side of farming), had led to a prominent social and political role for
the females. Whereas the Algonkians were patrilineal and patrilo-
cal, the Iroquoians were matrilineal and matrilocal. At times their
society approached the status of matriarchy. What these terms
mean is that a person in Iroquoian society traced his or her family
identity through the mother: one belonged to the family of one's
mother. Furthermore, when a man married, he took up residence
with the family of his bride. A household, which was the basic unit
of society among Iroquoians, consisted of a woman, her female
relations, their spouses and dependants. (An Algonkian band's
composition was a group of male kin who hunted together, their
spouses and their dependent families.) Among Iroquoians, chief-
tainship was hereditary among families of certain female lines, and
the prominent women of the tribe had much to say about selecting
the individual male who would become chief on the death of a
leader.

The large concentrations in which Iroquoians lived had also led
them to develop sophisticated instruments of social control and
political decision-making. For example, each Iroquoian belonged
to a clan (eg, Turtle) as well as a nation (eg, Rock). Villages
consisted of representatives of each of the clans, meaning that
every Iroquoian had potential hosts in other villages and that there
was a disincentive to war with other villages or nations of the
confederacy. Paralleling such ingenious social institutions were
political structures that enabled the relatively large Iroquoian
nations – and the Huron and Iroquois confederacies in particular –
to reach and carry out agreements. A tribe or nation possessed its
own territory and its own council of sachems (chiefs). A confederacy had a representative council; the grand council of the Five
Nations consisted of fifty chiefs representing the different tribes
roughly according to their size. An insight into the values of
aboriginal society resided in one of the grand council's practices: all
decisions had to be unanimous.

Algonkians and Iroquoians might have differed greatly in social
and political structures; what they had in common was commerce,
warfare, and religion. Long before the European intruded in North
America, the indigenous inhabitants had developed patterns of
trade, patterns of commerce based on considerations of geography
and economics. Particular tribes such as the Huron found them-

selves well placed athwart or adjacent to water transportation routes to exact a toll from those who wished to travel through their territory; they could also initiate commercial transactions with those traversing their region or with people to whom they could travel themselves. Similarly, some Algonkians, such as the nation that controlled the Ottawa River, found that their locations near travel routes induced them into commerce. The other major factor was possession of goods of particular importance. One such was the copper that the Indians on the shore of Lake Superior had and traded with other tribes to the east. This important metal – apparently the only metal known to Indians of eastern North America prior to contact – was used for both utilitarian and decorative purposes by tribes far from Superior. Other important trade items were tobacco and maize, both of which were the property of the agricultural Iroquoians. Surplus corn was the basis of Huron influence long before the European came; tribes that wanted tobacco for both ritualistic and recreational purposes found themselves trading with the Petun nation or with intermediaries such as the Huron, who were located between the Petun and most of the Algonkian peoples.

Trade had critically important social aspects for the Indians. The right to trade with another tribe was a customary property right of certain families, usually prominent families who had initiated the commerce. Such commercial rights were an important factor in the affluence and prominence of the leading families, a reservoir of wealth that fed their prestige and influence. But in Indian society this prestige was established and maintained not by piling up and hoarding wealth but by distributing it among one's followers. Sharing and redistribution of material goods were not just admired but required; acquisitiveness and selfishness were abhorred and shunned. Another important social aspect of native commerce was the exchange of people that accompanied it. Those families of different nations that engaged in trade exchanged people, usually sons, to cement the commercial association. Having a fellow tribesman living with a family in another tribe was both a surety of continuing commercial intercourse and a deterrent to friction and conflict between the two groups.

Commercial motives, however, were not infrequently a cause of warfare in Indian society. It was not rare for one group to attack another to acquire food or products, or to force acquiescence in the aggressor's use of hunting or fishing territories. It is possible that warfare based on such motives was responsible for the dispersal of the St Lawrence Iroquoians in the sixteenth century. The other principal cause of warfare in pre-contact times was retribution. In societies without coercive authority and police functions, a major deterrent to violence against people was the requirement that those whose kin or tribesmen were killed avenge the fallen. The family that lost a member to another in the tribe theoretically had the obligation to kill a member of that other family, though in practice such obligations were transmuted into acceptance of a compensatory payment for the loss. No such transformation of the duty to seek vengeance occurred in the case of violence by a member of one tribe or nation against a different people. Most of the non-commercial warfare that pre-existed European incursions was attributed by Indians to retribution and vengeance. Warfare was not racially or ethnically motivated. One nation warred with another for revenge or for commercial reasons; it did not fight the other simply because it was a different people. There was no normal relationship between nations of the same linguistic family; nor was it true that there was some normal, hostile relationship between Algonkians and Iroquoians. An Iroquoian people was as likely to fight another Iroquoian group as an Algonkian.

Although warfare was common before the coming of the European, it was not usually very extensive or destructive in those times. Non-commercial war in particular tended to be focused narrowly on a particular family or village, and its objectives were satisfied with the death of relatively few people. Once members of another tribe were killed or captured to be tortured to death later, the need to engage in violence was satisfied, although admittedly a new obligation to spill blood would have been created in the other group. The other important feature of this warfare was that the tactics and weapons employed were not especially destructive. Attacks from hiding and lightning raids by small parties that used arrows and clubs were the norm. Both the style of their attack and the weapons they used meant that warfare did not lead to wholesale slaughter. No doubt such considerations were little solace to prisoners as they trudged back to their captors' village.

Among some Indians the death of captives taken in battle was not just expiation of the obligation to seek retribution but also a religious rite. Torture was commonly employed among both Algonkians and Iroquoians, and for the Iroquoians torture was a type of religious observation in honour of the sun. Captured prisoners – men of young or middle age were particularly important – were taken back to the village of the successful raiding party. Prisoners were adopted by a family in the victors' village, and in some cases the adoptees were taken into the family to replace someone who had died or been killed in battle. More often the male captive was subjected to lengthy and ingenious torture in which fire and knives were extensively employed. The prisoner was expected to bear pain without crying out or showing any sign of suffering. It would be even better if he laughed at his torturers and told them that he was enjoying the treatment that he was receiving. Such stoic and defiant behaviour was greatly admired; those who manifested it would receive special attention later.

The usual practice was to torture the prisoner intermittently, reviving him from time to time and ensuring that he survived the night. The Iroquoians followed the practice of finally putting the prisoner to death at the rising of the sun, proof that the torture was in part religious ritual.[5] In the case of a prisoner who had been particularly brave, the captors would roast his heart and apportion it among the young men of the village. 'The prisoner's body was then cut up in order to be cooked and eaten. Some ate the body with horror; others relished the taste of human flesh. We are again dealing with an act that was primarily of religious significance.'[6]

Religious beliefs underlay this ritual cannibalism. All the indigenous peoples of North America held metaphysical, theological, and ethical ideas that are categorized as animistic. Animistic religions place humans in the physical environment without drawing any distinction or barrier between them and the physical world. Creation myths could vary from one nation to another, but the underlying understanding of what constituted being was the same for all Indians. All people, animals, fish, and physical aspects of nature were animate; all had souls or spirits. Even items of human manufacture had souls. And souls required respectful treatment at all times, expiation and placating at particular times. There were rituals or prayers to show respect to animals and dangerous passages in the river, invocations to ensure that the animal about to be taken and eaten would not avenge itself on its takers by warning away its brothers and sisters in future. Similarly there were numerous taboos that had to be observed to placate spirits: fish bones should not be thrown into the fire lest the fish be angered at this humiliation and prevent its kin from being caught in future. Such a belief system was based on the assumption that all the world was a continuum, that everything was animate, and that humans held no special place on Earth and in the cosmos.

Other religious rituals had more specific purposes than showing respect for the souls of creation. The torture of prisoners was both a tribute to the sun and a part of the male cult of prestige through battle. Iroquoians believed that by eating a portion of the heart of a captive who had borne torture with great courage they would gain a portion of his bravery. Some rituals, such as the Huron Feast of the Dead, had social purposes. Every ten or twelve years, probably when the village changed locations to get fertile land, the Huron disinterred the corpses of those who had been buried in the burial grounds of their village, cleaned the bones, wrapped them with gifts in fine beaver pelts, and reinterred them in a common ossuary. The ten days of preparation and ceremony were marked by feasting and exchange of gifts, and the entire ritual had the effect of bonding the different clans and families, and even tribes, of the Huron more closely together.[7]

Other rituals aimed to ward off or cure disease, and in some nations curing societies had an important social and religious role. There was no distinction whatever between medicine and religion for the simple reason that disease was believed to be caused by evil spirits, some of them implanted by witchcraft. All religious behaviour was closely associated with the giving of feasts and presents, an important redistributive and bonding process that was vitally important to Indian society. Selfishness was considered not just antisocial but also evidence of witchcraft. Witchcraft was one of the few charges in Indian society that justified putting someone to death. Though religion permeated every aspect of life, there was no separate religious institution or priestly class. Shamans, who oversaw ritual and carried out curing rites in most Indian nations, were 'part-time specialists' who were employed as occasion required to deal with the spirit world.[8]

Indian communities, then, were highly diversified societies of people who had adapted to their environment and worked out a code of behaviour for living compatibly with their world. There was no monolith called 'Indian.' There was wide variety depending on the topography and fauna of the region in which the people lived and the consequent nature of their economy. The Indian nations that occupied the northeastern part of North America 600 years ago had evolved to accommodate themselves to their world and to one another. Their values and institutions were still experiencing slow change at the time of the first contact with Europeans. Though they had pronounced differences, they also shared some features. They participated in some activities, such as commerce and warfare, and thereby learned of different ways. Their theology and ethics were roughly similar. But in spite of these significant similarities, it made little sense to regard them as one, undifferentiated human community. To label all the indigenous peoples simply 'Indians' and treat them as though they were the same made about as much sense as naming all newcomers 'Europeans' and pretending that there were not sharp differences among them. Any newcomers to North America would have to take the distinctive nature of Indian societies into consideration; immigrants, too, would have to adjust.

It was not 'Europeans' who came to North America but Basque whalers, west-country English fishermen, Dutch traders, and French missionaries. Though it would take the indigenous populations some time to understand this diversity, the differences among the intruders were pronounced, and their different natures and purposes had much to do with the type of relations they established with the inhabitants of the continent they began to reach in the late fifteenth century. And yet, like aboriginal communities, the Europeans had common features that united them and distinguished them from the Indians. These included their social and economic structures, their political systems, and their beliefs.

European societies of the sixteenth century were highly stratified and their governments were coercive in nature. In all the Western European states there was a well-established hierarchy of nobles, gentry, burghers, and common people. Though those of higher rank could have obligations to the less fortunate, individualism was more deeply ingrained among them than it was among the peoples of North America. The ethic of sharing was not as important and all-pervasive among these European peoples as it was in North American societies. Their polities, though they varied in detail, all employed coercion to enforce decisions. Absolutism was firmly entrenched in some countries, while the beginnings of parliamentary government were stirring in others. But in all it was expected that policy, once arrived at by debate or fiat, would be enforced. The king's troops, the local militia, or the community's tiny police force would impose the decisions of court, parliament, or magistrates on people. From the standpoint of those that gave the orders for enforcement, the only problem was that military and police power did not reach nearly as far as the ambitions of the rulers. Often what freedom people enjoyed in these societies was a function of the inability of the powerful to exert coercive power effectively.

European countries were not just structured societies and authoritarian polities; they were also acquisitive economies. By the sixteenth century the beginnings of a market mentality could be detected in some of them, particularly Holland and England. The significance of capitalism lay in its psychological character: capitalists both acted on and promoted a desire to acquire material goods, not simply for consumption and other social purposes but for reinvestment for the purpose of acquiring still more property. This economic motive also encouraged the development of an individualistic spirit that was beginning in economically advanced countries to erode communal ties of village loyalty and clan solidarity. In time this impulse, strengthened by the individualistic intellectual traditions that were a product of the European Renaissance, would remake the social ethics of Europe. The same forces, abetted by economic motivation, were bringing about a new reliance on machine technology and novel forms of energy. This revolution, like the impact of the Renaissance and the expanding grip of capitalist ethics, was turning Western Europe into an increasingly individualistic and acquisitive human community. At its best this process would lead to considerable prosperity and a high degree of personal liberty; at its worst to unbridled selfishness and yawning chasms between affluent and poor.

Though the Western European countries had economies that

were diversified, and though the primary economic ambitions of these peoples differed widely, there were but a few economic reasons for the Europeans' approach to North America. After the era of abortive Norse exploration and settlement, the first contacts were made by fishing boats sometime in the fifteenth century. Although many European countries sought protein in the waters of North America, the Basques, Spanish, French, and English emerged as the most numerous and prominent of the fishermen off Newfoundland and Nova Scotia. They were in search especially of whales and cod, which were found in incredible profusion on the Grand Banks.

Although the fishing boats of the various European countries all sought mainly the same product, they would do different things with it. By an accident of geography and history, fishermen were forced to ply their trade in different ways in North America. Those from the more southerly regions had quantities of solar salt that they could use to preserve the fish on board their vessels before returning to Europe. Those from more northerly areas, particularly Normans, Bretons, and English, did not have access to a supply of salt from the Bay of Biscay. They could not use the 'green fishery' of their southern competitors, but had to follow the dry fishery. As a result, Europeans from more northerly countries began the practice of landing for protracted periods to erect the stands on which they dried the cod they had cleaned before packing it on board ship for the return voyage. These stays ashore meant that they came into contact, and conflict, with the indigenous inhabitants to a much greater extent than those who landed less frequently for shorter periods in search of fresh water, food, and wood for repairs. If the contact with aboriginal peoples in the future Canada revolved around northern French and British rather than Spaniards and Basques, the explanation lies to a great extent in whose home territory yielded salt evaporated from sea water and whose did not.

In time, and for reasons that will be explained later, this first contact led to an extensive commercial relationship between Europeans and coastal Algonkians such as the Micmac. Occasional visits of fishermen produced meetings; meetings led to barter of tools and clothing for furs; and out of these encounters grew the second major Canadian economy of the European era, the fur trade. Two important aspects of both the fish and the fur trades helped to shape the ensuing relationship of European and Indian: the European was motivated by the desire for gain; and achievement of his economic goal required the cooperation of the indigenous peoples with whom he came into contact.

There were two other principal motives for European expansion to North America in the fifteenth and sixteenth centuries – exploration and proselytization. Europeans knew from the accounts of Marco Polo's voyages to the lands of the Great Khan and from other even more fabulous accounts that regions with great riches in the form of spices and precious metals lay in the east. Thanks to the discoveries of science and the speculations of navigators, it was thinkable and feasible to sail west in hopes of finding these riches. Many of the early European explorers, in part at least, sailed to North America in search of Asia. Some of them thought that these western lands were the east, as the application of the term 'Indians' to the people of what explorers thought at first were the Indies graphically illustrates. Navigators and ship captains in the fifteenth and sixteenth centuries probed westward in search of the Orient, and, later, when they realized that North America was not Asia, in hopes of finding a waterway through this land mass to the lands of the Khan. They, too, like the fishing-boat captain and the fur trader who followed in his wake, would discover that they needed the cooperation of the indigenous peoples whom they encountered on their voyages of exploration.

Finally, there was also a non-monetary reason for European countries to send people to North America from the seventeenth century onward: religion. Europe was Christian, and from that simple social fact many important consequences followed. For one thing, Christians, like the Hebrews from whom they were historically and theologically descended, held a worldview that contrasted sharply with the animistic beliefs of the indigenous peoples of North America. Amerindians believed that they were only one species among many. An Indian's spirit was but one among a myriad of spirits of people, animals, fish, flora, and minerals. In contrast, Christians believed that they held a special place in creation. At the irreducible core of Christianity was the dictum that God created man in the deity's image, and that the non-human world was available for human use and God's glorification. While

Christianity recognized a duty of stewardship in the use and exploitation of the non-human things that God had put on earth for Christians' advantage, it also confirmed that human beings were on a higher level of existence than animals, fish, and the rest of the natural world. This worldview had fuelled Western society's development of science and subjugation of nature by means of technology ever since the Renaissance. By the sixteenth century it had so shaped Christians' attitudes that they saw themselves as the more important part of a duality – humans and nature. It was an interpretation of reality and the place of human beings in creation that differed fundamentally from that of the indigenous populations of North America.

The significance of religion to the early contact between Europeans and aborigines did not end with Christianity's influence on the European view of the world; Christianity also had a bearing on which European peoples would undertake the exploration and economic development of the northern part of what would later be known as North America. The Vatican had decreed that all new lands were to be divided by the Christian nations of Spain and Portugal. Francis I of France did not accept his exclusion from the potential riches of the Western Hemisphere. 'Show me Adam's will!' he is supposed to have said of the papal edict.[9] In practice, France secured Rome's acquiescence in French efforts to find new lands to the north of those already being exploited by the Iberian states. It was politic and convenient to direct most of the voyages that the French crown sponsored to the northerly latitudes. So, in part, it was that the French concentrated many of their attentions on the region that would later become Canada. Certainly that was true of state-sponsored evangelical efforts, which were themselves another manifestation of the Christian nature of Europe.

It was a historically important coincidence that much of the early period of European exploration and penetration of North America was an era of intense religious feeling. The Catholic church had been wracked and divided by a drive for reform led by those who protested against the spiritual flabbiness and fleshly venality of an institution that had held a monopoly of religious services for centuries. The emergence of various forms of Protestantism would play a profoundly important role in the relations of indigenous peoples and European newcomers in many of the Anglo-American colonies that would develop. In the Roman Catholic church in general, and in France in particular, the rise of a Protestant challenge provoked both a Counter-Reformation and the emergence of a newly militant spirit of Catholicism. Both Catholic renewal and Catholic militancy were to have profound effects on the Indian peoples of North America.

The upheavals within the ranks of European Christianity stirred renewed desires to take Christ's message to all the world and new vehicles for taking it at precisely the moment France was poised to explore North America. The year of Jacques Cartier's first voyage, 1534, was also the year in which the Spaniard Ignatius Loyola established the Society of Jesus. Just as the Catholic revitalization motivated both clerics and rulers to follow the biblical injunction to evangelize, new missionary organizations emerged to fulfil this aim. The Recollets, a particularly strict branch of the Franciscans, and the Jesuits, an aggressive and militant order, were but two of the many orders that were founded or renewed in the aftermath of the Protestant Reformation. The Jesuits in particular moved eagerly to spread the Christian Word, and by the seventeenth century they were ministering to the Chinese and other Asians. It was the presence of groups such as these missionary orders that was to make the seventeenth century, the period of intensive and concerted efforts to explore and develop Canada, a century of faith. Without this recent evolution in Christianity in Western Europe, the early history of Canada, and the first stages of Indian-European relations, would have been vitally different.

It would have been difficult at any time and in any part of the globe to have found two such different human communities as the Micmac band and Cartier's men who came together at Gaspé in the summer of 1534. The indigenous inhabitants consisted of a multitude of bands and nations of hunter-gatherers and agriculturalists who had adjusted to their environment and lived in harmony with it. They had, especially the agrarian Iroquoians among them, developed elaborate social and political institutions and practices to cope with their large concentrations of population. Their technology and value system made their pressure on the resources of their world light. Lacking iron and firearms, they were unable to inflict much damage on fellow humans and animals; their animistic religion restrained them even from developing the desire to do so. Their economic organization meant that they lived in smaller population concentrations than did Europeans, often faced more threats to their physical well-being, and were forced to coexist with one another and with nature. While they shared a rudimentary form of commerce, similar motives for engaging in warfare, and an essentially similar cosmology and ethics, they had never experienced any need or occasion to combine for economic or political purposes.

The Europeans who came to North America also shared certain characteristics. In Europe, population concentrations were large compared to those in North America; political systems had developed that were authoritarian and coercive rather than communitarian and consensual; and the various economies were increasingly driven by the capitalistic motive of acquisition and investment. European nations also shared a common Christian faith, and, while differences of theological and ecclesiological detail might in the sixteenth century cause them to war with one another, that common faith gave them a similar attitude towards the environment. Their outlook was that of scientifically inclined creatures of God, who were beginning to believe not only that the world was created for their enjoyment but that the rules governing it were knowable and exploitable for economic purposes. Perhaps the different arrangement of the Europeans' mental furniture was the thing that distinguished them most from the indigenous peoples of America.

When Europeans began to undertake voyages to the new world they were setting in train a process that would bring these two contrasting communities out of solitude and into contact. The wonder of it was that early contact between two such different societies should have been so cooperative.

PART ONE

COOPERATION

2

Early contacts in the eastern woodlands

The earliest European ventures in North America proved abortive. About the first millennium after the birth of Christ, Norsemen attempted to colonize parts of Newfoundland and Labrador from Iceland and Greenland. In the latter place the Norse had already encountered an Inuit population they called *skraelings*. They applied the same name to the natives of Newfoundland, but the population they encountered was probably Beothuk or some other Algonkian people. Little is known of the relations between the would-be settlers and the natives save that there was conflict that led to the abandonment of European settlements at such places as the present-day l'Anse aux Meadows. This first failed attempt at colonization set a pattern for aboriginal-European relations in both the Atlantic and continental areas of Canada. Penetration of Newfoundland for agricultural settlement led to resistance and repulse by the indigenous people.

After the unsuccessful Norse attempt, contacts apparently became intermittent and commercial, rather than systematic and agricultural, for almost five centuries. The Norse continued to visit the coast of North America in search of timber for use in Greenland and Iceland, and probably also for fish, walrus, and even the polar bear. North America was part of the vast northern European trade that the Norse maintained for several centuries. Although this trade declined in the fourteenth century, and the Norsemen's control of commerce was replaced by that of the Hanseatic League of German states, the voyages and meetings would be important later on. The Norse had established sailing routes that others would follow and thereby encounter North America's indigenous peoples.

These early European contacts were motivated by the search for the products of the sea. Fish was extremely important in the European diet. The Catholic calendar's fifty-seven fast days and numerous other days (including each Friday and Saturday) on which the faithful abstained from consuming meat meant that during the equivalent of almost five months of the year no flesh was to be eaten.[1] The paucity of other inexpensive sources of protein ensured that there would be a heavy demand for fish, such as cod, that was nutritious and relatively inexpensive. There was also high demand for the great sea mammal the whale, whose meat, fat, and oil were all valuable. The importance of the prosaic cod can be seen from the fact that Azorean fishermen called Newfoundland the Land of the Baccolos (codfish).

Through the latter years of the fifteenth century, ships came from many European countries in search of sea products. The Basques became noteworthy for whaling, while the French and English were particularly interested in cod and other fish of the Grand Banks. The continuity between these increasingly frequent voyages and the earlier Norse approaches lay in the fact that all followed a northerly route across the Atlantic to the Western Hemisphere. Such a route not only took advantage of what knowledge endured about the sea-lanes developed by the Norse but also kept ships as close to land for as long a period as possible. Equally important for the later history of North America, these routes also ensured that the European vessels would come into contact with the indigenous peoples of Canada.

Late in the fifteenth century another motive began to incite the Europeans to explore the Western Hemisphere. In the 1490s merchants from Bristol began to underwrite the voyages of a Venetian navigator whom they called John Cabot, a man who argued that one could reach the Orient by sailing to the northwest. Probably in 1494 Cabot's ship poked about part of the Atlantic region and possibly also Cape Breton, and in 1497 he made a landfall on what he called New Found Land. Cabot, like Christopher Columbus who had reached the region he called the Indies by a southern route in 1492, was seeking the riches of the Great Khan that Europe had been informed of by Marco Polo. Even when Cabot and others finally realized that Newfoundland was not Asia, their voyages in search of eastern riches would persist and be imitated. North America would at first be mistaken by French explorers as well for Asia, and, once they realized their error, would be regarded as a land mass barring the way to the fabled East. When European navigators gave up on Canada as the Orient, they would continue for some time to search for a northwest passage through it to Asia. Like the fishing ships, they would come principally by the northern route; like them, they would encounter the natives in the process.

As the sixteenth century rolled on, the approaches of the different European countries to North America began to fall into a pattern. To a great extent the efforts of the English and the Basques remained focused on Newfoundland, Labrador, and the north shore region of what the local inhabitants called the River of Canada. The English and northern French fishing captains, who did not have large supplies of cheap salt to practise a green fishery, were forced to land to dry their catch on stages (or flakes) that they erected. What inclinations they might have had to turn these brief landings into the beginnings of settlement were discouraged, first, by the natives' resistance and, later, by an English policy forbidding settlement. More southerly Europeans who did have large quantities of salt made less use of the shore and, consequently, had little land-based contact with the Algonkians of the Atlantic region. When the French began to direct serious attention to North America in the sixteenth century, they focused on the mainland and became involved in extensive contacts with the natives. As events would soon demonstrate, all these voyages of exploration and for food from the sea had, in the meantime, been encouraging the growth of yet a third form of contact that pushed the French in particular to undertake unprecedented efforts to voyage to Canada.

This new form of contact was a commerce that had grown up spontaneously between the Europeans and the indigenous peoples. When the French navigator Jacques Cartier was cruising the coast in 1534, he met some Algonkians in the area of the Bay of Chaleur. The encounter was instructive. The Micmac 'set up a great clamour and made frequent signs to us to come on shore, holding up to us some furs on sticks.'² Since the Indians initiated both contact and commerce, and since they hid the females among their group in the woods before approaching the Europeans, it is clear that there had been considerable interaction between new-comers and themselves sometime previously. The inhabitants 'showed a marvellously great pleasure in possessing and obtaining these iron wares and other commodities, dancing and going through many ceremonies and throwing salt water over their heads with their hands.' They 'bartered all they had to such an extent that all went back naked without anything on them; and they made signs to us that they would return on the morrow with more furs.'³

Cartier had learned, as no doubt other voyagers had before him, that out of occasional contact in the fishery was emerging a commerce in the region's animal pelts. For both sides this was an attractive and mutually beneficial sideline. To the Indians the trade represented an opportunity to barter their used skin clothing for ornamental and utilitarian European products; for the newcomers it was a chance to develop a lucrative ancillary activity in the midst of fishing and exploring.

Other European activities apparently were less welcome and beneficial to the Indian inhabitants of the Atlantic region with whom Cartier and others made contact. The fact that the Micmac hid their womenfolk when they spied Cartier's ship hints at one problem that had ensued from contact. Another European activity that would have mixed results was presaged in Cartier's conclu-sion after a few days' observation that the natives 'would be easy to convert to our holy faith.'⁴ Yet another problem was the Euro-peans' presumptuous behaviour in ignoring the indigenous people's control of the territory, as in erecting a cross.⁵ Indubitably, the Indians rejected European attempts to proclaim their control by right of discovery of these lands.

Further problems arose when Cartier kidnapped Domagaya and Taigoagny, sons of the Iroquoian chief Donnacona, to take them back to France. Donnacona was a leader of some of the St Lawrence Iroquoians who in the sixteenth century dominated the River of Canada from present-day Lake Ontario to Gaspé. As later Indian leaders were bitterly to observe, the white man 'began by stealing the people from their land, and were to end up by stealing the continent from the people.'[6] In this instance the boys returned the following year on Cartier's second voyage. But other navigators and explorers kidnapped or persuaded Indians to return to Europe as living proof of what they had found in the west, and often the North Americans did not survive.

Cartier's subsequent voyages also began the process of European penetration of the northern part of the continent by means of the River of Canada. In 1535 Cartier probed to Stadacona, or Quebec City, and then onward over the protests of the Indians of that region to the upriver village they called Hochelaga, the future site of Montreal. The Stadaconans tried unsuccessfully to deter the Frenchmen from sailing past their village because they wanted to prevent the Hochelagans from getting access to European technology. Already the indigenous population was tending to try to monopolize trade in the interests of maximizing profits, a tendency that would develop on both the European and Indian sides of the commercial frontier at regular intervals. Cartier's westward voyage in the interior was undertaken in search of the region that the Indians called the Kingdom of the Saguenay; it ended at the rapids in the river that became known by the ironic title of La Chine (China).

During the Frenchmen's overwintering at Stadacona, new patterns were established within the developing relationship. The initial good relations between Cartier's men and Donnacona's people gave way to suspicion, to the point that the French fortified their winter quarters against the natives. Moreover, the winter brought dreadful suffering to the Europeans in the form of scurvy that killed almost one-quarter of them and left most of the remainder gravely debilitated. Then, although extermination of the sojourners would have been child's play, the Indians instead saved them from illness and possible death by showing them how to make a tonic containing ascorbic acid from bark, cedar needles, and water. Without this help, Cartier's party well might have perished.

By the end of Cartier's third voyage to the new world, 1541–2, the relationship had been established and attitudes formed. The Europeans had settled on the motives that would drive their contact until the eighteenth century: fish, furs, exploration, and evangelization. The indigenous people had tolerated the first, eagerly embraced the second, cooperated in the third when doing so did not threaten their interests, and still remained blissfully ignorant of the fourth motive.

Attitudes had begun to form, too. At first Cartier thought that 'This people may well be called savage, for they are the sorriest folk there can be in the world, and the whole lot of them had not anything above the value of five sous, their canoes and fishing-nets excepted.'[7] The Europeans initially formed a poor impression of the native peoples, though on longer and closer contact they would moderate the severity of their judgment. How negative the Frenchmen's view was has been exaggerated by translators who have not always understood fully the words that people like Cartier used. Usually, the French referred to the indigenous people as *sauvage*, a term which could have the English translation 'savage.' But *sauvage* did not always mean 'savage': it could have a more neutral meaning, such as someone who resided in natural surroundings. Or it could mean something that was not domesticated, something occurring naturally in nature.

What *sauvage* meant depended completely on the context. Cartier in 1534 probably meant that the people he encountered were in a rude and impoverished state. Later missionaries would refer to an Indian convert as 'un bon sauvage vraiment chrétien' (a good, truly Christian —), a use of the term *sauvage* that could not translate as 'savage' and still make sense. In such a case it obviously was merely the term for the native inhabitants of the woodlands. At other times Frenchmen who referred to indigenous people as *sauvage* meant that they were primitive and barbarous by French standards. Which meaning was intended could only be understood from the context, a subtlety that was too often missed in the direct and blunt translations into English that rendered every Indian a 'savage,' whether he was a 'truly Christian' convert or a warrior torturing prisoners. Later generations, both Indian and Euro-Canadian, would pay dearly for this use of language as a blunt instrument.

Such concerns lay far in the future in the aftermath of the French explorations of the early sixteenth century. For reasons largely having to do with political and religious affairs in Western Europe, the French crown was distracted from the 1540s onward from further explorations. The fact that Cartier had brought back only people, fool's gold, and worthless quartz rather than spices, gold, and diamonds meant that there was little incentive to continue the voyages. In any event, there occurred an interruption of European explorations of the northern portion of the continent and contact with the natives that would last until the early seventeenth century. In the latter half of the sixteenth century the contacts that persisted were the now familiar ones of fishing and whaling vessels, who presumably continued the ancillary enterprise of trading in furs as opportunity in America and markets in Europe were available.

When French voyages of exploration resumed early in the seventeenth century they focused primarily on the Maritime and St Lawrence regions, and they had significant differences from the tentative probings of the previous century. In the first place, when Champlain and his ships poked their way up the River of Canada they discovered that the St Lawrence Iroquoians had disappeared, most likely dispersed by the incursions of other Indian nations. The Indians with whom Champlain came most frequently into contact were Algonkians, whether Micmac of the Maritimes or Naskapi and Montagnais along the north shore of the river. The second major change was found in the Europeans who came, rather than the indigenous people who met them. French efforts in the seventeenth century differed from those of the previous century in their greater emphasis on evangelism.

If the sixteenth century had been the century of religious wars in Europe, and if the eighteenth would be the century of the enlightenment, then the seventeenth was the century of faith. In the case of France's Most Christian Majesty there was a greater emphasis on spreading the Christian Word, and the crown's support of exploratory voyages to North America now was conditional on the willingness of the ships to carry missionaries. Since France was still an absolute monarchy, the church in no way was exalted above the station and prestige of the monarch. On the contrary, in any battles with the crown's representatives the agents of the church would invariably lose. But France and its royal head nonetheless supported and promoted missionary efforts as part of the outreach program France was beginning to North America.

The addition of a new motive, faith, for European contact to the familiar triad of fish, fur, and exploration did not change the nature of the relationship between Europeans and Indians. Nor did it change the pattern of contact to any great extent. If the French in the seventeenth century had begun to concentrate their efforts on the Maritime area they called Acadia and on the St Lawrence region for which they would adopt the Indian name Canada, other nations maintained the kinds of contact they had earlier. The English continued to journey annually to the Grand Banks off Newfoundland and Acadia, and their government's prohibition on settlement in this part of the new world meant that they continued to land and encounter the indigenous population intermittently as they sought supplies or a place to dry their fish. The Spaniards and the Basques similarly kept up their practice of regular, brief voyages to the Strait of Belle Isle, the Gulf of St Lawrence, and portions of the river estuary such as the Saguenay near Tadoussac where the whales gathered. In other words, the seventeenth-century pattern of European contact ensured that it would be the French who most regularly and most persistently encountered the indigenous populations.

The reasons the French had for coming ensured that their attitude towards the Indians would not change fundamentally in the seventeenth century, whether they were exploring and settling in the Bay of Fundy area or pushing their way up the St Lawrence. The French who came for fish, fur, faith, or more knowledge of the geography and topography of this strange new land soon discovered that they needed the people they met there. Even in the fisheries off the east coast, and even for those fishing boats that practised the green fishery, a minimal level of tolerance towards them by the native population was an essential precondition of their success. Should the newcomers irritate and offend the more numerous Indians, they would soon encounter both maritime and land-based assaults that would make catching and processing the cod impossible. Since the Indians possessed canoes, they were capable of depredations on the isolated vessels. And for those, such as the English, who had to land to pursue the dry fishery, the threat of native hostility was very serious. Even as things were in the seventeenth century, the occasional landings caused some annoyance and much curiosity among the Indians. From the English fishermen's point of view, the light-fingered Beothuk who helped themselves to some of the things that the fishermen left behind were a nuisance. But these irritations only underlined the degree of dependence on Indian tolerance under which the Europeans laboured.

The same was true of the relationship between the Indians and those French, such as Samuel de Champlain, who coasted the Maritimes and sailed up the St Lawrence in search of a passage through this landmass to Asia. They were dependent on Indian informants for knowledge of what lay beyond the next hill or lake, and the fact that the Indians – polite people – tended to respond to their questions with the sort of answers they thought these newcomers wanted to hear meant that much confusion occurred. French explorers and cartographers heard a great deal about a western sea and a so-called Kingdom of the Saguenay that owed more to their own desires and Indian politesse than fact. In addition to being dependent on the Indians for knowledge, the explorers relied on them for safe conduct and for the means to travel in the interior. As was the case with the fishing captain, if the European navigator alienated the Indians he would find himself completely frustrated in his efforts to do his job. Moreover, the explorer soon learned that he required Indian canoes – especially the birchbark canoe that could carry a heavy load but was still light enough to portage – to get beyond the rapids at the place they called Lachine. Champlain and those who came after him would learn that they needed other Indian tools such as the contraption they called a toboggan and the gear they put on their feet to travel over snow during the long winters. Those who came to explore and map found themselves even more dependent on the goodwill and assistance of the indigenous populations than did the fishermen.

But the most dependent of all were those who came, not for fish or geographical knowledge, but for fur and faith. The Indians would not have allowed European fur traders to come in large numbers to take the furs and process them themselves. In any event, conducting the fur trade principally with European labour would have proved so prohibitively expensive that the commerce would quickly have been abandoned. It made much more sense, to both the indigenous harvesters of fur and the foreign purchasers of pelts, to practise a division of labour in the fur trade. The Indians collected the furs in large quantities and brought them to the European. The Europeans, for the most part, purchased furs gathered by others and transported them to overseas markets. This arrangement made the commerce in fur symbiotic: each party to the exchange of pelts needed the other.

This relationship of mutual dependence particularly characterized the branch of the fur trade that was to dominate in the seventeenth and eighteenth centuries – the trade in beaver fur. The fickle winds of fashion and the physiology of the *castor canadensis* combined to ensure that Indians and Europeans were bound by ties of mutual self-interest. In Europe in the seventeenth century the broad-brimmed, shiny hat made of felted fur was all the rage. Since the Baltic supplies of suitable fur were largely exhausted, it made perfect sense to seek a replacement in North America, whence fishing boats had been bringing back packets of fur for decades. And certain characteristics of beaver fur ensured that it would become the fur of choice for felters and hatters. Beaver fur consisted of two types of hairs or filaments. One was a soft, downy hair that had tiny hooks or barbs at the tips. This construction meant that the soft, shorter hair of the beaver's pelt made an ideal felt – smooth, shiny, flat – for hatters. Barbed filaments linked and locked, producing a felt that stayed flat and thin.

The other type of hair in the beaver's pelt ensured that there was an essential role for the native North Americans to play not just in catching the beaver and taking its pelt, but also in giving it its preliminary processing. In addition to the down, the beaver pelt had longer, coarse hairs known as guard hairs. The best beaver pelt for felting purposes was one from which the guard hairs had been removed, leaving the soft, lustrous down. Fortunately, the Indians removed the guard hairs before trading the pelt. They 'processed' the beaver fur simply by wearing it next to their skin in garments consisting of several pelts sewn together with leather thongs. After a year's service as a garment it ceased to be a simple beaver pelt; it became what the French called *castor gras*, or greasy beaver. The skin was soft and supple; and the guard hairs had been removed by abrasion, sweat, smoke, and heat.

But the French fur trader did not refer to the most highly prized beaver fur simply as *castor gras*; the fur that he wanted above all others was what he called *castor gras d'hiver* (greasy *winter* beaver). The best pelt was the one taken in the winter, when the beaver's natural insulation against the cold – the down – was thickest. But the fur traders hoped to be safely and profitably back home by winter, and they would have had an extremely difficult time taking the prime winter beaver even if they had – lamentably, from their point of view – still been in North America. The beaver inconsiderately spent the winter in remote lakes and streams, under the protection of a lodge it built of branches and mud. These lodges were extremely hard, and their underwater entrances were difficult to detect. Naturally, the Indians, who for centuries had been catching the beaver for fur and meat, knew how to reach the ponds where lodges were to be found, how to locate the entrances, and how to destroy the structures so as to get at the inhabitants. Consequently, the Indians were essential to taking the *castor gras d'hiver* in its prime, just as they were to its proper processing. A trade in the beaver pelts that furriers craved in seventeenth-century Europe was simply impossible without the cooperation of the indigenous North Americans. Europeans who came in search of prime furs needed the native population's knowledge, skills, and cooperation.

Obviously, the Frenchmen who came to harvest souls rather than skins were also dependent upon the people whom they sought to proselytize. In the earliest years of French contact in the seventeenth century, down to the late 1620s, it was particularly a branch of the Franciscans known as the Recollets who carried the evangelical message to Algonkians in Acadia and to Iroquoians and Algonkians along the St Lawrence and in the interior. From the 1620s onward, however, they were replaced by the Society of Jesus, or Jesuits, one of the most formidable teaching and missionary orders of the Roman Catholic church. (The Recollets would return to share the mission field in 1670, concentrating on Acadia. Sulpicians moved into the Montreal area in 1657.) New France was officially closed to Protestants, and although many individual Huguenots came as fur traders and merchants, Protestantism had no official presence in France's colony. Certainly, no Protestant missionaries were allowed in.

Recollets differed from Jesuits in that they believed that Indians had to be remade into French persons before they could be turned into Christians. In other words, the Recollet approach usually was to try to assimilate the Indians in order to Christianize them. But the Jesuits, who had had considerable cross-cultural experience in Asia, took a less assimilationist approach. Jesuits believed not only that it was unnecessary for Indians to adopt European ways in order to come to accept Christ, but also that there were some native beliefs that could be incorporated into Christianity, thereby making the new dispensation both more intelligible and attractive to the intended proselytes. Moreover, prolonged experience in New France persuaded the Jesuits that contact with Europeans often debased the Indians they wished to convert. Eventually they concluded, as a Jesuit historian put it in the 1740s, that 'there was no longer any doubt that the best mode of Christianizing them, was to avoid Frenchifying them.'[8] Jesuits wanted to convert; they did not usually consider it necessary to assimilate Indians as well.

Whatever the missionary order and whatever its approach to proselytizing the North American Indians, the evangelists needed cooperation. They were as dependent on the Indians as they were on the French crown that encouraged their work and the ship captains and fur traders who had, often reluctantly, to carry them to North America and into areas where Indians were to be found. If Indians refused to tolerate the presence in their canoes of black robes, as they called the Jesuits, the priests simply would never gain access to the regions where Indians dwelt in large numbers. And if the Indians declined to trade for food and shelter, then the missionaries could not stay among them even after they reached their villages. If the indigenous population was hostile, missionaries could quickly find themselves achieving not their primary objective, conversion, but the second of their priorities, personal martyrdom. And, as the Jesuits quickly discovered, unless Indian converts cooperated by becoming lay missionaries or catechists, the spread of Christianity throughout the Indian nations would be slow.

The missionaries soon discovered that they could no more realize their North American objectives by themselves than could their fur-trading compatriots or the navigators or fishing captains. European presence in North America was dependent on native goodwill and cooperation because the Indian was vital to the realization of all the purposes the European had in coming to the continent. Whether the European came for fish, fur, to seek a passage to Asia, or to find a place in the people's heart for his god, the newcomer was totally dependent on the native. It was not just that the Indians greatly outnumbered the Europeans – though that also was important; it was that the interloper could accomplish nothing without the help of the host society.

Why did the Indian cooperate with the fisherman, the fur trader, the explorer, and the black robe? Indian motives were many and varied. The fishing boats rarely threatened them or their resources. There was a bountiful supply of fish, and, besides, sharing was an ethical imperative. Moreover, in the Atlantic region the presence of European fishing boats soon led to the development of a trade in furs from which the Indians derived benefit. From the Indian side of this commercial nexus the advantage in the fur trade was access to European technology. It must have been, as the behaviour of the Indians whom Cartier encountered in the 1530s illustrated, strange and wonderful to discover that these hairy strangers were eager to get their hands on the old furs that the Indians wore. That these fools would take worthless hides in exchange for wondrous things such as mirrors, glass beads, and items made of iron was amazing.

The only metal that these Indians had previously known was the copper from the shores of Lake Superior that had been diffused throughout eastern North America by well-established trade routes. But copper, though useful for many decorative and a few utilitarian purposes, was too soft to be of much use in those things that mattered most to Indians. The other elements that Indians used were bone for pointed items, wood for clubs and clumsy kettles in which liquids were heating by immersing a series of heated rocks, and stone as an edge in clubs and some scraping tools. Iron was an ideal substitute for weapons such as arrow heads and spear tips, for tools such as knives used for skinning and cutting, and, perhaps above all, for containers. The difference in household and village routine between being able to carry pots on trips and having to adjust the band's itinerary to reach the large, fixed wooden vessels in which food preparation was often carried on must have been monumental.

The Indian reaction to kettles amused the French, who took such vessels as much for granted as Indians did greasy beaver pelts. The

Huron thought that among these *gens du fer* ('iron people'), as they took to calling the French, 'the greatest captains in France were endowed with the greatest mind, and possessing so great a mind they alone make the most complicated things, such as axes, knives, kettles, etc.' Accordingly, they 'concluded therefore that the King, being the greatest captain and chief of them all made the largest kettles.'[9] An Acadian visitor to Paris was certain that the street 'where there were then many coppersmiths' must contain the establishments of 'relatives of the King.' He asked 'if this was not the trade of the grandest Seigniors of the Kingdom.'[10] But it was hardly strange that Indians seemed overwhelmed by the iron kettle; little wonder that the proud possessors of them would use and patch these wondrous vessels nearly to the point of destroying them – and then trade them to members of some less fortunate band that did not have direct access to such goods. The chance to obtain iron, brandy, and decorative items constituted an important reason for Indian cooperation in the fur trade.

For some tribes the fur trade offered enormous commercial potential. Iroquoian nations, especially, found that their geographical locations put them into advantageous positions for trading both with other nations and with the French. Moreover, their possession of such important goods as a portable supply of protein (corn) and tobacco made it possible for them to journey far afield to trade and to have important commodities to trade once they got there. The greatest profits on the Indian side of the trade were realized not by those who caught and processed the furs but by those who gathered the pelts from other Indians by commerce or war and then traded them to the newcomers. Whether the pre-contact commerce in food, copper, and other goods had conditioned the Huron and others, or whether they responded rapidly to the creation of market conditions, there is no doubt that the Indians reacted quickly and shrewdly to the opportunities that the fur trade created. The development of middleman strategies by such groups as the Huron, and the emergence of the practice of refusing to trade with the first vessels of the season were immediate adjustments to the economic opportunities created by the European presence. Indians of the lower St Lawrence and Acadia understood that two or more ships full of traders at anchor meant higher prices for furs than one shipload of would-be purchasers. Indians were as swift to exploit their advantages as any European.

And there could be no doubt about who was the dominant partner in this commercial relationship. The Indians dictated that the trade should follow forms that had existed among them for centuries. For example, trade did not begin immediately after an encounter; exchange was preceded by speech-making and gift-giving. In some cases, the trade ostensibly took the form of an exchange of presents, a fiction that conformed to Indian usages and ethical imperatives much more than European proclivities towards market behaviour. Particularly well-situated groups, such as the Algonkin of Allumette Island in the Ottawa River, used their position and power to exact tolls from canoe brigades, including those of traders, who passed through their territory. The mastery they exercised was demonstrated graphically by their leader Le Borgne in 1650. Offended by the efforts of a group of Huron under Jesuit leadership to evade his toll collection, Le Borgne had the priest 'suspended from a tree by the arm-pits.' He told 'him that the French were not the masters of his country; and that in it he alone was acknowledged as chief.'[11] The clearest evidence of where the power truly resided in the commercial relationship was found in the communications between Europeans and Indians, especially French fur traders and the Huron. The affluent and proud Huron refused to lower themselves to learn the newcomers' language. If the French wanted to trade, they could speak the Indian language. They did.

The Indians also used the valuable trade goods they derived from the fur trade in a network of exchanges among themselves. Though Indian ethical systems emphasized sharing, such values did not extend to giving away valuable goods to people from other nations. Iroquois or Montagnais middlemen were perfectly capable of exploiting their monopoly of European goods by exacting high prices for kettles or knives when they passed them on to less favoured tribes in the interior. In these transactions, as in the various techniques they used to monopolize the trade and exact the best terms for themselves, the Indians demonstrated shrewd commercial instincts as well as the fact that they controlled the trade. If they participated in commerce, it was because they benefited substantially from it.

To a considerable extent the Indians' desire to maintain the commercial link to the French explains both their cooperation with explorers and their toleration of missionaries. Natives recognized quickly that the former posed a threat to their commercial well-being, but they had to accommodate the cartographers to maintain friendship with their compatriots. The missionaries posed a less obvious, longer-term threat to their spiritual health and their cultural identity; the Indians were less successful in developing strategies to counter this menace.

From the earliest times Indians had to balance their wish to retain access to European goods against their desire not to allow the Europeans direct contact with their trading partners. The St Lawrence Iroquoians had tried to discourage Cartier's penetration of the upper St Lawrence, first to Hochelaga and later beyond present-day Montreal. Similarly, in the seventeenth century Champlain and others frequently found that their desire to be escorted into the interior so they could explore and map the water routes was frustrated by natives' unwillingness to take them into these regions. But even those Indians who were reluctant to jeopardize their control of the interior trade by allowing Europeans direct access usually had to give in. Accordingly, Champlain was accompanied into Huronia in 1616, and many after him were guided to the northern interior as well. The Indians' concern not to undermine the trading partnership usually persuaded them to accommodate the Europeans.

But the commercial nexus did not operate only to the advantage of the Europeans; the desire for good relations with the Indians could lead the explorers to accommodate Indian wishes as well. A clear, early example of the way in which the desire to maintain good relations with the Indians induced the newcomers to take actions they might otherwise have avoided was Champlain's participation in 1609 in an Algonkian raiding party into the territories of the Iroquois, in which firearms were employed deliberately for the first time against surprised Indian forces. As Cartier's penetration of the River of Canada and Champlain's use of muskets on the shores of the lake that was to bear his name showed, the cooperation of Europeans and Indians in a commercial relationship facilitated other activities.

If it is obvious why Indians helped the Europeans to fish, trade in furs, and explore, why did they tolerate the fourth of the newcomers' activities? Why did the Huron in the 1630s and 1640s agree to allow Jesuits to reside in Huronia and to proselytize? The key to understanding the reluctant agreement to play host to missionaries, whether in Huronia or among the nomadic Algonkian bands, was the Indian conception of the commercial alliance. In trade between Indian peoples of different villages and nations there were well-established ground rules. One was that the family or band that initiated exchange with an outside group enjoyed a monopoly of access to that group. Such behaviour was continued in trade with the French: families who traded first with the Europeans controlled the right to trade with them.

A second feature of Indian commerce was an exchange of personnel. When different bands or nations traded regularly, it was common for them to exchange members of their comunities. These hostages to commerce, usually sons of families active in the trade, resided in the village of the trading partner. So, too, it would appear, did the Huron regard the young French fur traders, such as Etienne Brulé, and the missionaries. It was logical enough for the Indians to assume that Europeans practised this form of exchange, too. Did the intruders not persuade the Indians to allow a few of their young men, and occasionally even a chief, to return with them across the water, promising that their people would come back when the big ships returned the following year to trade? Missionaries were simply another form of hostage to the trade. The French, under the pressure of the government in France, wanted the Huron to accept missionaries among them. To maintain the commercial alliance, and assuming that the arrival of missionaries represented a continuation of the tradition of exchanging personnel, the Indians accepted the strange black robes among them.

For their part, the missionaries but dimly perceived how the Indians regarded them. The Jesuits knew they were dependent on the fur trade in the sense that without the trade and without commercial voyages from the interior to the St Lawrence, the means for them to minister to the inland nations would not exist. But the priests rarely comprehended that they were dependent on the trade in an even more fundamental sense: without commerce their Indian hosts would have spurned their presence.

In short, when contact resumed in the seventeenth century it was principally the French who came to mainland northern North America, and they came for four reasons. From the time of Champlain's voyages till the dawn of the eighteenth century, the French came for fish, fur, exploration, and evangelization. The Indian was an indispensable partner – frequently a dominant as well as necessary partner – in all these activities. To preserve fish, to gather fur, to probe and map the land, and to spread the Christian message, cooperation by the Indians was essential. For their part the Indians found it acceptable, and occasionally desirable, to humour the newcomers. To a minor degree the explanation could be found in Indian traditions of sharing and avoiding coercion of others. A more important reason for their toleration of and cooperation with the French was that the newcomers' activities were compatible with the continuation of Indian ways. Fishing boats were no threat, given the rich stocks of fish and the brief landfalls by fishermen. Fur traders were a source of valued goods, and their activities did not require much change in Indian economic activities. Explorers and cartographers were less obviously useful, and might have posed a long-term threat if they expanded the French acquaintance with tribes that were dependent on middlemen such as the Montagnais or Huron. But cooperation with them was necessary to maintain the commercial relationship. The same consideration explained the grudging acceptance of missionaries in Indian villages.

In the seventeenth century the Europeans came to North America in pursuit of goals that could not be reached without Indian cooperation. The Indians found good, practical reasons for cooperating with the newcomers. In short, the relationship in these early decades was one of mutual benefit. Certainly it posed no threat to the Indians, who were more numerous, more at home in the North American environment, and capable at any moment of repelling the few thousands of French who at first came to their shores. Accordingly, Indian-European relations in this initial period were not just mutually beneficial but also harmonious. European motives and Indian interests were largely compatible.

3

Commercial partnership and mutual benefit

Harmonious relations did not mean that there were no problems, much less change. For both Indians and Europeans, constant interaction in the fur trade and in missionary settings brought rewards and problems, advantages and setbacks. For the European there were more of the former than the latter: they prospered, acquired new tools and techniques, and were influenced positively by Indian customs. But for the Indian, association with the European was a mixed blessing. Undoubtedly the new technology based on iron greatly improved everyday life and hunting, but it also made warfare more destructive. The Frenchmen's brandy also was a popular means of recreation, but it wreaked a fearful havoc at times. More serious still were the scourges of disease and religion. One killed the bodies of thousands of Indians; the other eroded the belief systems that were both a reflection and a support of their relationship with the cosmos and with each other. If the seventeenth-century relationship was mutually beneficial, it was also influential.

On the European side the most obvious consequences of their contact with the indigenous population were profit and expansion. Down to the late decades of the seventeenth century the fur trade was sufficiently profitable to bring a series of French companies to New France. Another manifestation of the success of the trade was the competition that it brought. If the French formed trading links with Algonkians such as the Montagnais and with Iroquoians such as the Huron, rivals from Holland and later England set up offsetting partnerships with the Five Nations of the Iroquois. Each European power developed a trading network based on the geography of the continent and the Indian nations with whom geography brought them most readily into contact. For the French this meant a close association with the Micmac of the Maritime region, with the Algonkian along the St Lawrence, and with the agricultural Huron of the interior who were accessible by way of the St Lawrence drainage system. The topography of North America drew the French in by the St Lawrence, up the Ottawa River, across Lake Nipissing, and through the French River to Lake Huron and, finally, Georgian Bay. This natural line of water approach largely determined the groups with whom the French would cooperate commercially.

Similarly, for the Dutch and English traders who entered North America by way of the river that Henry Hudson named, a different path of approach and a different set of alliances and partnerships were developed. For fur traders and explorers in these more southerly areas, penetration of the continent was achieved by ascent of the Hudson River, and then either transfer into the Mohawk River that would take travellers eventually to the lower Great Lakes, or overland travel to Lake Champlain and to the Richelieu River that emptied into the St Lawrence above Donnacona's village. Fairly quickly a rival fur-trade network of Iroquois and Dutch or English developed with strategic centres at Fort Orange (Albany) and New Amsterdam (New York). The Iroquois, especially the Mohawk whose easternmost position drew them into earliest and most frequent contact with the newcomers, were as essential to the European traders south of New France as the Montagnais and Huron were to the French. Between the rival networks that developed along their respective drainage systems grew a fierce and unremitting competition for mastery of the trade.

This competition had both benign and malignant consequences. Among the positive effects of the struggle for furs was the compulsion to push ever further inland in search of newer sources of pelts, better furs, and unspoiled trading partners. It was the goad of the fur trade and the profit motive that drove French traders and military officers to probe the lower Great Lakes, the Ohio and Mississippi rivers, and the network of rivers in present-day northern Quebec and Ontario. In the process of pursuing furs they also induced the Maritime Indians to exhaust the fur resources of their region. Before the seventeenth century was over the Micmac found their role as fur traders destroyed by the efficiency with which they and other nations had trapped the beaver. By the end of the century, the fur resources of the interior were by no means exhausted, but much of the European's ignorance of the interior lands was dissipated. Thanks to fur-trade exploration, most of the principal arteries of the eastern half of North America had been tested and the results recorded; and the restless European was beginning to cast wondering eyes westward in search of the vast body of water the Indians had described and they, hopefully, had named *la mer de l'Ouest* (the western sea). Without the fur trade there would have been no stimulus of competition to search out new fur lands, and without the profits to underwrite the voyages there would have been no means to carry out the search. Most important of all, without the Indian, the canoe, maize, and other products of the indigenous society, none of the great exploratory trips would have got much further than Lachine.

It was more difficult to measure other effects of this seventeenth-century relationship on Europeans. The need to support the fur trade and the missionary effort induced the French crown to end administration of New France by a succession of commercial monopolies and to establish it as a crown colony in 1663. The desire to promote the missionary drive contributed to the decision to found the religious settlement of Ville Marie near the confluence of the Ottawa and St Lawrence rivers in 1642. As Montreal it was to develop as a thoroughly secular fur-trade centre, largely supplanting Trois-Rivières in that role. And the need to overawe if not conquer the Iroquois who did so much damage to Montreal and the fur trade in the 1640s and 1650s induced France to send several regiments of troops. But none of these initiatives fundamentally changed the nature of the French presence in Acadia and Canada, or greatly swelled the population. And what areas of French settlement there were occurred in regions that the Indians used only in transit.[1] There were but a few thousand permanent residents in the French settlements in the St Lawrence valley when royal rule and the Carignan-Salières regiment arrived in the 1660s, and agriculture and manufacturing were still minor adjuncts to commerce. Throughout the seventeenth century, New France remained in essence a commercial colony rather than an expanding agricultural settlement. As such it was not a major threat to the Indian population with which it traded, for fur traders did not cut down trees or drive off game. The European presence, and hence the impact on North America and its indigenous population of Europeans, remained small-scale, commercial, and compatible with the customs and economic activities of the continent.

Even harder to gauge than expansion through exploration and the planting of small commercial and administrative centres were the effects of contact with the indigenous population on the Europeans' manners, customs, attitudes, and mores. There were some physical signs of transferring Indian values and practices to the European that were unmistakable. The French women's adoption of the short skirt that Indian women wore was one that scandalized many a clerical visitor from France. Similarly, the use of the canoe in summer and the toboggan and snowshoes in winter demonstrated that the European was as capable of adopting usable technology as the Indian woman who now cooked in an iron kettle. Food was another area of transfer from the indigenous to the outsider. Corn was merely the most prominent item in a list that included beans and squash as well. Also among the crops that the French bartered for with the Indian was one plant that was to have a devastating effect on the European. Tobacco from the area north of Lake Erie was traded throughout eastern North America by the Petun (Tobacco), Huron, and other commercial nations. Ontario tobacco made its way to France as Virginia tobacco did to England, in both cases with deadly long-term consequences.

But it was perhaps in the area of values and attitudes that the Indian peoples had their greatest, though least measurable, effect on the Europeans. Particularly among the young men who voyaged into the interior in search of new routes or furs there was a tendency to emulate Indian ways. The Europeans greatly admired the Indians for their hardihood, their dignity, their skills in coping with the environment, and their sophisticated ways of dealing with one another. A perverse manifestation of this respect, as well as a product of the motive of conspicuous consumption, was the development of an Indian slave trade. Indians were especially coveted as slaves by French merchants and administrators in the towns precisely because slaves had almost no economic value in New France. The fact that the colony was not an agricultural settlement that grew large surplus crops for export on plantations that required a great quantity of labour, as well as the independence and pride of the Indians, ensured that there would be neither need for unfree labour nor available, tractable slaves. The Indians who were enslaved after battles among the tribes were useful only to demonstrate their owner's affluence and status. When these slaves or *panis* (apparently a corruption of the name for the Pawnee) were traded to the French they became a bizarre product of Indian independence and French snobbery, a decorative slave caste with no economic purpose.

But it was the independence and other positive characteristics that most affected the European youths who worked in close proximity to the Indians. The young voyageurs struggled to imitate the Indians' stoicism in the face of adversity and their endurance when confronted with hardship, deprivation, and pain. They also copied as much as they dared of the autonomy that Indian society inculcated in its young. French males found the liberated sexual attitudes of young Indian women prior to matrimony as attractive as the missionaries found them repugnant. Many of the French formed liaisons with Indian women, but, since most of the intermarriage and interbreeding took place in the interior, the results of this miscegenation were largely concentrated in the Indian villages. Over time, the mixed-blood population was reabsorbed into Indian society. But what was definitely brought back to Montreal and Quebec were the Indians' independent attitudes.

It would not be accurate to attribute all of the independence or insolence that French visitors increasingly noticed in the *Canadien* population to the influence of the Indians. Other contributing factors were the scarcity of labour and abundance of arable land in New France: the former made ordinary Canadian labourers and tradesmen affluent, and the latter gave what would in Europe have been an impoverished peasantry the opportunity to reach the same heights. But the fact that the young Canadian always had the alternative of escaping to the *pays d'en haut* (the fur-trading country in the interior) gave him an option his more constricted European counterpart did not enjoy.

By the end of the seventeenth century Canadians were developing their own ways, not always to the satisfaction of Frenchmen who persisted in thinking of themselves as the betters of these colonials. Land, affluence, the open fur-trade frontier, and the Indian role model all contributed to the emergence of a distinctive Canadian. Neither French peasant nor Indian brave, he was a bit of both. He called himself a *habitant*, and many of his habits were those of the Indians he admired. Over the decades these people were becoming, thanks in part to the Indians, *Canadiens*.

The Indians did not reciprocate French admiration. On the whole, though the Indians respected European technology and were prepared to associate themselves with those who produced it, they were unimpressed by Europeans. The ambivalence of many indigenous people towards the newcomers was expressed by the grandmother of convert Pierre Pastedechouan, who described natives' reaction to the appearance of a French ship. 'They thought it was a moving Island,' and 'their astonishment was redoubled in seeing a number of men on deck.' But when the Frenchmen in their armour gave them ship's biscuit and introduced them to wine, they were appalled. They dismissed the intruders as people who 'drank blood and ate wood, thus naming the wine and the biscuits.'[2] Indians' appreciation of the French did not necessarily improve over the decades. Natives considered many white men ugly, and Indians' impression of Europeans' physiological features was not at all aided by the fact that many Indians considered facial hair a sign of stupidity.[3] The newcomers had big canoes and weapons, but they could not mend their own kettles or survive unaided in the North American environment. They did not know even elementary things about how to greet people and parley before engaging in commerce. And these strangers had a distressing and repugnant tendency to behave selfishly. In their own societies people who behaved as the hairy interlopers did would be labelled witches and put to death.

To some degree the increasing reliance of Indians on the trade goods they gained through the fur trade could have led to a dependence that might cause problems. There is scattered evidence that some bands relied on European goods so thoroughly and so long that they lost the ability to make similar items of bone, wood, or stone that they had used before the white men came. The Jesuits and some other observers claimed that Indians who traded intensively with the French became dependent on the flow of European goods and experienced hardship when the supply was temporarily interrupted or permanently choked off. But too much should not be made of these kinds of comments. For one thing, Europeans often mistook the passing hardship caused by a temporary pause in supply for real suffering that resulted from a permanent loss of skills. Over the centuries, of course, these skills would be lost.

It is even more important to remember that European observers often failed to distinguish between Indian use of trade goods that undermined traditional ways and Indian usages that merely reinforced the old beliefs and values. (A contemporary analogy might be the war veterans who become upset at teenagers' use of war medals as decorations: the veterans are transferring their understanding of the meaning and proper use of the medal to the adolescents, who almost certainly are ignorant of the former combatants' assumptions and feelings.) Europeans often noted the Indians' eagerness to accumulate iron goods and other products of European technology; what they failed to notice was the traditional uses to which these items were put. In European society accumulation was motivated primarily by the desire to consume and to reinvest; in Indian society accumulation was but the prelude to consumption and redistribution. So it was with a vast quantity of trade goods that ended up not being used by the Indians who traded for them, or passed on at a profit to other Indians, but interred in elaborate funerary rites such as the periodic Feast of the Dead. As well, many prominent Indians desired goods only to give them to their followers, an act that was both their duty and an opportunity to reinforce their status. Such uses of European goods, far from undermining Indian values and carrying with them capitalist notions, reinforced traditional values.[4] What mattered about the Indians' participation in commerce and acquisition of European goods was not that they traded or even that they made profits. What counted was the fact that they did so for traditional reasons.

As long as these motivations remained dominant, trade and European goods did not fundamentally remake Indian societies.

What did alter Indian society were some other things that came along with commerce: disease, alcohol, and Christianity. Although Indians were hardy and knew how, by using clothing adequate to the weather and religious rituals equal to the task of placating the spirits, to cope with their world, they had no immunity to many of the diseases that the Europeans unwittingly brought with them. Centuries of exposure to such contagious diseases as measles and smallpox had produced a high degree of immunity in Europeans, but Indians soon fell victims to such diseases in large numbers. Estimates vary widely and precision is impossible, but it seems reasonably clear that those Indian nations who came into frequent contact with the newcomers suffered dreadful losses. The Huron who harboured Jesuit missionaries and French traders probably lost half of their population to measles between 1634 and 1640. Since the new diseases tended to strike disproportionately at the old and the very young, these sudden losses meant that the Huron were deprived in great numbers of both the preservers of their traditions and their future soldiers. And it is quite likely that at least half of the 200,000 to 300,000 aboriginal inhabitants of Canada at contact were removed by disease over the ensuing 300 years.[5] Canadian history lacks the instances of germ warfare that disfigure the history of the Thirteen Colonies and the United States, but disease nonetheless wreaked havoc among the Indian populations of the future Canada.

Though one might expect that the disease of alcoholism was a serious threat, such was not the case even though alcohol was a social problem. There can be no doubt, given the plethora of horrified accounts by officials and missionaries, that alcohol often had devastating effects upon Indians. The descriptions of the scenes that unfolded at the Montreal fur fair each year when the Indian canoe brigades arrived leave little doubt that consumption of brandy led to acts of violence against their own families and others, particularly those from other nations.

But there are several aspects of these oft-observed problems that need to be taken into account so as not to gain a distorted perception of the alcohol problems among the vast majority of Indians. In the first place, those Indians who drank to excess in

Montreal after trading their furs might not have touched brandy since their last visit to the fur-trade emporium. Alcohol was a bulky, heavy product to transport by canoe and over portages the 1000 kilometres to Huronia, not to mention the greater distances to the more northerly fur-bearing areas south of James Bay. The French crown and Catholic missionaries discouraged the use of brandy as a trade item, although the competition from the English in the south and the Englishmen's apparent willingness to use the vast supplies of cheap rum they possessed for trade often meant that gubernatorial and clerical prohibitions were ignored. Still, the quantity of brandy reaching the more distant Indians could not have been very great during most of the seventeenth century. Finally, in interpreting the significance of the use of alcohol, it is important to consider the motives the Indians had in using it and the manner in which they employed it. To many the intoxication that could be derived from ardent spirits was merely an aid in the vision quest, a religious obligation. And Indians tended not to drink, whether in moderate or excessive amounts, regularly and persistently; they inclined more to the 'binge' style of consumption. While such habits were conducive neither to the imbibers' health nor the tranquillity of their neighbours, these ways of handling alcohol did not of themselves lead to alcoholism.

In fact, the role of alcohol in the erosion of Indian societies in this early period of contact is one fraught with confusion and contradiction. Some observers argue that alcohol brought on social disintegration and psychological collapse. Others argue that alcohol was the symptom rather than the cause of these social and personal debilities. Their argument is that the abuse of alcohol was motivated by a desire to escape the frustrations of a society already experiencing collapse, an implosion of values and social glues.[6] In some accounts the excessive use of alcohol is a subconscious act of rebellion: the Indian is an adolescent; the bottle is rock music; consumption is protest.[7] Whether Indians became demoralized because they drank too much, or whether they drank too much because they had been demoralized by other influences can never be known for sure. What is beyond doubt is that alcohol, whether cause or effect, was associated with demoralization.

Almost as imponderable is the therapeutic use that Indians may have made of the Europeans' alcohol. Indian societies were, perforce, close-knit and intense. Peoples living and working together found themselves in steady, intimate, and perhaps stressful relations. The need for occasional release from these pressures would have been great. There is some evidence to suggest that Indians sometimes used alcohol for such purposes, or, if they did so and transgressed, excused themselves by blaming their misbehaviour on the alcohol. The Jesuit Le Jeune reported that a Montagnais rebuffed an accusation from a French official that he was responsible for killing an Iroquois prisoner and thereby spoiling chances of making peace by saying, 'It is thou ... and thine, who killed him; for, if thou hadst not given us brandy or wine, we would not have done it.'[8] Alcohol served as a licence to permit, and an excuse to expiate, actions against people that in a normal, sober state would be unacceptable. As such, it might have served a therapeutic function in close-knit Indian communities.

The effect of the introduction of European firearms into Indian society was equally difficult to determine. Again, as with alcohol, the French made greater efforts than did the English to restrict the dissemination of muskets, trying so far as possible not to trade them with any but converted Indians. Even if this policy was effectively and consistently followed, it had to be abandoned as competition from the English who traded weapons freely drove the French to make muskets, powder, and ball available to their commercial partners too. These weapons had an important impact on Indian warfare and on the Indians' ability to kill animals and fowl. Prior to the intervention of Europeans there certainly had been war, but it had been small-scale, localized, and not very destructive. The introduction of firearms changed this pattern by making warfare more devastating. Now an opponent or rival could be killed more easily than would have been the case had it been necessary to stalk him and strike with arrow, club, or bone-tipped spear. However, given the unreliability and inaccuracy of the musket of this era, care must be taken not to overestimate how much damage Indians could do with the new weapon.

Similarly, the musket made depredations on the animals more effective just as extensive commerce created new incentives to kill more animals in search of furs to trade. What is obvious about this change is that Indians with muskets had greater capability to kill much larger numbers of birds and animals more easily. What seems almost as obvious is that they employed the new technology to harvest more furs, a response to the incentive of the new commerce. What is not as clear is the effect of these changes on the Indians' relationship to the natural world. Did the introduction of commercial motivations and large-scale harvesting dilute or destroy the Indians' perceptions of the animals they killed as fellow sojourners on earth? Did the fact that they were now, apparently, taking many more animals, and taking them for commercial reasons rather than subsistence, destroy the mammals', rodents', and fowls' place in the Indians' mental map of the cosmos? The evidence on this point is neither clear nor unequivocal, but it is difficult to imagine how such large changes in the Indians' treatment of the creatures of the natural world could not have led to alterations of their interpretation of animals' role in the universe.

As the interpretive puzzles surrounding alcohol and Indians' relations to animals hint, one of the areas of greatest potential influence was religion. The Indian peoples of North America were not religious ignoramuses, not spiritual blank sheets of paper on which missionaries wrote their Word. Theirs was an animistic religion: they believed that creation was inhabited by spirits that had to be treated according to rituals passed from generation to generation. Human beings had no distinctive or elevated role in the world. Indians' relationship to the spirits and to the Great Spirit was no different from that of the beaver or the stream or the trees. Closely associated with such beliefs was a system of ethics that espoused communalism, consensual practices, and a high degree of tolerance. All such tenets of Indian religion would come under systematic attack.

Missionaries differed among themselves, as did Frenchmen in general. There were those in both the mercantile and clerical communities in New France who regarded the Indians as *ni foi, ni roi, ni loi* – as people without religion, without a political system, and without the restraint of a code of law.[9] There were others who appreciated, especially after prolonged exposure to Indian communities, that the indigenous population had religious beliefs and their own codes of conduct and political decision-making. The problem was, so far as these observers were concerned, that the beliefs were those of the devil and the legal and political codes were wrong-headed. Whether Indians held wrong beliefs or no beliefs, they should be exposed to correct beliefs and converted. Or so missionaries believed.

The impact of the missionary thrust in New France was significant. In both Acadia and in the interior of the continent, Catholic missionaries worked assiduously under trying circumstances to spread their message. Their first success came in 1610 when the Micmac chief Membertou and twenty of his family were converted. This was the beginning of the extensive, enduring conversion of the Micmac. Throughout New France, missionaries faced a language barrier that could be surmounted only if they learned the Indian language. In the case of the nomadic Algonkian, this was very difficult, as ministering to them generally was. Missionaries who wanted to preach to them had to travel and live with them. Those who did so in Acadia or far north of the River of Canada found their desire for martyrdom largely met by the living hell they experienced. The hardships of travel, the privations of hunger, and the inconveniences of living in close proximity with people whose customs differed greatly from those of the European were all trials for the missionaries.

Things were little better for those Jesuits who resided with sedentary Iroquoians such as the Huron to learn the language and propagate Christianity. While living in a Huron longhouse was not as difficult as living with a small band of nomadic Algonkian, it was not easy either. Even after the Jesuits secured permission to establish separate dwellings in Huron villages, the black robes found their life a trial. Hostile Indians ridiculed them and embarrassed them by teaching the priests obscenities while supposedly introducing them to the Huron vocabulary. Youngsters frequently bothered them, and the sociable Indians thought nothing of entering their dwellings at any hour of the day. The fact that Indians indulged their children much more than Europeans did simply made the pestering of the children all the more difficult to end. (For their part, the Indians were aghast at the firm discipline Europeans exercised on their children, to the point that they called French mothers 'porcupines' because of their apparent lack of tenderness towards their children.)[10] Many would-be converts drew back when they learned that conversion meant that they would spend the after-life apart from their kin. Converts could not participate in rituals such as the Feast of the Dead; they became outcasts in their own villages.

The chief obstacle to the black robes, however, was not hardship or boisterous children; it was their professional rival, the shaman. Priest and shaman quickly sized each other up for the competitors that they were. These tribal curers and invokers of the spirit world sought at every turn to undermine the authority of the European preachers. The missionaries quickly learned to turn their knowledge against the shaman in the battle for followers. What medical training they had came in handy in curing the sick, effecting cures where shamanistic rituals and prayers had proven unavailing. When the black robe succeeded in curing someone from whom the shaman's incantations had failed to drive the evil spirit causing the malady, the efficacy of the missionary's spirit or *manito* rose in the estimation of the natives. If the missionary could – as Jesuits in Huronia did on one occasion – predict accurately an eclipse of the sun, the Indians would be impressed. And if the black robes prayed for rain for the crops prior to a shower, again their prestige rose and the power of the spirits they invoked became more obvious to the Indians.

The effects of the religious relations, as well as several other dimensions of the seventeenth-century relationship between indigenous Indians and French newcomers, can be seen in microcosm in the history of the Jesuit missions in Huronia in the 1630s and 1640s. This formidable effort was by no means the only evangelical project the Europeans undertook. There were priests working steadily in Acadia and in the north of the interior, and priests and nuns also carried out educational and medical efforts in Quebec. The Jesuits even experimented with a boarding school for Indian youths, but quickly gave it up in face of the boys' unhappiness. The creation of hospitals and provision of medical care, however, were successful and permanent missionary efforts carried on by both priests and nuns in the settlements. But the experiment in Huronia was nonetheless instructive about the Indian-European relationship.

In Huronia the Jesuits had to combat hostility, indifference, and hardship. They were tolerated at first only because they were essential to the fur trade. Their peculiar habits, such as an apparent aversion to women and their obsession with privacy, made them suspect in the eyes of many Huron. When disease began to ravage the Huron villages, the Jesuits responded by baptizing as many as possible in the hope of ensuring their place in heaven. Quickly Indians noted that those on whom the Jesuits sprinkled water and over whom they said incantations all too frequently died. The Jesuits were widely suspected of practising witchcraft against the Huron, and they might well have been murdered had their Huron hosts not feared that violence against them would destroy the commercial connection.

In the 1640s the fortunes of the Huron declined while those of the evangelists were in the ascendant. The ravages of disease were now exacerbated by a series of raids on Huronia by the Iroquois from south of Lake Ontario, who sought apparently to disperse the Huron as they had the Mahican earlier in order to gain unchallenged access to hunting and fur-bearing territories. The fact that the Iroquois were armed with muskets from Albany made their attacks all the more destructive. Within Huronia there were two quite different responses to the twin scourges. Many Huron accepted conversion to Christianity, or at least apparent conversion. How far these conversions were motivated, subconsciously perhaps, by the fact that converts enjoyed a privileged trading relationship with the French and could barter with the newcomers for firearms is impossible to know. The wave of baptisms divided the Huron Confederacy just as disease and Iroquois attacks seriously threatened it. Among Huron traditionalists – the unconverted whom the Jesuits termed pagans – it became a moot point whether succumbing to the Iroquois quickly was worse than eventual collapse as disease and conversion proceeded apace. The presence of convert and traditionalist factions within the villages loosened the cohesive bonds among the Huron. Converts could not join in rituals, would not travel or work on their sabbath, and frequently refused to participate in the sharing practices that were essential to Huron life.

As events transpired, baffled traditionalists found that the question was settled for them by the Iroquois. In 1648 and 1649 the Five Nations conducted extensive campaigns that destroyed Huronia. Hundreds were killed, several Jesuit priests were martyred, and the advanced and sophisticated civilization that was Huronia was terminated. Some Huron were absorbed voluntarily or as captives into the Iroquois villages to replace lost soldiers, others fled southwestward to link up with other Indian groups, and some returned eventually to the French towns in the St Lawrence valley for refuge.

The settlement of the refugee Huron at Ancienne Lorette near Quebec constituted the second Indian reserve in New France. Earlier a group of Algonkian had unsuccessfully tried to develop an agricultural settlement under Jesuit leadership at Sillery. Later, refugee Abenaki from the Maritime region and Mohawk converts from Iroquoia would form the basis of two more reserves, those on the Chaudière River and at Sault St Louis, or Caughnawaga, southwest of Montreal. The various reserves were under both the spiritual and material direction of missionaries, and, while the purpose of the priests was to convert the inhabitants to Christianity and agriculture, other aspects of native culture, such as language, were not attacked. Reserve settlements at St Regis, west of Caughnawaga on the south shore of the St Lawrence, and Oka, on the confluence of the Ottawa and St Lawrence rivers that was known as Lake of Two Mountains, rounded out these groupings of what became known as the 'praying Indians' of New France.[11]

The unhappy experiences of such groups as the Huron and the Abenaki were instructive about the relationships of Europeans and Indians in seventeenth-century Canada, but care should be taken not to draw too drastic conclusions from the fact that the Hurons' fate was destruction, dispersion, and death. Commercial wars were not new; they did not arrive with the Europeans and their trade goods. There was considerable evidence of both trade networks and commercial warfare from the period before European contact. Just as it is essential to avoid concluding that the contact was utterly negative for the Indians, it is important to appreciate that the changes that the Europeans brought with them were merely another in a long series of evolutionary phases that Indian societies – like all human societies – experienced. As Trigger has argued, Indian societies were not static but dynamic before contact; they continued to evolve after the white people came. Europeans did not introduce change into Indian society; they were merely the latest form of change.[12]

And what sorts of modifications, on both sides of the relationship, did the meeting of indigenous peoples and Frenchmen in North America produce in the seventeenth century? As has been noted, most of the changes that the Europeans experienced were positive. As a result of interaction, profits from fishing were possible. Thanks to the cooperation of the Indians there emerged a thriving fur trade that underwrote most of the settlement and development that occurred in New France. And yet it is important not to exaggerate the size of this French presence. As Eccles has observed, fur traders were like mariners rather than farmers: they ranged over the territories from which they extracted riches without changing those regions to any great extent.[13] Moreover, the commercial frontier was dependent for its continued success and profitability on not allowing agricultural settlement, which threatened the ecology on which traditional Indian economies and ways of life depended, to flourish. A commercial New France was a colony with low population, a colony that bore lightly on the land and its native inhabitants.

Indian participation in the vital commerce in fur also extended the French presence and influenced its reshaping into something discernibly Canadian. It was thanks to the fur trade and its Indian participants that French exploration of the interior networks of waterways was possible. If at the end of the seventeenth century the French commercial empire stretched from the Gaspé to Louisiana and from Tadoussac to the regions south of Lake Superior, it was because Indians made that expansion possible. They permitted it; they helped by serving as guides; their native means of transportation and food supplies enabled the French to traverse their commercial hinterland. None of this would have been possible without Indian cooperation. And the close and constant proximity to Indian society that this cooperation brought about caused the French, or *Canadiens* as they preferred to be called, to change in attitudes and practices. The European new-comers adopted many elements of Indian dress, language, and spirit of independence and aversion to coercion. A large part of the emerging Canadian identity that French officials decried in the eighteenth century had its roots in contact with Indian society.

And, of course, Indians changed, too, as a result of contact with the *gens du fer*. They now had access to weapons, household goods, decorative items, and alcohol, all of which they embraced with enthusiasm. In some cases they may have developed a dependence on these goods and allowed their customary techniques and equipment to fall into desuetude. The strengthening of the commercial motive for hunting may have begun to reshape their attitudes towards the creatures of the natural world. Certainly firearms and iron tools made it possible to harvest larger numbers more quickly. And the Indian nations were dramatically affected by the diseases that the Europeans unwittingly introduced. In some cases, as in Huronia in the 1630s, the impact of disease was horrendous.

But while the European presence undoubtedly worked changes on Indian society as early as the seventeenth century, it did not fundamentally remake it. Even the use of iron goods did not mean the adoption of European attitudes towards those items and their accumulation. The devotion of the new articles to such old practices as funerary rituals is a strong argument against exaggerating the degree of change. Even the notorious alcohol in some cases was used as an aid to conventional Indian religious practices. In the language of the anthropologists, European technology brought about 'non-directed change': it was change that affected surface appearances but did not alter underlying attitudes.[14] The most important thing about non-directed cultural change was that it did not disrupt the bases of society or alter its internal relationships.

It is easy to explain why European influence in this early period was limited. The Europeans were too few to force much change; and most of them had no reason to want change in Indian society. French cartographers lacked a reason to try to transform Indians into bronze Frenchmen. Explorers needed knowledgeable and skilled people to guide them; they had no reason to get them to alter the very ways that made them successful navigators and guides in the wilderness. Similarly, fur traders wanted to exploit, not modify, existing hunting methods and dress. And, finally, the French military presence was one that lived in 'creative symbiosis' with the Indians as well.[15] The Indians were valuable allies precisely because of their ability to survive in and fight effectively from the woods. The frontiers of commerce and navigation created no impetus to remodel the natives, and, in any event, the newcomers were too few to effect change.

But what of the missionaries? Did they not want to bring about a transformation of Indian society? Some, such as the Recollets in the early years, did. Others, such as the much more numerous Jesuits, did not believe that assimilation was a necessary precondition to conversion. But did missionaries not want to change Indian belief systems, and did they not succeed in the many cases of conversion that they recorded with prayerful thanks? Certainly, missionaries hoped to implant Christian beliefs in Indian minds or souls. And certainly many Indians said that they accepted those beliefs. But what is impossible to determine is how deep conversion went.

The test of a shaman's claims to authenticity was whether or not his dreams were proved valid, whether his cures were effective, and whether his placating of the spirits was efficacious. When the black robes were proved by subsequent events to have predicted or prayed effectively, their credibility as shamans and the stock of their god rose. When they failed, they often found their new converts lapsing. Many so-called Indian converts simply incorporated the Christian god into their religion alongside the many other spirits. Some were thoroughly converted, no doubt, but many probably were only partial or temporary converts.[16] And, since the missionaries were few in number relative to the Indians, they could not have had much effect on Indian societies in general. It is important not to exaggerate the long-term impact of the evangelical efforts, just as it is essential to keep perspective on the limited changes that the fishermen, traders, administrators, and soldiers wrought.

During the seventeenth century, then, French and Indians interacted along commercial, evangelical, and navigational frontiers. The results of that encounter were mainly beneficial because the Europeans were few and because the interactions took place over the astrolabe, across the trading counter, and within the rustic chapel. In the eighteenth century, military cooperation, which had been a minor aspect of the relationship in the seventeenth century, would become much more important. The consequent emergence of the Indian as ally would profoundly alter Indian-European relations in North America.

4

Military allies through a century of warfare

Of the many aspects of Indian-European relations, none is more misunderstood than the military. Europeans often claimed that Indians' destructive style of warfare proved that they were inherently barbarous and savage. These condemnations reached a crescendo during the American Revolution, when both American propagandists and British opposition politicians accused the English military of 'loosing' Indians on innocent farmers in the Thirteen Colonies. The Indians were said to be gorily addicted to scalping and torturing prisoners. These charges were unfounded.

Indian warfare was different from European warfare not because it was Indian but because it was North American. Indian nations had not had long periods of familiarity with explosives that led to the development of strategies that employed artillery, infantry, and naval vessels in complicated schemes of attack, siege, and defence. Nor did Indian societies have complex dynastic relationships among them that were, as in the European case, based both on blood and marriage. Finally, Indian societies did not have a rigid hierarchical organization and coercive system of decision-making and enforcement that allowed rulers and generals to throw thousands of common people into bloody confrontations. Indians simply did not fight as the Europeans did, with large formations of infantry backed up by artillery in structured clashes that resulted in enormous loss of life.

The North American environment and the nature of Indians' social and political structures ensured that their approach to warfare would be small-scale, relatively bloodless, and usually of short duration. North American geography led the Indians to concentrate their efforts on what the French called *la petite guerre*, or guerilla warfare. The difficulties of travel and of maintaining supply lines ensured that war parties were usually small. They travelled quickly to the target, fell on the enemy, and retired swiftly with their trophies and prisoners. In many cases, warriors were motivated by a desire to prove their manliness as much as anything else, and here small-scale raids satisfied them, too. Indian warfare consisted of ambushes from forest cover, raids on unsuspecting encampments or travelling parties, and brief clashes. To European military officers such warfare was cowardly and treacherous; to Indians it was sensible, suited to their world, and appropriate to their military objectives.

Much of the misunderstanding over Indian warfare stemmed not just from Indians' style of battle but also from the way they treated their captives. Europeans accused Indians of barbarity for their torture and scalping of victims. People from the patriarchal old world were particularly aghast at the prominent role that women played in torture: 'You should have seen these furious women,' they said, 'howling, yelling, applying fire to the most sensitive and private parts of the body, pricking them with awls, biting them with savage glee, laying open their flesh with knives; in short, doing everything that madness can suggest to a woman. They threw fire upon them, burning coals, hot sand; and when the sufferers cried out, all the others cried still louder, in order that the groans should not be heard, and that no one might be touched with pity.'[1] Such practices shocked French and British alike.

The Europeans' revulsion arose from an ethnocentrically inspired misunderstanding. In the first place, many of the captives whom Indian parties took in battle were not tortured or killed but adopted by families of the victorious nation to replace fallen kin. Other captives were enslaved, either used as drudges in the victors' camp or bartered to the French. Those who were tortured were part of a religious ritual that honoured the sun, the patron of war. The purpose of torture was in large part to break the enemy's spirit and reassure the victors that they were braver and hardier than their foes. In the treatment of female prisoners, Indians were much more humane than victorious Europeans, among whom brutal rape and collective violence were common. When a female Iroquois prisoner who had been handed over to the French was asked if she feared mistreatment, 'She replied that she was now of their Nation; that she did not fear they would do her any harm.'[2] Her reaction reflected attitudes that had been built up in response to Indian treatment of female prisoners.

When cannibalism and scalping occurred, the newcomers failed to understand the significance of what was taking place. Eating the flesh of the captive – especially the heart of an enemy who had endured torture with particular stoicism – was a means of absorbing the spirits that accounted for the victim's more laudable qualities. And, as Jaenen has pointed out, it was somewhat obtuse of Europeans 'who believed in transubstantiation and literally eating their Lord in their communion service' to miss the spiritual significance of native cannibalism.[3]

Scalping, like ritual cannibalism, was misunderstood by the Europeans. The taking of trophies had, after all, been a common enough practice among all armies at least since records were kept. Indians took heads, scalps, individual limbs, or even a quarter of the body as evidence of their victory. Scalps were particularly useful to record the triumph and for later use in taunting the comrades of the fallen enemy. There were few things better to wave in front of a captive who was being tortured. Scalps were also conveniently portable and could be carried on future raids, both to reassure the attackers and, if opportunity arose, to taunt the attacked. Surely the people of countries who guillotined, hanged, drew, and quartered those guilty of any of hundreds of offences, and who put heads on pikes as a warning to others, should have been able to understand the symbolic, cheer-leading, and deterrent purposes of such native North American practices.

In any event, as is well known, it was the Europeans who encouraged and promoted the growth of scalping by offering bounties for enemy scalps. Moreover, the existence of iron knives made scalping – never an easy physical feat – less difficult than it had been. There is even some evidence that European bounties encouraged the adoption of scalping where it was previously unknown. The Micmac of the Maritimes, for example, apparently did not scalp captives until their French friends taught them to do it.[4] Where scalping had previously existed, it grew thanks in large part to bounties that the English and the French began to pay in the late seventeenth century. Killing and scalping captives became the favoured procedure; taking them back alive to be ransomed by the Europeans was now uneconomic as well as dangerous.

Above all, Indians did not engage in warfare because it was endemic to them; they had no more blood-lust than any other human community. Indian warfare was motivated by desires for revenge, for commercial advantage, and to replenish populations lost to disease and battle. From the first French martial encounter, Champlain's participation with Algonkians against Iroquoians, to the protracted wars between French and Iroquois in the late seventeenth century, the underlying motive on the Indian side was commercial. The French, the Huron, and most northern Algonkians were commercial rivals of the southern Iroquoians and their Dutch and English trading partners at Albany; raids and battles were merely commercial 'policy by other means' for the Iroquois. The Five Nations warred systematically against the neighbouring Mahican in the 1620s and 1630s, against the Huron and other northerly Iroquoians in the 1630s and 1640s, and against the other trading partners of the French intermittently from the 1650s until a treaty of peace and neutrality was concluded in 1701. The principal purpose of these campaigns was to eliminate rivals, as well as to gain access to their hunting territories and transportation routes. The French sometimes considered the Iroquois especially barbarous, but the Five Nations were simply acting as did Algonkian allies of the French, often with French support and encouragement. Indian warfare had limited objectives; it was not the manifestation of some insatiable blood-lust.

Indian warfare and European attitudes towards it became more important in the eighteenth century than they had been earlier because the Age of Reason, ironically, turned out to be a century-long battle for control of North America. During the first six decades of the century a struggle between France and England for supremacy embroiled a number of Indian nations in the toils of European dynastic and national ambitions. During the next sixty years, from the Peace of Paris in 1763 to the end of the War of 1812, the victorious British and Anglo-Americans decided, and then reconfirmed, a subdivision of the continent they had wrested from the French earlier. In all these phases of the struggle for America, from the War of the Spanish Succession to the War of 1812, the Indians played a vital role because of their numbers and because most of the struggles took place in Indian-controlled territory. During this century of continental war the three principal arenas of struggle were Acadia, the interior region south and southwest of the lower Great Lakes, and the valley of the St Lawrence.

The shift of emphasis from the Indian as navigator, trader, and proselyte to the Indian as warrior and ally began in 1700 because of French strategic considerations. Rivalries over succession to the Spanish throne led France to prepare for war with other European powers. To guard against the eventuality of war with England, French officials began to strengthen their strategic position throughout the world, including North America. Orders were issued to build a string of military forts along the interior track of fur-trading posts through the Ohio and Illinois country, linking up with France's southern colony of Louisiana to create a military chain-link fence that would pen in the Thirteen Colonies east of the Allegheny mountains.

Such an ambitious plan, the North American facet of a global strategy, could only work if France neutralized England's principal Indian ally and turned its own commercial links with a variety of tribes into a military alliance. The first of these policies, neutralizing the Iroquois, was accomplished temporarily by a critically important treaty with the Five Nations that was concluded in 1701. The Iroquois signed because their position between Canada and New England made them potential targets of both European powers. Since they stood to gain little from the victory of either state, they sought neutrality. By the treaty of 1701 the Iroquois promised to remain neutral in any conflict that might break out between England and France. This was important for the French not only because it ended the wars with the Iroquois that had been going on since the 1640s, but also because it deprived England of its most formidable ally in North America. In the past the French had regarded the Iroquois as both the greatest enemy and the essential protection of their commercial empire in New France. The Iroquois raids so overwhelmed the French settlements and their fur-trade

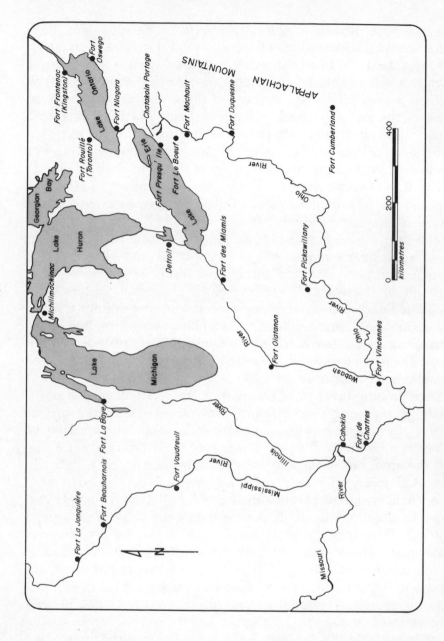

The Ohio and Illinois country, 1754

network that at their height, as an Iroquois chief boasted, 'they were not able to goe over a door to pisse.'[5] But as threatening as the Iroquois were, they were essential to the French fur trade: if they had not blocked the path to Albany, tribes in the interior would have been able to go to the English post there. The 1701 treaty removed the Iroquois as a military threat, though they still acted as a barrier to commerce between Indians of the interior and the English merchants. For the Iroquois, this treaty marked a shift to a strategy of neutrality in the struggles of the Europeans.

The tactic of neutralizing the Iroquois by treaty did not have a lasting effect. The Iroquois became once again, at least nominally, allies of the British by the Treaty of Utrecht (1713), by which France recognized British suzerainty over the Iroquois Confederacy. (The Iroquois Confederacy consisted of Six Nations now that the Tuscarora had been incorporated into it.) To a great extent this setback was mitigated by two factors. France blithely ignored its commitment to treat the Iroquois as subjects of the British whenever it suited French military interests to do so, and the Iroquois' behaviour was predicated on the assumption that they owed obedience to no other power. The Six Nations continued to pursue their own interests, as they always had done.

During the remainder of the struggle between France and Britain for control of North America, Indian alliances were vital in all areas of the contest. In the north, where France occasionally captured Hudson's Bay Company posts such as Fort Prince of Wales, the assistance of their Indian allies was important both to journey overland to the marge of James Bay and to hold the fort once they had taken it. In the Maritime region, France officially conceded 'Acadia with its ancient limits' to Britain by the Treaty of Utrecht, but fortunately no one knew where those limits lay, and the Micmac and other Indians of the region did not regard themselves as bound by any agreement European powers made. From 1713 to the fall of Acadia in 1758, French strategy in the Maritime theatre relied on the Micmac as well as their naval base on Cape Breton, Louisbourg. Louisbourg, as its repeated capture by American colonial and British forces illustrated, possessed more the illusion of strength than the reality, but the Micmac alliance was a real source of military advantage to France in its confrontation with the British in Acadia. Finally, the French were able to use their

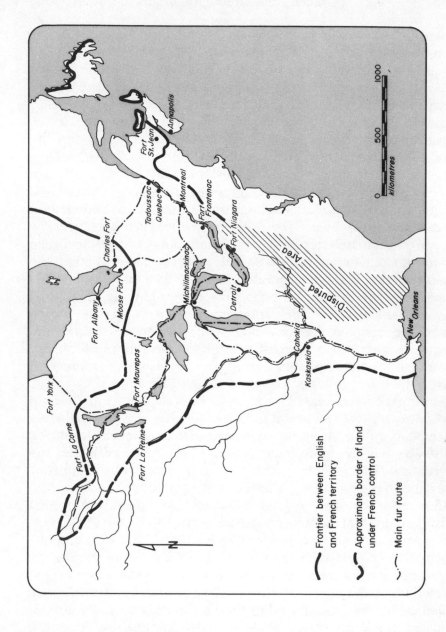

French possessions in North America, 1750

Fort St. Jean
Annapolis
Montreal
Tadoussac
Quebec
Fort Frontenac
Fort Niagara
Charles Fort
Michilimackinac
Detroit
Moose Fort
Fort Albany
New Orleans
Cahokia
Kaskaskia
Fort York
Fort Maurepas
Fort La Corne
Fort La Reine

Disputed Area

1000
500
0
kilometres

N

—— Frontier between English
and French territory

) Approximate border of land
under French control

–·– Main fur route

commercial links with Indian tribes as the basis of military alliance in the southwest interior, the Ohio-Illinois country south of the lower Great Lakes.

But why did the Indians respond to the European struggle by siding largely with the French? In the first place, it is important to note that there was no uniform Indian reaction, no single pattern of Indian military behaviour. The Micmac were solidly pro-French, the Iroquois sought to play French and English off against each other to their own advantage, and the tribes of the southwest interior were usually pro-French. The Iroquois strategy was easily understood: given their vulnerable location, and given their exhaustion from the protracted struggle with the French in the seventeenth century, it made perfect sense for them to try to sit out the wars and to profit as much as they could from the European rivalries that lay behind them. To both British and French, this brinkmanship often made the Iroquois look treacherous and unreliable. Such judgments misunderstood Iroquois motives and underestimated Iroquois strategic sense: the Six Nations were jockeying for position just as the British and French were.

The Maritime and interior Indians tended usually to side with the French and *Canadiens* in these territorial struggles. They acted from self-interest, and pursued their own objectives. In the eastern region that is today mainland Nova Scotia and northern New Brunswick, there were two factors that accounted for the solid support of the French. The first was religion: the long-standing presence of Catholic missionaries in the region had led to the development of close ties between Micmac and the French. The descendants of Membertou were the Indian people who, in the seventeenth and eighteenth centuries, seem to have experienced the most extensive and thorough conversion to Christianity. In the eighteenth century Catholicism would be both a continuing link between Indian and European, and the Indians' badge of defiance against the British who, after 1713, claimed their territory and tried to force them to acknowledge the suzerainty of the Protestant power. Maintaining the Catholic faith, like refusing to take an oath of allegiance to the British crown, was an effective manner of expressing Micmac support of and identification with the French. The French, in turn, used Jesuit agents to maintain the Indian alliance in Acadia and to encourage Micmac hostility to the British.

Underlying the Micmac predisposition towards Catholic France rather than Protestant Britain was another factor that had nothing to do with denominational loyalties. Indian nations in general perceived the two European powers in North America differently because they were different economically. 'In the seventeenth century, the Amerindians seem to have stereotyped the Englishman as a farmer or town-dweller whose activities gradually drove the original agriculturalists deeper into the hinterland, whereas the stereotype of the Frenchman was a trader or soldier laden with baubles and brandy who asked only for furs and hospitality.'[6] Or as Iroquois converts to Catholicism put it in 1754: 'Brethren, are you ignorant of the difference between our Father [the French] and the English? Go see the forts our Father has erected, and you will see that the land beneath his walls is still hunting ground, having fixed himself in those places we frequent, only to supply our wants; whilst the English, on the contrary, no sooner get possession of a country than the game is forced to leave it; the trees fall down before them, the earth becomes bare, and we find among them hardly wherewithal to shelter us when the the night falls.'[7]

To many Indian nations the French were merchants and soldiers who did not want to take possession of their lands but merely to trade for the fruits of the forest; the British, though some of them were merchants, were also largely agricultural settlers who inexorably dispossessed the original inhabitants with their expanding farming settlements. Even in the Maritime region, where the Acadians were also farmers, the distinction held, because the settlers of French descent had farmed principally on diked and reclaimed land, not seriously infringing on traditional Micmac territories, while the British who moved into the peninsula in the eighteenth century established their farms on Indian land and across Indian transportation and hunting routes.[8] The French followed up on their religious links and on Micmac opposition to British possessiveness about the land by making generous presents to the Indians in order to maintain their support. Even so, the French sometimes complained that they were 'trahis par nos plus affidés Sauvages,' a complaint that testified to the Micmac's 'determination to make their own decisions despite the exhortations of French officials and missionaries.'[9] The Micmac pursued their own objectives, but given the differences in the forms that

British and French presence took, and aided by the religious ties to the Catholic French, they tended to favour the French in Acadia.

In the interior the issue was clearer: the French were less of a threat and more of a benefit than the English to the tribes south of the lower Great Lakes and down the Illinois and Mississippi valleys. French settlement in the valley of the St Lawrence was small-scale, and the region itself was uninhabited at the time the French villages began to develop. Further inland, in the Ohio and Illinois country, the French presence was military and commercial, not agricultural. But in some of these regions the Anglo-American agricultural expansion that was trying to poke its way through the Alleghenies threatened the lands that traditionally belonged to hunter-gatherers. Particularly from New York and Pennsylvania southward, the heavy emphasis on agriculture in the economy meant that the local white population was unwelcome in Indian country.

The French, in contrast, were in the region primarily for strategic reasons. Their continuation of a fur trade when it was no longer economic was a consequence of their desire to maintain alliances with the interior Indians so as to deny the interior to the British. France built military posts and made lavish gifts of trade goods, weapons, and ammunition to the tribes of the region, not because French merchants had a lucrative market in Europe for the inferior furs that could still be gathered in this region, but because the French military encouraged and underwrote commerce for purposes of alliance. Trade was but a means to a strategic end for the French. To the Indians of the region it little mattered what French motives were so long as they were compatible with Indian interests. The military and commercial French were no threat.

But the Pennsylvanians and Virginians who wanted to invade Indian territories to plant crops had to be repelled. In 1748–9 the stage was set for a decisive clash of the agricultural and military-commercial frontiers. In September 1748 the new governor of New France recommended a policy of retaining interior posts and maintaining Indian allies in spite of the fact that the fur trade of the Illinois country was no longer economically desirable. A few months later a group of leading Anglo-American entrepreneurs and plantation owners formed the Ohio Company to purchase half a million acres in the Ohio valley and to sell it in turn to would-be agricultural colonists from the seaboard. 'The military fur trade frontier was about to clash, head on, with the Anglo-American land settlement frontier.'[10]

This clash occurred in the 1750s in what the French called the Seven Years' War and the Americans, significantly, termed the French and Indian Wars. This campaign was merely another phase of the struggle that had begun with the War of the Spanish Succession and continued with the War of the Austrian Succession (1744–8). It was a struggle that saw most of the Indians of the southwest interior align themselves with the French against the British and land-hungry Anglo-Americans. The fact that the French gave lavish presents and seemed to hold the winning hand for much of the 1750s also induced many Indian tribes to support them. The French victories were attributable to their superior colonial military organization and to the Indian alliances. The Canadians might number only about one-tenth of the half million or so Thirteen Colonists, but every *Canadien* male was a trained militiaman. Repeatedly the Indians and French in the interior thrashed both British and American colonial troops that were sent into the region: Washington and his ragtag militiamen were sent packing from the Ohio valley in 1754; Braddock's forces were almost wiped out the next year by a combined Indian, Canadian, and French force that attacked his neat formations of red coats from forest cover.

What turned the tide against France and ensured the triumph of the agricultural frontier in Nova Scotia and the American interior was a shift not in the Western Hemisphere but in Europe. When Britain chose a 'blue-water strategy' that sought to take advantage of its superior naval power, it set in motion a series of events that starved the French and Canadian campaigns by interrupting the transoceanic flow of supplies from France. Victories of the British fleet off European coasts were more important than the tardy and dilatory taking of Louisbourg for the last time in 1758. Canada, with its support from France throttled by British dominance of the sea lanes, had to draw back from the interior. The line of forts was shortened, as French and Canadians fell back on their St Lawrence valley bastion. In Acadia, the British expelled the Acadians in 1755, took Louisbourg three years later, and established effective control of the region before the decade was over. Finally, in 1759 Quebec fell, and the following year British control of the seas ensured that France would not retake its colonial capital. When Montreal capitulated in 1760, the Seven Years' War ended in North America.

The arrangements that ended the struggle, the Peace of Paris of 1763 and the Royal Proclamation of the same year, fundamentally altered relations between Indians and Europeans. In the first place, by the Peace of Paris France ceded her title and claims to all territory in the northern part of North America save for a portion of the Newfoundland shore that her fishermen were accustomed to use. Second, the Royal Proclamation that the new rulers issued in 1763 laid down a number of limits and guidelines for all inhabitants of what had previously been France's interior colony, but had special interest for the Indians of the region south of the lower Great Lakes. The definition of the boundaries of the new British province called Quebec was a narrow one: the height of land north of the St Lawrence constituted the northern bound, and the southern was a line drawn arbitrarily and roughly parallel to the River of Canada that included the Gaspé peninsula but little else. The western boundary was another line drawn south from Lake Nipissing across the St Lawrence to the forty-fifth degree of latitude. Both the controversial 'Acadia with its ancient limits' and the southwestern hinterland were severed from their traditional commercial metropolis in the St Lawrence valley.[11] If France had abandoned Canada to the British by the Peace of Paris, then Britain had greatly trimmed the extent of its new possession.

But the section of the proclamation that had the greatest impact on the Indian peoples, both immediately and throughout the remainder of Canadian history, was not the boundary definition but the provisions concerning Indian lands: 'And whereas it is just and reasonable, and essential to our Interest, and the Security of our Colonies, that the several Nations or Tribes of Indians with whom We are connected, and who live under our Protection, should not be molested or disturbed in the Possession of such Parts of Our Dominions and Territories as ... are reserved to them, or any of them, as their Hunting Grounds,' therefore, any lands that had 'not been ceded to or puchased by Us as aforesaid, are reserved to the said Indians.' Furthermore, 'We do hereby strictly forbid, on Pain of our Displeasure, all our loving Subjects from making any Purchases or Settlements whatever, or taking Posses-

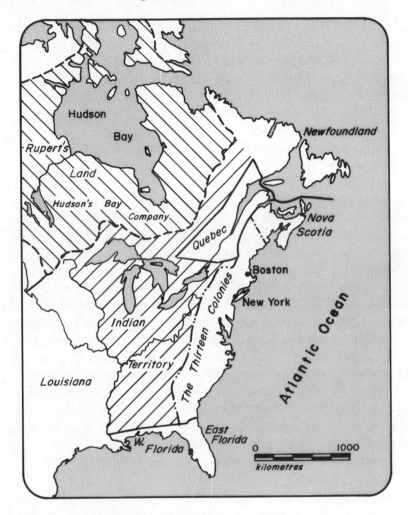

Effect of the Royal Proclamation of 1763

sion of any of the Lands above reserved, without our especial leave and Licence for that Purpose first obtained.' By the proclamation, 'no private Person' was allowed 'to make any purchase from the said Indians of any Lands reserved to the said Indians.' If Indians wanted to sell lands reserved to them, 'the same shall be Purchased only for Us, in our Name, at some public Meeting or assembly of the said Indians, to be held for the Purpose by the Governor or Commander in Chief of our Colony.' And, finally, the proclamation permitted trade with the Indians only to those who 'do take out a Licence for carrying on such Trade from the Governor or Commander in Chief of any of our Colonies.'[12]

These clauses of the Royal Proclamation were intended to avoid conflict between the indigenous population and land-hungry immigrants. The boundary definition, in combination with the restrictions on trade, meant that the interior hinterland was closed to agricultural expansion and subject only to limited commercial penetration. The provisions governing acquisition of Indian lands only by and through the crown were designed to prevent a species of semi-official fraud that had begun to develop in the Thirteen Colonies. The proclamation put a stop to schemes in which white land developers purported to purchase lands from dependent and/or unrepresentative Indians and then called on the colonial legislatures to make good their claim and protect the agricultural settlers who wanted to take up the newly acquired lands. That was the immediate purpose. In the longer term it would have even more profound implications. Indian organizations would later base part of their arguments for recognition of aboriginal title to unceded lands on the proclamation, which could reasonably be read to imply royal recognition that natives had rights to lands that pre-existed the assertion of British title. While this contention would by no means be the only legal basis of the twentieth-century arguments for aboriginal title, it would prove an important part of the modern case for Indian control of lands that had not been ceded to the crown.[13]

In 1763 and 1764 the interior Indians reacted to the French loss and the termination of their presents in an armed resistance led by Pontiac, a chief of the Ottawa. The immediate cause was a British decision to cut off the supply of presents that the French had employed to win and hold the allegiance of the Indians in the Illinois country. The fact that interior Indians had not been defeated in the Seven Years' War also spurred them. But underlying the conflict was the old antagonism between a frontier of commerce and an expanding margin of agricultural settlement. Pontiac's appeal to arms captured the conflict graphically: 'And as for these English, – these dogs dressed in red, who have come to rob you of your hunting grounds, and drive away the game, – you must lift the hatchet against them. Wipe them from the face of the earth, and thus you will win my favour back again, and once more be happy and prosperous. The children of your great father, the King of France, are not like the English.'[14] Before Pontiac and his warriors were cowed by British troops, they had taken several of the western posts and killed over 2000 settlers who menaced their lands. Even while making peace, Pontiac maintained that the Indians held title to the lands of the interior.[15] Although American historians would refer to the bloody and unsuccessful uprising as the 'Conspiracy of Pontiac,' it was only another angry response by hunter-gatherers to the encroachments of farmers.

The British military officials who now governed Quebec were not blind to either the restiveness of the Thirteen Colonies or the dangers of a full-scale Indian war in the interior. In part, the proclamation that closed the Ohio to settlement and outlawed entrepreneurial purchases of Indian lands was designed to prevent a clash between the Anglo-Americans and the Indians. Ironically, the British on the St Lawrence found themselves drawn into the same economic and military postures as the French and *Canadiens* they had ousted from power. In order to keep the interior tribes reasonably tranquil, the government of Quebec encouraged the resumption of the fur trade out of Montreal and cleared the way for continued Canadian commercial activities in the southwest interior. This British policy was confirmed in the Quebec Act of 1774, which restored the interior hinterland to the jurisdiction of Quebec. The adoption of this policy towards the Indians was instructive: it proved that the French had enjoyed better relations with the Indian nations than the British and Anglo-Americans, not because they were French, but because they were merchants and soldiers who did not threaten Indians and Indian lands as the Americans did. If there were any doubt of that fact, it was removed by the American Revolutionary War.

The rebellion of the Thirteen Colonies was partially incited by

British policy towards the interior Indians. Britain's policy was embodied in the Quebec Act, which the American rebels described as one of the 'Intolerable Acts' that justified their rising. Besides wanting to avoid an all-out Indian war in the interior, the British wished to retain the loyalty of the *Canadiens* and their traditional Indian allies in the event of an American rebellion. The restoration of the fur trade and the traditional pursuit of good relations with the Indians were components of this strategic plan. During the fighting after 1775, the British strategy of maximizing the advantages that its northern position and continued reliance on commerce in the St Lawrence colony gave it paid off. In the War of Independence, the alignment of the various Indian nations was extremely important. Thanks to the influence of geography and commerce, the British were supported by more of the Indian groups than were the land-hungry Americans.

There was no single pattern to the alliances between Indians and Europeans during the revolutionary war, and there was no truth to the charge that Indians made barbarous allies. The one consistent theme was that Indians chose their fighting partners, or in some cases chose not to fight at all, according to their own definition of where their interest lay. The erroneous notion that the British 'used' the Indians in the war against the colonists was articulated in the Declaration of Independence and reiterated by generations of American propagandists and historians. The Declaration of Independence charged that the British king 'has excited domestic insurrections among us, and has endeavoured to bring on the inhabitants of our frontiers, the merciless Indian Savages, whose known rule of warfare, is an undistinguished destruction of all ages, sexes, and conditions.'[16] And colonial propagandists put in the mouths of British officers such charming sentiments as:

I will let loose the dogs of hell,
Ten thousand Indians who shall yell,
And foam and tear, and grin and roar,
And drench their moccasins in gore.

They'll scalp your heads, and kick your shins,
And rip your guts, and flay your skins,
And of your ears be nimble croppers
And make your thumbs be tobacco-stoppers.[17]

Assumptions that Indians were 'used' and that their methods were barbaric were nonsense.

As the reaction of the various tribes of the Iroquois shows, the Indian response was based on a complex of factors, including the varied perceptions of Americans to the east and British and *Canadiens* to the north. The Iroquois minority who were most sympathetic to the rebels, the Oneida who advocated neutrality, were well disposed to the Americans principally because they had been ministered to for many years by Puritan missionaries from New England. And even the Oneida implied that Indians should consult their own self-interest when they pleaded, 'Let us Indians be all of one Mind & live in peace with one another, and you white people settle your own Disputes betwixt yourselves.'[18]

Those Iroquois who supported the British were motivated by a combination of personal ties and calculations that their lands would be better defended by the British, whose proclamation policy had kept back the land-hungry farmers, than by the colonies from which those American settlers came. In addition, the Mohawk were greatly influenced by their ties to the family of William Johnson, Britain's 'superintendent of Indian affairs for the Northern Department' after 1755, who from his base in the Mohawk valley of New York had distributed presents to the Indians and protected their lands from white encroachment.[19] Molly Brant, sister of the Mohawk leader Joseph, was married to William Johnson, and that connubial link serves as a reminder of the importance of personal ties, as well as the political role of women in Iroquoian society.[20] Also important was the Iroquoian perception that American power threatened them, a view that became embodied in their term for the commander-in-chief of American forces, the president. The Iroquois term for the president was, and is, 'town-destroyer.' This dubious title originated in the name they accorded George Washington, the future first president, after he marched through Iroquoia burning their palisaded villages.[21]

Finally, Indians such as the Mohawk and others to the south were motivated to support the British and Canadians by a desire to protect their lands. It was still the Americans who were trying to expand their agricultural frontier into what the proclamation had termed Indian 'hunting grounds,' and it was still the British who resisted that expansion. As some of the tribes in the Ohio country put it to a representative of the rebel Continental Congress: 'You have feloniously taken possession of part of our country on the branches of the Ohio, as well as the Susquehanna, to the latter we have some time since sent you word to quit our Lands as we now do to you, as we don't know we ever gave you liberty, nor can we be easy in our minds while there is an arm'd Force at our very doors.' They added, 'we now tell you in a peaceful manner to quit our lands wherever you have possessed yourselves of them immediately, or blame yourselves for whatever may happen.'[22] Those Indians, such as the Mohawk and some Cherokee further south, who allied themselves with the British were doing as Pontiac had a decade earlier. They threw their support behind commerce and against agricultural expansion. 'They were neither beasts howling for blood for its own sake, nor merely paid pawns of the whites. For them, the Revolution was another bitter episode in a struggle as old as European settlement in North America.'[23]

Much of the bitterness that Indians experienced in this latest phase of alliance with the Europeans in the north stemmed less from the destruction of wartime than the dispossession wrought in the peace. The group that had thrown its support to the victors fared worst of all. Although the Oneida were supposed to be conceded lands in their traditional territories, it was not long until the surging agricultural frontier overtook and dispossessed them. The Mohawk were at first chagrined to discover that their territorial claims had been abandoned in the talks that produced the 1783 Treaty of Versailles. British negotiators recklessly surrendered all claims to the lands south of the lakes that they, the Canadians, or the Indians had held. This betrayal prompted one chieftain to reprimand a British official: 'The King surely would not pretend to give the Americans that which was not his to give; and would not believe that the Americans would accept that which the King had not power to give. They were allies of the King, not subjects; and would not submit to such treatment ... If England had done so it was an act of cruelty and injustice and capable only of *Christians*.'[24] The anger of betrayed Indian allies was intense.

Britain's response was to make provision to resettle the principal of her Indian allies north of the lakes. Land was purchased from the Mississauga and other branches of the Ojibwa, and comrades-in-arms from the Six Nations were invited to share parts of the territory that soon would become Upper Canada with white-skinned Loyalists. A large group of Iroquois numbering over 1500 and led by Captain Joseph Brant settled a large tract along both sides of the Grand River in the vicinity of present-day Brantford, while a smaller number under the leadership of Captain John Deseronto established themselves on the Bay of Quinte. Britain was motivated to establish refuges for Iroquoian allies both out of a sense of obligation to them and out of a desire to retain their loyalty and military alliance.

For a decade after 1783 the British continued to shape their policy according to their desire to maintain peace while retaining the support of Indian nations both south and north of the lower Great Lakes. Fear of an Indian uprising that might embroil the British and Americans in another war accounted for the fact that, from 1783 to 1794, Britain violated the terms of the Treaty of Versailles by maintaining control of the posts in Indian territory. The pro-claimed, but in reality minor, reason for this retention of the western posts was the refusal of the American Congress to honour Loyalist claims for damages in their old home territories; the real motive was fear of an Indian uprising along the lines of Pontiac's campaign of 1763–4. At times British representatives even har-boured unrealistic hopes of encouraging the formation of an Indian buffer state between the United States and their own new settlements to the north of the lakes, but any chance of such a grand strategy's success collapsed thanks to events in Europe.

When Britain went to war with France in 1793, her planners felt compelled to normalize relations with the United States. One of the major outstanding issues was the illegal retention of the posts. Furthermore, the Americans had indicated by a series of Indian wars that they had fought since the 1780s, and which had culminated in a rout of the Indians in the Battle of Fallen Timbers in 1794, that the new republic was determined to take effective control of the lands that the Treaty of Versailles had, rightly or wrongly, given it. Britain, in search of peace with her former colonies, pulled back from her commitment to the Indians in the disputed region south of the lakes and concluded Jay's Treaty with the Americans in 1794. But even this pact had an interesting legacy for some North American Indians. Once again, Britain made some provision for its former Indian allies whose interests it was abandoning, this time by purchasing land for up to 3000 of them from the Ojibwa along the Thames River in southwestern Ontario. Jay's Treaty had other, longstanding consequences. Ever since 1794 some of the Indians affected by it, such as the St Regis band, have claimed the status of an independent nation. They insist that they are neither American nor Canadian, and claim that they have the right of free passage across the international border in such localities as Cornwall, Ontario.

Relations between Indians and Europeans in the eighteenth century revolved around military alliance. The fact that the European powers were engaged in a protracted struggle to determine the political affiliation of the northern part of North America meant that Indians were increasingly important to the whites as military allies. Indians did not cease entirely to play their customary roles as guides and navigators, commercial partners, and objects of proselytization. On the contrary, European exploration of the continent continued, although in the eighteenth century it was increasingly focused on the lands far to the west of the Great Lakes basin. The fur trade continued to draw Indians and Europeans into a mutually beneficial relationship, although its locus, too, after the 1780s was to be found increasingly in more northerly latitudes. And the missionaries certainly continued their ministrations in the eighteenth century, although for a time they were subordinated to military objectives. But, while the commercial, navigational, and evangelical contacts continued to be important, the relationship of allies largely predominated.

In the military relationship the Indian continued to play a major, perhaps even predominant, role. Particularly down to the end of the Seven Years' War, the desire to maintain Indian military support largely determined European actions. As the heavy flow of presents to the Indians clearly indicated, the Europeans badly needed the natives. But if the military relationship of the eighteenth century continued to be one in which the Indian was the dominant partner, it was a break with the seventeenth-century pattern of relations in that the results of the interaction were mainly negative for the Indians. Obviously, a century of on-and-off warfare meant major losses of life for the Indians. These were costs that the Indians reckoned before entering into military association. In the final analysis, however, the relationship was disastrous because the power that represented the agricultural frontier – first Britain and the Anglo-Americans, then the Americans – triumphed over the more northerly commercial frontier. Britain and the Anglo-Americans defeated the French and *Canadiens*; then the Americans defeated the combined forces of the British and Quebec. When the final reckoning came, the Indian allies suffered substantial territorial losses.

PART TWO

COERCION

5

From alliance to irrelevance

Between the 1790s and the 1830s Indian-white relations in the eastern third of the continent changed profoundly. In both the Maritime and central regions peace was followed by substantial immigration, first of Loyalists and later of British settlers. The bulk of this influx deposited itself in Nova Scotia and the region west of the Ottawa River, although some migrants entered Quebec and marginally affected relations there. As important as the influx of settlers destined to clear the forest and establish farms were two other factors: the end of the Montreal-based fur trade and the normalization of relations between the new republic in the south and Great Britain. The amalgamation of Montreal's North West Company with the Hudson's Bay Company in 1821 stopped fur-trade operations from Montreal. At a single stroke, commercial cooperation between eastern Indians and the European was drastically diminished. At about the same time, a smoothing of relations between the United States and Great Britain occurred first in the Maritime region and somewhat later in the central colonies of Lower Canada and Upper Canada. This reconciliation removed the threat from the south and diminished the military significance of Indians in the eyes of British planners.

The lessening of the American menace, the presence of greatly increased numbers of Anglo-American and British colonists, and the termination of the Montreal-based fur trade changed the

European's approach to the relationship with the indigenous population. The association was no longer one that emphasized military alliance, but rather one in which the dominant partner sought the removal of the Indian from the path of agricultural settlement. To both the British official and the frontier farmer the Indian became less desirable as a comrade-in-arms; increasingly the Indian was an impediment to the objectives that the white population had in an era of peace and settlement. In short, the Indian in eastern British North America declined in military importance. From 'the point of view of the European, the Indian had become irrelevant.'[1]

The most immediate problem after the close of the revolutionary war had been the angry reaction of Britain's erstwhile allies south of the lower Great Lakes. Provision had to be made for the allies, especially the Mohawk, who had been dispossessed. An obvious place to look for lands to replace the lost portions of Iroquoia was the vast tract north of the lower lakes and the upper St Lawrence River. Britain initiated a policy of purchasing lands by treaty from the Mississauga where there were established patterns of occupation and usage. The Mississauga, a branch of the Ojibwa who were found in several parts of northern Ontario and around the west end of Lake Ontario, readily parted with land to enable the relocation of former allies. One of these became known as the 'Gunshot Treaty,' supposedly because the depth of the land purchased back of the lake was the distance at which a shot could be heard on a still day.[2] In the eastern part of the future Ontario, where there was little utilization of the lands, the British simply put the wheels in motion to settle the Indian Loyalists, such as the bands associated with Captain John Desoronto, near the site of the town that bears his name.

By agreement with the Indians, Europeans were settled in this region too. When it became clear that white-skinned Loyalists were also attracted to the fertile lands west of the Ottawa River, Britain approached the resident Indians for permission to settle the new land frontier with disbanded Loyalist troops and their families. Accordingly, the settlements along the north shore of the St Lawrence and at the west end of Lake Ontario that began in 1784 were made up of a mixture of European Loyalists, such as

Johnson's Mohawk valley tenants who located in what would become Glengarry County, and Indian Loyalists, such as the Iroquois who established themselves on the Grand River, near present-day Brantford. This early establishment of the foundations of Ontario involved two practices that were to prove incompatible with and inimical to the interests of Indians: obtaining land, in accordance with the Royal Proclamation of 1763, by royal purchase; and attempting to settle white agriculturalists and Indians in close proximity.

British policy-makers had to worry about the Americans who stayed south as well as the Loyalists who came north. British Indian Department policy towards her Indian allies south of the lakes, a policy that included the continuation of giving presents at posts in British territory, was intended to maintain their friendly neutrality, while ensuring as far as possible that the Indians would side with Britain in the event of another war with the American republic.[3] The citizens of the United States remained suspicious and resentful of what they took to be British meddling with the native peoples in the United States. This phase of uneasy relations in the old northwest culminated in the War of 1812, the final chapter of the long struggle for control of the continent that had begun a century earlier.

In Upper Canada (the future Ontario), the main prize coveted by the War Hawks from land-hungry states who were largely responsible for the Congressional decision to go to war against Britain, the Indians would once again play a vital military role. Upper Canada, which stretched west from the Ottawa River along the north shore of the St Lawrence and the lower lakes, was the most vulnerable of the British North American colonies. Overconfident American expansionists predicted that taking it would be a 'mere matter of marching,' thanks to the inadequacies of British defences, the feebleness of its long supply line from Quebec, and the nature of the Upper Canadian population.[4] Since the 1790s there had been such an influx of American agricultural immigrants that the populace was as much American as British, both in its sentiments and its leanings. The British worried about the ability of Upper Canada to withstand the anticipated American invasion, and would have despaired altogether were it not for the fact that many Indians were prepared to side once again with the British.

The principal Indian groups to whom Britain looked were the Loyalist Mohawk and the western tribes in American territory who were led by Tecumseh of the Shawnee and his brother the Prophet. Once again, the Indians fought not as instruments of European policy but as agents in pursuit of their own interests. The fundamental reason for Indian support of the British cause in the War of 1812 was simply explained: 'Tecumseh and his followers had not yet given up hope that an Indian state could be created in the Ohio Valley and that the continuous stream of white settlers from across the mountains could be checked. Alliance with the British in the War of 1812 offered the opportunity that alliance with France had offered some of the same people in the time of Pontiac.'[5] To the Indians, the War of 1812 was merely a continuation of earlier hostilities.

The British enjoyed their greatest successes in the land war in Upper Canada as long as the Indians fought in large numbers alongside them. At the outbreak of hostilities a small British force seized Michilimackinac, an early indicator that caused the Indians to flock to the British colours. In the words of an American general, the 'surrender of Michilimackinac opened the northern hive of Indians and they were swarming down in every direction.' Almost 'every tribe and nation of Indians, excepting a part of the Miamis and Delawares, north from beyond Lake Superior, west from beyond the Mississippi, south from the Ohio and Wabash, and east from every part of Upper Canada and from all the intermediate country, joined in open hostility, under the British standard against the Army I commanded.'[6] Soon after the fall of Michilimackinac, Detroit surrendered without a shot because its American commander believed the rumours that the British forces facing him included 5000 Indians and because his line of communications to the east had been cut by Tecumseh and his warriors. Britain's Indian allies fought bravely and effectively in the southwest portion of Upper Canada until Tecumseh's death at the Battle of Moraviantown in the autumn of 1813 disheartened them and caused the force slowly to melt away.

The Indians in the southwest interior were not the only ones to flock to the British colours. The Six Nations also fought effectively in the Niagara peninsula, as did some detachments of the 'praying Indians' from such Lower Canadian reserves as Oka, Caughnawaga, and St Regis. So too did a contingent of Ottawa under another famous war chief, Blackbird. The battle of Beaver Dam in the Niagara region, like the battle of Moraviantown in the southwest, was an Indian, not a British or Canadian, victory. Without the contributions and sacrifices of these Indian groups, Upper Canada might well have proved 'a mere matter of marching' before reinforcements of British regulars could arrive and the will of the Upper Canadian population to resist their invading cousins could establish itself. When Indian support dissipated late in 1813 and in 1814 as a consequence of Tecumseh's death at Moraviantown and British naval losses on Lake Ontario, the British cause suffered a serious setback.

The end of the War of 1812 meant the defeat of the Indian strategy of resistance and the onset of a long period of peace in the interior of the North American continent. In talks that led to the Treaty of Ghent, the British tried to obtain terms that would protect their Indian allies, but their efforts to secure a territory south of the lower lakes exclusively for the Indians, a sort of Indian buffer state, failed in the face of American determination not to consider any such arrangement. The peace treaty restored the boundaries that had existed before the outbreak of hostilities, and the text also created a moral obligation – unenforceable and unenforced – to restore to the Indians those lands and rights they had possessed in 1812. The war and the Treaty of Ghent meant that the strategies of those tribes that had supported first the French and then the British from the north against the Americans were now rendered inoperable. The region south of the lakes had become decidedly American and agricultural, and after the War of 1812 the region north of Lakes Ontario and Erie began to undergo the same sort of development. The Treaty of Ghent was reinforced in 1817 by the Rush-Bagot Convention, which furthered continental peace by severely restricting naval forces on the Great Lakes and Lake Champlain. The War of 1812, then, marked the end of an important phase of relations in the interior, an epoch in which the Indian and the European were allies in a common cause.

The pattern of relations after 1783 was different in the Maritime colony of Nova Scotia because immigration and peace came to that region sooner than they did to Upper Canada. The dominant factors in the Maritimes were the arrival of thousands of Loyalists, most of them white-skinned, and the non-arrival of the War of 1812. The migration of the Loyalists meant the creation of a new province, New Brunswick, in 1784, and consequent pressure on Indian groups such as the Maliseet, Penobscot, and, of course, the Micmac, as agricultural use of the land expanded. Agrarian development was greater in Nova Scotia than in New Brunswick, which had relatively little land suitable for agriculture, but even in the Loyalist province the arrival of the Euro-Americans meant pressure on the Indians because of the rapid development of an export trade in timber. The fact that the New England states were opposed to the War of 1812 meant that the final phase of the struggle among the Europeans for the continent bypassed the Atlantic region. The Maritime colonies sat out the War of 1812; the Indian inhabitants did not have this last chance to play their role as allies.

What occurred instead in the Maritime region, especially in Nova Scotia and New Brunswick, was a discouraging pattern of Indian-European relations that was to become all too familiar elsewhere during the nineteenth century. As the immigrants moved in, they dispossessed the original inhabitants, in spite of pledges to respect the relatively small areas of land set aside for natives. Colonial governments in the three Maritime colonies never found it convenient to use the limited forces at their disposal for the protection of Indian lands, though it was easy enough to persuade them to have British troops or militia sent in when hard-pressed Indians resisted.[7] Squatters simply encroached on Indian encampments, improved their property with buildings and agricultural development of the land, and then defied efforts to make them move. Colonial judges and legislators had neither the will nor the means to protect the Indians. The consequence of these developments was that as agricultural and forestry development proceeded in the Maritimes in the early nineteenth century, the indigenous population was dispossessed and reduced to scratching out an existence with hunting and handicrafts.

The Maritime region, and Nova Scotia and New Brunswick in particular, was the site of the earliest examples of a common nineteenth-century occurrence: futile efforts by overseas organizations to protect and assist North American Indians. In the nineteenth century, as a sort of obverse of British imperial expansion, there developed bodies that sought first the emancipation of non-white colonial populations and later the protection of them from whites in their own homelands. The humanitarians came to the Maritimes initially in the form of the non-denominational Protestant missionary New England Company, which sought between the 1780s and the early nineteenth century to provide assistance and education to the Indians of the region.[8] Efforts to provide education were diverted, however, when colonial administrators used missionary funds to support schools for white children. And programs of apprenticing young Indian children to Euro-Canadians in order to assimilate and train them often became a means for colonists to acquire cheap labour and hard cash.

The New England Company's abortive effort in New Brunswick was as revealing as it was unavailing. A program intended for humanitarian purposes was distorted in the hands of a colonial population unsympathetic to Indians into a source of British funds and a means to exploit the Indian population. It was in part thanks to the ineffectiveness of such missionary initiatives in the face of colonial hostility and cupidity that the Indian population of the Maritimes went through a degrading and debilitating evolution in the last decades of the eighteenth century and first half of the nineteenth century. An Indian population that had ceased to have commercial and military utility to the Europeans became, at best, irrelevant and, at worst, an obstacle to the settlers who now outnumbered them.

In Newfoundland, humanitarian efforts to mitigate European depredations were more belated and even less successful than in the mainland Maritime colonies. It was only in the second and third decades of the nineteenth century that government and colonials became alarmed at the rapid decline of the indigenous people and made efforts to protect them and to learn from them. The Beothuk had probably numbered between one and two thousand when Europeans began to make contact with them in the fishery in the fifteenth and sixteenth centuries. Initial interactions had produced some conflict, as the Indians pilfered from shacks in which the fishermen left equipment after using the shore to dry their fish. But the opportunities for extended conflict had been limited by two factors. In the first place, the policy of the British, who were the Europeans who made most use of the shore in the dry fishery, had forbidden permanent settlement in what they called the New Found Land. Second, after initial clashes, the Beothuk had adopted a strategy of withdrawal from contact with the Europeans. The Beothuk, who did not possess firearms, retreated to the interior of the island. But such a strategy proved no more successful in protecting them than the cooperation of the Huron or the policy of resistance pursued by the Indians in the Ohio and Illinois country.[9]

Although there was no record of conflict between Beothuk and Europeans from the sixteenth to the eighteenth century, the Beothuk nonetheless suffered. European diseases probably reduced their numbers to five or six hundred before contact and conflict resumed. The occasion of this renewed contact was the increasing use of the island by settled Newfoundlanders, and in particular their pursuit of fur-bearing animals. Their hunting and trapping activities brought them into occasional and bloody contact with the Beothuk. Again, since they had firearms and the Indians did not, the results were devastating to the Beothuk. A final factor may have been the increased use of the southern part of Newfoundland by the Micmac after 1713, although the evidence for this is inconclusive. The effects of tuberculosis and other diseases caused the Beothuk population to continue to dwindle throughout the eighteenth century. By 1811 there were only seventy-two Beothuk left in two camps; by 1819 the number had declined to thirty-one, even though efforts were now being made to befriend and protect remnants of the Beothuk people. Too little, too late. The Beothuk population was reduced by disease to thirteen by 1823, and in 1829 Shawnadithit, the last survivor, succumbed to tuberculosis. The original 'red Indians' were no more.

The fate of the Beothuk has been the subject of much controversy and misinformation. Older notions that the Europeans somehow 'used' the Micmac against the Beothuk are invalid, as is the controversial charge that Europeans hunted Beothuk for 'sport.' It seems almost certain that they were not systematically hunted down, nor were they the object of a campaign of genocide. Since their fate was extinction whatever the intent of the Euro-Canadians who deliberately or unwittingly were the cause of that end, such a distinction might seem irrelevant. But such is not the case. It is no fairer or historically valid to accuse Newfoundlanders of deliberately eliminating the Beothuk than it is to allege that 'using' Indians in forest warfare was defensible because of their 'blood-lust.' The latter suggestions, now largely discredited by military historians, demean Indians who pursued their own objectives. Accusations of genocide in Newfoundland similarly diminish Europeans' humanity by accusing them of actions they did not perform. The fate of the Beothuk was a tragedy, not proof of European malevolence.

By the time Shawnadithit, the last of the Beothuk, succumbed to disease in Newfoundland, relations between Indians and Europeans in central Canada were about to enter a new and significantly different phase. In Lower Canada the impact of the changing order on the aboriginal population was relatively slight. Immigration to the francophone colony after the revolutionary war was small in comparison to that of Upper Canada, and the European immigrants settled mainly in areas where they did not come into contact and competition with indigenous populations. The arrival of some Loyalist Indians did increase the numbers of Indians in the enclaves at Caughnawaga and Lake of Two Mountains, and St Regis got its real start as a consequence of the arrival of Mohawk moving out of the way of the victorious Americans. White-skinned Loyalists and later British immigration, however, tended to focus on Montreal and the Eastern Townships, where land was held in familiar freehold tenure rather than the *seigneurial* system that *Canadiens* used in most of the settled parts of the province. As a consequence, their arrival hardly disturbed the largest numbers of Lower Canadian Indians, who were scattered in small hunting bands in the Shield country north of the arable region as well as in the even more northerly areas. In Lower Canada in the early nineteenth century, Indians either continued to live in a traditional way based on a wilderness economy, or they dwelt as Christian converts in the reserves presided over by Sulpicians, Jesuits, and other priests.

The post-1783 influences were felt in the part of the old province of Quebec that lay west of the Ottawa River, the area that became the colony of Upper Canada in 1791. In Upper Canada the

Europeans' impact was considerable; vast numbers of them in a short period of time invaded an Indian-controlled area that had previously had few whites in it. As already noted, the relocation of Loyalist Indians had required the British authorities, following the policy of the Royal Proclamation of 1763, to secure Indian agreement to access to lands by purchase and treaty. The fact that Loyalists were followed in the 1790s and 1800s by large numbers of so-called Late Loyalists – really just land-hungry American farmers – meant that this policy had to be continued.

After the conclusion of the War of 1812 the only change in this pattern involved the country of origin from which the immigrants came: from the 1820s onward most new Upper Canadian settlers came from the British Isles rather than the United States. Regardless of their point of origin, these farmers and townspeople soon swamped the indigenous population. Upper Canada's population increased by a factor of ten – from 95,000 to 952,000 – between the end of the War of 1812 and the census of 1851. (The total population of British North America went from approximately 750,000 in 1821 to 2.3 million by 1851.) Whereas in 1812 the Indian population in Upper Canada had already been reduced to about one-tenth of the total population of the colony, the inundations of the 1820s and 1840s reduced them to demographic insignificance.[10]

Attempts to remove the Indians from the land and the initiation of a policy designed to change them from Indians to modified Europeans were the consequences of the Upper Canadian population shift. The policy of acquiring title to Indian lands by purchase was continued after 1815, with one important modification. In the past, land surrender treaties had involved the exchange of title and claims to tracts of land for lump-sum payments. But in postwar Upper Canada, continuation of such a policy seemed prohibitively expensive to British administrators. Now that the Rush-Bagot Convention had brought real peace to North America and made the Indians less important for military purposes, British authorities were increasingly preoccupied with the cost of Indian affairs.

From 1818 onward a new land-purchase policy was followed. Instead of outright purchases, a system of acquiring the land in return for smaller, annual payments, or annuities, was pursued. The theory behind the scheme was that the lands would be sold to settlers who would make a downpayment of 10 per cent and

mortgage the remainder. In reality, mortgagors were only expected to pay the annual interest, not the principal. The revenue
derived from the settlers' annual payments in turn was used to pay
the annuities to the Indians from whom the tract had been
purchased in the first place. From the British viewpoint the policy
had two attractions: it eliminated most of the large expenditures on
land surrenders; and the Indians indirectly funded most of the
purchase price of their land through instalment payments made
from revenues derived from the land.[11] To the Indians such
payments probably seemed familiar and welcome, resembling as
they did the annual presents that many of them had been
accustomed to receive from the British in the days when military
alliance had been important and that some of them continued to
receive in the decades after the War of 1812. In this way, during the
fifteen years after the War of 1812, vast areas of Indian lands in
Upper Canada were transferred to agricultural settlers in seven
land treaties. While there certainly were instances in Upper
Canada of the Maritime pattern of Euro-Canadian encroachment
on lands under Indian control and subsequent dispossession of the
Indian occupants, most of the land settlement in the new colony
took place with legal fastidiousness on the part of the whites, but
little profit to the account of the Indians.

Closely associated with the evolution of land policy in Upper
Canada was a shift of responsibility for Indian matters from the
British military to the civil authorities. Once a lasting peace was
established in North America, it was merely a matter of time until
Britain recognized that its erstwhile Indian allies were now an
expensive encumbrance and an obstacle to agricultural expansion.
In the age of the Indians' military irrelevance they became a social
responsibility. In 1830 Great Britain transferred jurisdiction over
Indian affairs in Lower and Upper Canada from military officers to
civilian administrators in each colony. Significantly, the Americans
in the same period shifted responsibility for Indians in the republic
to the War Department.[12]

This reassignment of jurisdiction in 1830 reflected the past
changes in the Indian's relationship with British Americans and
presaged still more novelties in the way in which the two
associated. The transfer of jurisdiction over Indian matters from
military to civil administration, like the policy of removing Indians

from the land through treaties and annuities, led to attempts to refashion the Indians. After all, if they were no longer useful militarily and could pose an obstacle to settlers' development of an agricultural economy, why not simply eliminate the Indians completely? But how could such a thing be done? The obvious choices were extermination or assimilation, eradicating the Indians through violence and disease, or coercively remaking them into bronze Europeans who lived and behaved as Euro-Canadians did. The former option, extermination, was not really open to either British officials or colonial settlers. In the first place, such an approach involved endless warfare and horrific expense, not to mention loss of life. Such a policy would provoke the increasingly numerous humanitarian organizations in Britain to create enormous political problems for any imperial government that followed such a bloody approach.

Furthermore, there was little in the Canadian tradition that would have created a desire to exterminate Indians. Colonial societies in British North America did not have a history of bloody conflict with the Indians in what they regarded as their part of North America. The fact that hitherto the relationship had been a cooperative one that had taken place along frontiers of exploration, commerce, and alliance meant that the Indian had been perceived positively on the whole. Without an entrenched attitude of hostility and fear of Indians in British North America, there was no colonial predisposition in favour of coercion or elimination of the indigenous population in Canada.

The political culture that was already well developed in Canada was one in which government played an active role in economic development and social policy. Government authority had preceded settlement and economic expansion from the days of the French intendants to the era of agricultural settlement when public funds were paying for development projects such as the canalization of the St Lawrence. Since it was the British-Canadian state, not individual settlers or local groups, that took the initiative in dealing with the Indians, the likelihood of conflict was reduced. The state acted in a more restrained manner in dealing with Indian populations than did mobs of frontiersmen or rude local assemblies. The prominent role of the state and the tradition of cooperative relations between Indians and newcomers explain why the Indians were not subjected to a strategy of extermination when they ceased to be militarily and economically useful in the early nineteenth century.

Not extermination, then, but assimilation became the method that British and British-Canadians employed. The approach was implied in the words that the British secretary of state for war and the colonies used when explaining the shift of jurisdiction to the civil authorities in 1830: 'It appears to me that the course which has hitherto been taken in dealing with these people, has had reference to the advantages which might be derived from their friendship in times of war, rather than to any settled purpose of gradually reclaiming them from a state of barbarism, and of introducing amongst them the industrious and peaceful habits of civilized life.'[13] The words 'gradually reclaiming them from a state of barbarism' and 'introducing amongst them the industrious and peaceful habits of civilized life' constituted the key element in Indian policy as it was developed and implemented under civilian control. 'Thus British policy changed at this time from a utilitarian plan of using Indians as allies to a paternal programme of gradually incorporating the Indians into white society.'[14] The significance of this change was that it meant a shift from non-directed cultural change to coercion in the form of directed cultural change.

Social scientists distinguish carefully between non-directed and directed cultural change. The former was the sort of changes – borrowings and adaptations – that had occurred on both sides of the relationship in the seventeenth and eighteenth centuries. The Indians might adopt European goods, but frequently used them to strengthen traditional practices. The Europeans might borrow the Indians' dress or style of forest warfare, but employed both costume and *la petite guerre* within a framework that remained recognizably European. Adoption of the abbreviated skirt was not accompanied by acquisition of the Iroquoians' distinctive views on the role of women by the *Canadiens*. And employment of Indian fighting tactics was undertaken within a grand strategy that was based on European perceptions and interests. On the whole, the adoption of European goods had not meant profound changes in the values, rituals, and beliefs of the Indians before the nineteenth century. This non-directed cultural change remained the pattern as long as the Indians outnumbered the newcomers, and as long as the Indians could maintain their traditional economies.

Directed cultural change, which usually set in when the immigrants outnumbered the indigenous population, meant a very different type of adaptation. It was the assertion of the ideas and values of the more dominant party in the relationship over the dependent one; it involved deliberate and systematic attempts by the dominant to change the culture of the weaker; and it subjected the more vulnerable of the two parties not just to the rules and sanctions of their own society but also to the taboos and requirements of the more powerful group. It was, in short, coercion. The consequence of such a pattern of change was usually the undermining of the weaker party's beliefs, social and political structures, and psychic well-being. The will to resist directed change often collapsed under the onslaught of increased numbers of newcomers, disruption of the traditional economy, and the ministrations of humanitarian groups that sought to inculcate their religion and secular beliefs in the minds of the indigenous population. It was not the fur trader or even the soldier who worked the worst damage on Canada's Indians; it was the missionary, the school-teacher, and the bureaucrat who thought they knew better than the indigenous peoples what was good for them.

If changed demographic and military conditions made the shift from non-directed to directed cultural change possible, the introduction of new European ideas provided the momentum to carry the transition on. These novel ideas included, but did not end with, the Christianity and associated beliefs of the humanitarian organizations that were springing up in Britain. An important adjunct to the growth of British humanitarianism was the development of scientific racism. The belief that various races had distinct qualities, particular virtues, and different vices was hardly new in nineteenth-century Britain or British North America. The British had long tended to regard non-white populations that they encountered throughout the world as beneath them. Indigenous populations were, after the initial phase when they outnumbered and overawed the British, usually looked down upon as economically, socially, and politically inferior. What was different in the nineteenth century was that the development of a series of schools of scientific and pseudo-scientific thought meant that such prejudices acquired a veneer of scientific legitimacy. Now the crude habit of judging other societies by one's own had the gloss of respectability.

Phrenology and the early stages of cultural anthropology, to mention but two types of this scientific racism, emerged within just such an ethnocentric framework. When Europeans began reading people's heads for clues to their nature or cataloguing their physical features and behaviour so as to understand them better, they simply assumed that Europeans were the norm against which everything else human in the world was to be measured. The appropriately named Charles White put the point well when, in defining the highest physical type, he asked where but among Caucasian societies in Europe one could find 'that nobly arched head, containing such a quantity of brain ...? Where that variety of features, and fulness of expression; those long, flowing, graceful ring-lets; that majestic beard, those rosy cheeks and coral lips? Where that ... noble gait? In what other quarter of the globe shall we find the blush that overspreads the soft features of the beautiful women of Europe, that emblem of modesty, of delicate feelings ...? Where, except on the bosom of the European woman, two such plump and snowy white hemispheres, tipt with vermilion?'[15] Where, indeed! Given such ethnocentric attitudes it was hardly surprising that those whose skulls differed from the Caucasian or whose social rituals were unrecognizable were regarded in the nineteenth century not just as different, but as inferior.[16]

The tendency to rank all other peoples below Caucasians was strengthened by the development and perversion of the evolutionary ideas of Charles Darwin and certain of his intellectual predecessors. The theories of natural selection, competition, and survival of the fittest were improperly transferred from the non-human to the human world by enthusiasts, who also usually managed to change 'fittest' to 'best' in the process. This was a gross distortion of what evolutionary theorists had in fact argued. This Social Darwinism, as it became known, was used to legitimize the tendency of Caucasians in Europe and North America to regard other peoples as inferior. Familiar, ugly racism was refurbished with scientific cosmetics; prejudice became scientific truth. In Britain these ideologies were used to justify expansion and domination in Africa and Asia; in the United States they were employed to defend first the institution of slavery and later the 'Jim Crow laws' that succeeded it; and in British North America and Canada they served as handy rationalizations to justify attempts to coerce and change Indian societies.

Between the American Revolutionary War and the aftermath of the War of 1812, the relations between Indians and Europeans in the eastern portion of Canada underwent a profound change. Warfare ceased to figure prominently in government planning after the Rush-Bagot Convention of 1817 demilitarized the Great Lakes, and the commerce in animal furs collapsed after the amalgamation of fur-trade companies in 1821. The Indians' utility as allies and trading partners was destroyed from Upper Canada to the Atlantic. Into the vacuum created by these changes moved, first, large numbers of immigrants who dispossessed the Indians of their lands in one fashion or another. As the Indians ceased to be allies and economic partners they increasingly assumed the roles of obstacle to development and consumer of public funds. Chief Golden Eagle of the Lake Simcoe Ojibwa in Upper Canada complained as early as 1805 that the authorities had 'told us the Farmers would help us, but instead of doing so when we encamp on the shore they drive us off & shoot our Dogs and never give us any assistance as was promised to our old Chiefs.'[17]

The response by Euro-Canadians to this changing relationship was to begin to develop Indian policy as part of the work of civil government and to mount numerous and extensive programs to assimilate the Indian. As the Indian moved from alliance to irrelevance, the European responded with a change of attitude from eager gratitude to pity and contempt. Cooperation was giving way to coercion. A disgruntled young Mississauga chieftain eloquently expressed the native reaction to a group of Englishmen: 'You came as a wind blown across the Great Lake. The wind wafted you to our shores. We rcd. you – we planted you – we nursed you. We protected you till you became a mighty tree that spread thro our Hunting Land. With its branches you now lash us.'[18] Unfortunately, there was worse to come.

6

Reserves, residential schools, and the threat of assimilation

The shift of responsibility for Indian affairs from military to civilian officials foreshadowed a major change in the relationship. Prior to 1830 the men who dealt with Indians had acted diplomatically, treating the Indians as powerful nations with whom they had to parley to achieve agreement on a course of action. This diplomatic mode had been a natural outgrowth of the underlying character of the relationship – military alliance. The new approach was based on an official view that:

the most effectual means of ameliorating the condition of the Indians, of promoting their religious improvement and education, and of eventually relieving His Majesty's Government from the expense of the Indian department, are, – 1st. To collect the Indians in considerable numbers, and to settle them in villages, with due portion of land for their cultivation and support.

2d. To make such provision for their religious improvement, education and instruction in husbandry, as circumstances may from time to time require.

3d. To afford them such assistance in building their houses, rations, and in procuring such seed and agricultural implements as may be necessary, commuting where practicable, a portion of their presents for the latter.[1]

The intention of civil government, now that Indians no longer were militarily useful, was to concentrate Indians in settled areas, or reserves; to subject them to as much proselytization, schooling, and instruction in agriculture as 'circumstances' made necessary; and to do these things at least in part with the Indians' own funds. The strategy was based on an assumption that complete assimilation was 'the only possible euthenasia of savage communities.'[2]

Existing Christian missionary endeavours provided the foundation for such a policy in Upper Canada. Since the 1790s the Moravian Brethren had been working among Indians that one of their leaders had brought from United States, and the Church of England's Society for the Propagation of the Gospel in Foreign Parts, by virtue of the Anglicans' lengthy ministry to the Mohawk, was well established on the Grand River. Anglican ministrations to the Bay of Quinte Iroquois were more modest and intermittent. However, the most extensive and effective evangelical efforts among the Indians of Upper Canada were those of the Methodists. Especially after a mixed-blood Mississauga named Peter Jones was converted to Christianity in 1823, the Methodists enjoyed considerable success at a number of centres. Indeed, Jones was but one of several native clerics and missionary workers – others included John Sunday, Peter Jacobs, and George Copway – who accounted for many of the advances that the Methodists made in places such as the Credit Mission near Toronto, Grape Island, Rice Lake, and Lake Simcoe. As well as securing the adoption of Christianity, the Methodists were particularly successful in promoting abstinence from alcohol and the adoption of sedentary agriculture and literacy among their followers. Later, the Catholic church's Society of Jesus began a long and moderately successful ministry to the Indians of Manitoulin Island at Wikwemikong.[3] These religious agencies stood ready to assist officialdom with its new policy in the 1830s.

Government intended to participate directly in carrying out the policy of peaceful 'euthenasia' in Upper Canada as well as in using missionaries to foster assimilation. The government's desire to reduce its expenditures for annual presents by encouraging the Indians to become economically self-sufficient through agriculture was one motive for its pursuit of the policy in the 1830s. Another reason was found in the new generation of officials who supervised Indian policy after 1830: these men, who had not been trained in the Johnson tradition of treating Indians as military allies, tended to regard them as social and economic problems who would benefit from Christianization and the adoption of sedentary agriculture. Moreover, Indian officials in Upper Canada wanted to settle Indians on reserves with schools and farming to counter the Americans' provision of schools and missions in regions where some of the 'wandering tribes' affiliated with the British resided.[4]

Finally, many of the Upper Canadian Indians recognized that they needed new skills and economic pursuits in an era of increasing Euro-Canadian settlement and agricultural development. A northern Ojibwa, Ashagashe, in 1827 told officials at Drummond Island, in the Michilimackinac area:

Father, we have observed with some degree of jealousy the establishment of a place at Michilimackinac, at which [missionary school] the children of our great father [Indians] are taught the means of living in the same way the whites do, where they also learn to *mark their thoughts* on paper, and to think the *news from books* [to read and write] as you do; ...

Father, tell our father that we squeeze him hard by the hand, and trust that he will assist us; tell him that we want some hoes and spades to dig with; don't leave our father until you get him to say yes.[5]

And Yellowhead, head chief of the Lake Simcoe Ojibwa, also reported that:

Our native brothers are desirous of forming a settlement, and we avail ourselves of this opportunity to address our great father on a subject of such deep interest to our tribe.

...

Father, should our great father agree, we are desirous of being settled together, we shall then be enabled to pursue a regular system of agriculture, and greater facilities will be afforded us in following the precepts of our religious teachers. Those that have embraced christianity [sic] already feel its happy effects.[6]

In short, the rising cost of distributing presents, the pro-assimilation attitudes of a new generation of Indian Department officers, American missionary enterprise, and the desires of some of the Indians combined to push government into an experiment in reserves and agriculture in the 1830s.

Reserves were established at Coldwater, near Lake Simcoe, and at Sarnia, and efforts were made to provide both education and practical instruction in farming methods. In sharp contrast to such church-directed efforts as the Methodist enterprise on the Credit River, however, the Coldwater-Narrows experiment at settling Indians proved unsuccessful. Clearing for settlements began in 1830, but by 1837 the enterprise had collapsed. In part, the explanation of failure lay in the fact that Indian Department officials expected too much too quickly of the Indians. The Ojibwa were reluctant to give up a mixed economy of hunting, fishing, and gathering for sedentary agriculture exclusively. Moreover, in contrast to the Methodists, who at settlements such as the Credit Mission worked through native missionaries, bureaucrats attempted first to direct and then to dominate the Indians and their traditional leaders. Finally, the experiment was troubled by denominational conflict between Methodists and Catholics, and by the encroachments of white settlers who coveted the lands set aside for Indians.[7]

A key component of the experiments at Coldwater and the Narrows, one whose results satisfied neither Indians nor Europeans, was schooling under the control of missionaries. Three partners who had different, though partially compatible, objectives were involved. From the government standpoint, education was a desirable adjunct to attempts to assimilate the Indians culturally and to teach them alternative skills such as agriculture. From the viewpoint of the churches – principally Catholic, Anglican, and Methodist – reading and writing in a European language were also essential to conversion and living as practising Christians. In the optimum case, education was an essential means of obtaining native missionaries and catechists. Finally, so far as the Indians were concerned, the motive for participating in schooling was to acquire the knowledge that they recognized as essential to their continued survival and success at a time when the literate Europeans were becoming dominant. Hence, all three groups could agree on the desirability of providing schooling for Indians, the government and missionaries for reasons that were compatible if not exactly identical. Indians often wanted the services of teachers, too, but for their own purposes: they wanted learning, but not the accompanying assimilationist efforts that were central to the purposes of officials and preachers.

In the 1830s in Upper Canada there was a considerable effort to provide day schools in or near Indian settlements where Indian groups indicated a desire for them or a willingness to accept them. Efforts were already in place in such centres as the Credit River settlement of Mississauga, and numerous others were established on the reserves and in other locations. The Methodists in particular were noteworthy for their efforts to teach trades, crafts, and agriculture along with basic formal education by means of teachers, usually whites, and 'native exhorters and class-leaders.'[8] Government efforts tended to segregate the formal schooling and the efforts to inculcate agriculture, and in neither were they especially successful. What advances the government and churches claimed in native education in the 1830s were primarily in the superficial manifestations of assimilation, such as the Indians' adoption of the clothing and domestic arrangements of Euro-Canadian society.

The efforts to use schools as instruments of assimilation and for teaching alternative economic skills were disrupted in the mid-1830s by two important events. The first was a growing realization among Methodist missionaries that the day schools were not as successful as they had hoped. The event that prompted this discovery was the second disruptive force, the efforts of a new lieutenant-governor to alter the policy of 'civilization' that had been in place since 1830. The arrival of Sir Francis Bond Head as lieutenant-governor of Upper Canada in 1836 unsettled many groups in the colony, not least the Indians. Bond Head, who had worked as a mine manager in South America and had served as a commissioner under the new Poor Law of 1832 in England, considered himself a thoroughly qualified expert on natives in the new world and on social engineering. Making up in self-assurance what he lacked in knowledge and experience of North American conditions, Bond Head urged that the policy of reserves-education-assimilation be dropped in favour of a different approach. He proposed – and, more important, acted on his own proposal – that the Indians not be converted to Christianity and a European way of life but that they be left alone to live out their days in isolation and peace. Bond Head had a different approach to the 'euthanasia' of the indigenous population in Upper Canada. He was convinced, he said, that the Indians were dwindling in numbers and were destined to die out completely. On this assumption he began to implement a policy of taking land surrenders from as many Indian groups as possible and relocating them on the Manitoulin islands where they would live out their remaining days.

The response to Bond Head's initiative was a clear indication of how much conditions had changed in Indian affairs. Although the British Colonial Office initially evinced cautious enthusiasm at the lieutenant-governor's course, it was forced to back down swiftly and completely in the face of an angry protest from religious and humanitarian groups both in British North America and the United Kingdom. The Wesleyan Methodists claimed that the Indians were greatly disquieted at this threat to their lands, and they objected to the proposed policy as an abandonment of the indigenous population. They secured the cooperation of English groups such as the recently founded Aborigines Protection Society (1836) and the Society of Friends in lobbying the imperial government against Bond Head's proposals. The combination of outraged public opinion and strategic concerns in 1837–8 about armed risings in both Canadas and about the danger of incursions by American brigands reminded British officials that abandoning and removing the Indians of Upper Canada was militarily foolish and politically dangerous. Britain countermanded Bond Head's suspension of the policy of settling Indians and encouraging the adoption of agriculture, although the land surrenders that Bond Head had arranged with Indian bands stood. Officialdom began again to look anxiously for a policy to replace that of the early 1830s.

The new policy consisted of a commission of inquiry and a revision of the assimilationist educational program. The commission, known usually as the Bagot Commission for the governor who established it in 1842, laid down many of the key elements of colonial policy that would govern Indian affairs up to and beyond Confederation.[9] The Bagot Commission reaffirmed the crown's obligations to the Indians, in particular in relation to the important question of land and land tenure. It acknowledged the Indians' 'right of occupancy' and 'claim to compensation for its surrender' that had been embodied in the Royal Proclamation. But at the same time it proposed changes that would move in the direction of eliminating the distinctive style of Indian use of land and reduce the government's obligations, financial and otherwise. Indians would be provided with the means to become successful farmers and artisans, and they would be encouraged to adopt individual ownership of plots of land in the British freehold system, rather than the communal reserve ownership that had been used to that point. Efforts would be made to reduce financial obligations by taking a census of Indians and restricting recipients of annual presents to those on it, and by stipulating that those who acquired sufficient education would no longer be eligible to receive presents. At the same time, administration of the payment of annuities would be tightened up, both to protect the government and to provide Indian leaders with a proper accounting of their funds.

The government's decision to implement the Bagot Commission's recommendations led to the reorganization of the Indian Department, a new thrust in Indian education, and significant Indian resistance. The offices were moved from Kingston to Montreal, and several somnolent officials were replaced with a set of new, presumably more energetic, 'Indian visitors.' But the recommendation to curtail the giving of annual presents remained a dead letter because Indians strongly opposed any step in the direction of terminating the symbol of their relationship with the crown. Similarly, the plan to grant individual Indians deeds to separate plots of reserve land encountered strenuous opposition from Indian leaders, who regarded the scheme as antithetical to their own traditions of communal ownership of land. Significantly, the Indian response to the other principal recommendations, those dealing with education, were initially much more positive.

The reorientation of schooling for Indians from day schools to residential institutions in the 1840s was an important change. In 1828 a Methodist missionary on Grape Island had begun to provide instruction to four Indian girls who boarded with him and his family. Another Indian school had been set up on the Six Nations reserve near Brantford in 1829 by the English non-denominational missionary organization, the New England Company. Though called at first a 'Mechanics' Institution' in recognition of its attempt to emulate metropolitan efforts at educating the lower orders of an industrializing society, it soon became known as the Mohawk Institute, and in 1833 it took its first boarders, ten boys and ten girls from the Six Nations reserve. The cost of lodging, feeding, clothing, and teaching the children was borne by the English missionary body.[10] Thus, when Bond Head denounced the lack of progress in Indian reserves and forced missionaries and teachers to reassess their methods, a model on which to base a new approach to schooling was available.

The Bagot Commission concluded that the failure of the day schools was rooted not in inadequate funding or assimilationist pressures on Indians, but on the influence that parents exerted when the young scholars returned from class. It recommended the establishment of boarding schools with farms in which the children could be taught agriculture or a trade, assimilated in the absence of Indian parental influence, equipped to forgo annual presents, and readied to take up individual plots of land in freehold tenure. These 'manual labour schools' should be funded by government and operated by all Christian religious groups willing and able to play a role in this important work. That groups such as the Methodists who had been active in education agreed with such notions was perhaps not surprising. In 1838 they had opened a small boarding school for girls at Alderville that grew to an enrolment of thirty by 1845.

What seemed more surprising was the initial Indian cooperation with and support for these boarding schools that were designed for the thorough assimilation and education of their children. Indians in the Alderville area supported the Methodist establishment there with £100 from their annuities.[11] In these same years Ojibwa were encouraging one of their own, Methodist minister Peter Jones, to raise funds in the United Kingdom for another Indian residential establishment at Munceytown.[12] Hence it was not surprising that when the government decided to implement the Bagot Commission's recommendations on residential schooling, it got support from some of the Indians.

At a conference at Orillia in 1846, most of the chiefs in attendance approved the plan of creating residential schools and promised the Indian Department one-quarter of their annuities for twenty-five years for support of the institutions. But their reasons for wanting these schools were different from the government's: they wished to acquire the Euro-Canadians' learning in order to survive, but they had no wish to assimilate. That they did not accept the whole assimilationist policy of the government was made clear by at least two developments. After the Orillia conference some bands refused to send their children to the residential schools at Alderville,

Munceytown, and the Six Nations reserve. And at the conference the chiefs' stout resistance to the idea that they give up their lands and congregate in the three sites that were proposed for such schools made it clear that they wanted only schooling, not a fundamental change in their way of life.[13]

This departure in education was to prove important for more than the Indians of Upper Canada, and for a longer period of time than the chiefs at Orillia in 1846 could have foreseen. During the 1850s and 1860s the system of boarding establishments in the future Ontario was extended, as government and churches co-operated in the program. Moreover, the theory and practice of these residential schools were elaborated in an important statement by the chief superintendent of common schools, Egerton Ryerson. His recommendations laid out the complete assimilationist theory and methods that had lain implicit in the experiments at Coldwater and elsewhere in the 1830s as well as in the Bagot Commission report of 1842–4.

The purpose of the schools, said Ryerson, was 'to give a plain English education adapted to the working farmer and mechanic,' it being understood of the Indian that 'with him nothing can be done to improve and elevate his character and condition without the aid of religious feeling.' The 'animating and controlling spirit of each industrial school establishment should ... be a religious one.' The system of removing the children from the home and Indian village, and subjecting them to constant indoctrination in Christianity and the three R's became well established. Combining a half-day of classroom work with a half-day in the shops or fields, an approach that was borrowed in part from similar institutions in the United States, would teach useful trades by practical experience while simultaneously supplying many of the basic needs of the school. 'I think,' concluded Ryerson optimistically, 'with judicious management, these establishments will be able in the course of a few years very nearly to support themselves.'[14]

This system of residential schooling would persist in Upper Canada to and beyond Confederation, and after the acquisition of the Hudson's Bay Company lands in the northwest it would be transferred there. What the missionaries and administrators responsible for this extension of residential schooling sometimes forgot was that Indian resistance to the assimilationist purpose of these schools appeared almost immediately in the 1840s and 1850s. As the chiefs at Orillia had tried to make clear, they wanted schooling, not refashioning.

There were other important developments in Upper Canada besides the creation of a reserve and educational program in the years between the transfer of policy to civil government in 1830 and the 1860s. Chief among these changes were modifications in the treaty-making process and in legislation dealing with Indians. In 1845 the government of the united Province of Canada, which consisted of the former colonies of Lower and Upper Canada, granted permission to mining companies to explore along the northern and eastern shores of Lake Superior for minerals. Not for the first – nor, for that matter, for the last – time, Indians of the region complained to the man who represented the crown, the lieutenant-governor, that the men employed by these companies were actually 'trespassing on their property.' Before an investigation into the complaints could be fully carried out, the Indians began to threaten to attack one of the mines on the eastern shore of Lake Superior. A worried lieutenant-governor sent troops to the site to end the conflict, with gratifying results. As Lord Elgin was driven to observe, 'I cannot but think that it is much to be regretted that steps were not taken to investigate thoroughly and extinguish all Indian claims before licences of exploration or grants of land were conceded by the Government in this Territory.'[15]

The readiness of some of the Indians in the territory to assert their rights in the face of white encroachment led to the negotiation of the Robinson treaties in 1850. The Robinson-Huron and Robinson-Superior treaties with the Ojibwa of northern Ontario were unusual in that they secured Indian agreement to Euro-Canadian penetration of a much larger region than was immediately needed for the economic purposes of the white entrepreneurs. In addition, the Indians showed a lively concern to secure recognition of their title to tracts that would be reserved for their exclusive use in the pursuit of traditional economic activities. As Robinson reported to his superiors: 'In allowing the Indians to retain reservations of land for their own use I was governed by the fact that they in most cases asked for such tracts as they had heretofore been in the habit of using for purposes of residence and cultivation, and by securing these to them and the right of hunting and fishing over the ceded territory, they cannot say that the Government takes from their usual means of subsistence and therefore have no claims for support, which they no doubt would have preferred, had this not been done.'[16] In their retention of annuities as the means of payment, the 1850 treaties were a continuation of the traditions of the Upper Canadian era; in the Indians' desire to hold on to large tracts that would permit them to maintain a traditional way of life, they were a harbinger of developments in the 1870s.

In the same year that the Robinson treaties were negotiated, the legislature of the Province of Canada undertook important initiatives in dealing with Indians. In 1850 Canada passed 'An Act for the better protection of the Lands and Property of Indians in Lower Canada' and 'An Act for the protection of the Indians in Upper Canada from imposition, and the property occupied or enjoyed by them from trespassing and injury.' As the titles of the measures indicated, the legislation was intended to protect the Indians' established right in both sections of the Province of Canada to the lands that had been set aside for them.

But the long-term significance of the measures lay in one particular feature of the legislation. The act that applied to Lower Canada, or Canada East as it was now known, purported to define 'Indians' as 'persons of Indian blood, reputed to belong to the particular Body or Tribe of Indians interested in such lands and their descendents [sic] ... persons intermarried with any such Indians and residing amongst them, and the descendents [sic] of all such persons ... persons residing among such Indians, whose parents on either side were or are Indians of such Body or Tribe, or entitled to be considered as such: And ... persons adopted in infancy by any such Indians, and residing in the village or upon the lands of such Tribe or Body of Indians and their Descendents [sic].'[17]

In comparison with later 'Indian Acts,' this 1850 definition was fairly broad. Anyone in Canada East who was reputed to have Indian blood and to be living with a band, anyone married to such a person, anyone residing with Indians either of whose parents was Indian, and anyone adopted as a child by Indians and still living with them was considered to be Indian. The truly significant feature of this statute was that civil government, an agency beyond the control of Indians, a body in which Indians were not even eligible to have representation, arrogated to itself the authority to define who was or was not Indian. This was a development that could have occurred only in a period when the original population had become marginal to the needs and aspirations of the immigrant population that dominated the territory. Earlier it had been neither possible nor desirable to treat commercial partners and military allies in such a high-handed fashion. Later the government would expand this intervention by defining and distinguishing between 'status' and 'non-status' Indians.

The Province of Canada now found itself on the slippery slope that led from the moral heights of protection to the depths of coercion. As the titles of the 1850 acts so plainly illustrated, the legislation was designed to protect Indians in Canada from the cycle of squatting-resistance-conflict-dispossession that had already begun in the arable portions of the Maritimes. This protective impulse was laid over top of the objectives of the Bagot Commission and missionaries to assimilate the Indians through education and adoption of agriculture. Given this background, it was only natural that the next step in the process was to provide for the legal emergence of the Indian who had been tutored and moulded from Indian status to full British colonial citizenship. In the process of making this transition, however, legislators ignored Indian opinion and introduced ominous provisions that threatened to undermine the base of Indians' identity and survival – their land.

The 'Act for the Gradual Civilization of the Indian Tribes in the Canadas' (Gradual Civilization Act) that was passed by the legislature of Canada in 1857 combined past assumptions and future objectives. The measure's preamble indicated that the legislation was built on the aspirations of the missionaries and the conclusions of the Bagot Commission: 'Whereas it is desirable to encourage the progress of Civilization among the Indian Tribes in this Province, and the gradual removal of all legal distinctions between them and her Majesty's other Canadian Subjects, and to facilitate the acquisition of property and of the rights accompanying it, by such individual Members of the said Tribes as shall be found to desire such encouragement and to have deserved it,' to that end the statute established ways in which Indians might become enfranchised.[18] The 1857 act spelled out how they might become full citizens and drop their Indian status.

The road to enfranchisement was not easy; the way of travelling it could be ironic. When Indians could meet the test of a special board and prove that they had been educated, were debt-free, and of good moral character, they would be enfranchised and given twenty hectares of land. It was expected that such progress would be the result of the work of missionaries and teachers in residential schools, with their Christian environment and model farms. The 1857 act thus created a paradox that persisted for a century: though the measure was designed to permit Indians to drop their distinctive status in favour of full British North American citizenship, it began by defining Indians as non-citizens. In other words, legislation whose purpose was 'to remove all legal distinctions between Indians and Euro-Canadians actually established them' in law. Furthermore, before Indians could overcome their status and realize the blissful integration that the preamble of the legislation contemplated, they had to meet a test that many – perhaps most – Euro-Canadians in the Canadas could not have satisfied in the 1850s.[19] That was plainly silly; but it was nonsense that would persist for more than a century.

Worse than the silly portions of the legislation were the serious ones that dealt with land. By providing that an enfranchised Indian would gain the right to freehold tenure of twenty hectares from reserve lands, this colonial measure presumed to set aside the policy of the Royal Proclamation. That earlier pronouncement had decreed that colonists, in their legislatures or otherwise, could not deal directly with Indians for land. Only the crown could alienate Indian land. But the 1857 statute breached that defence of Indian control of their lands by creating at least a presumption that a colonial legislature could interfere with reserve lands to the extent of parcelling out small plots to newly enfranchised band members. Ominously, in 1860 Britain transferred responsibility for Indian matters to the legislatures of her British North American colonies. In accordance with the canons of responsible government, which meant colonial self-government, the mother country was transferring control of an important subject to Canada. But that meant that jurisdiction over Indian matters was transferred to the legislative representatives of a settler society that had even less sympathy for Indians than did imperial Britain.

The measure of 1857 also ran counter to the clearly expressed wishes of the Indians. Though they had said on many occasions – and frequently backed up their assertions with their money – that they wanted education, they rejected the total assimilation that missionaries and officials intended to be the final outcome of schooling and evangelization. Similarly, the chiefs of Canada West had made it clear in the meeting at Orillia in 1846 that they wanted no part of provisions that would allow the conversion of lands that bands held in common to individual plots held in freehold tenure. The Gradual Civilization Act deliberately ran counter to those wishes by making provision for the conversion of reserve lands into alienated plots in the hands of men who would cease to be Indians upon enfranchisement. The reaction of the Indians to at least these provisions of the act was swift and blunt. It was, said a tribal leader, an attempt 'to break them to pieces.' It did not, he continued, 'meet their views' because it ran counter to their wish to maintain tribal integrity and communal land ownership. Equally revealing was the response of the Indian Department: 'the Civilization Act is no grievance to you,' it replied brusquely.[20]

What the 1857 Gradual Civilization Act and its aftermath illustrated very clearly was that Indian-government relations were changing dramatically in the era of extensive European settlement in central Canada. After responsibility for Indian relations was transferred from military to civil authorities in 1830, government officials began to plan for the removal of Indians from the path of settlement. To a great extent that had been done in the land surrender treaties that preceded immigration to parts of Upper Canada, and it was continued in more northerly regions by means of the Robinson treaties. At the same time, a new alliance of church and humanitarian organizations, with government encourage-ment, promoted fundamental changes in those Indians who remained within or close to areas of the colony where agricultural and commercial development was going on apace. They tried to convert Indians in religious terms and to remake them culturally by the twin instruments of church and school. The effort began with a network of day schools, but shifted in the 1840s to reliance on residential schools. In these new institutions Indian children were insulated from the influences of their own people and subjected to a program designed to lead them to forget who they were and to adopt the ways and values of their teachers. The culmination of this process was expected to be their jettisoning of their Indian legal status in favour of enfranchisement. They would, once they had lost their Indian identity, become citizens, and they would remove both themselves and their land from the Indian world.

In the process of making this transition in policy, both churches and governments edged steadily from protection to compulsion and from cooperation to coercion. The shift from day schools to boarding schools was one symptom of that transition: residential schools were designed to enable missionaries to interfere with the character formation and identity of the young even though Indians had said repeatedly that they wanted not assimilation but schooling. Similarly, the pregnant provisions of the 1850 act governing Lower Canadian Indians and the 1857 Gradual Civilization Act that applied to all Indians in the Province of Canada were an assertion of legislative authority over and control of Indian peoples in Canada. The legislature now was saying that it would define who was an Indian as a preliminary to making it possible for the Indian to cease being Indian. And the 1857 legislation also violated the tradition of the Royal Proclamation of 1763 and contradicted Indian desires to hold their land communally. The Gradual Civilization Act simply brushed aside Indian wishes in the first of many coercive actions directed against Indian peoples. When the Indian Department stated that 'the Civilization Act is no grievance to you,' it was giving an answer that only a government embarked on legislated coercion of Indian peoples would have thought appropriate. That reply showed how far relations between Indians and governments had travelled in the few decades since the Rush-Bagot Convention had ended the military threat from the south.

In the decade after the Gradual Civilization Act a pattern that was to become depressingly familiar was established. Indians in Canada West responded with protest to the new assimilative program. Their cooperation in establishing and supporting manual labour schools that had begun to develop in the late 1840s and early 1850s was replaced with resistance. Indian bands came to regard missionaries and their schools as enemies in many instances, and some Indian parents withdrew their children and their financial backing from schools. It was significant that the Reverend Peter Jones, the convert who had been an early native advocate of boarding schools and who had served briefly as the superintendent of the Methodists' institution at Munceytown, refused to send his sons to boarding school.[21] Indians also protested against the 1857 legislation and demanded its repeal. They said that they would not sell any more of their land, and made plans to lay their grievances before the throne when the Prince of Wales visited Canada in 1861. They continued to support the objectives of using education and agricultural instruction to enable them to cope economically with the changes about them, but they emphatically rejected the Euro-Canadians' assimilationist strategy of which schooling and agricultural instruction were a part. Above all, in the highly symbolic area of enfranchisement, Indians simply refused to cooperate. Only one Indian was enfranchised between passage of the Gradual Civilization Act in 1857 and the codification of Indian policy in a new Indian Act in 1876.[22] The Indians resisted by refusing to comply.

The government's response, in turn, was to slide further from protection towards compulsion. By 1863 it was clear to the Canadian government that its policy of enfranchisement was a failure. Similarly, increasing Indian non-cooperation in the educational sphere was noted and led to demands for compulsory schooling legislation that would eliminate parents' ability to withhold or withdraw their children from the clutches of the preachers and teachers.

In 1869 the new Dominion of Canada moved the rest of the way towards coercion in another Enfranchisement Act. (At Confederation, jurisdiction for 'Indians and lands reserved for Indians' had been assigned to the federal level of government.) Under the guise of providing Indian bands with institutions of local self-government, the dominion established a mechanism that allowed Ottawa bureaucrats to interfere with the traditional leaders who had so often blocked their initiatives. They could be set aside for 'dishonesty, intemperance or immorality' by the Governor General in Council and replaced with elected officials. The 1869 act also continued the assault on communal land-holding by re-enacting provisions of an 1868 statute that had encouraged individuals to get 'location tickets' for their share of reserve lands. And, finally, the post-Confederation statute meddled still more in the definition of who was an Indian by stipulating that an Indian woman who married a non-Indian would lose her Indian status. Both she and her offspring would cease to be Indians and to qualify for annuities or band membership if she married a non-Indian. This measure expanded on the 1850 clause that had presumed to define who was an Indian; now Ottawa was distinguishing between 'status Indians' and a new category that would be known as 'non-status Indians.'

The federal government would later insist that it had no obligations to 'non-status Indians.' The 1869 provision, like the whole of the statute, was a gross interference in Indians' management of their internal affairs and a major escalation of the coercion that had been implied in assimilationist policies and the Gradual Civilization Act of 1857.

The downward slide of Indian policy between 1830 and Confederation was both a reflection of the changing relationship and a portent of things to come. The move towards interference and compulsion was intelligible only against a shifting background in which Indians became increasingly marginal to the desires of the newcomers, but in which Indians refused to concede their defeat. Indian resistance, however, merely served to provoke more coercive policies by missionaries and officials. The do-gooders concluded that Indian recalcitrance was the principal obstacle to the success of their policies. This evolution occurred because of two other factors as well, the rising influence of church and humanitarian groups in British North America and in the United Kingdom, and growing colonial control of relations with the Indians. The influence of the humanitarian groups discouraged the use of the worst forms of force, but the alternative was merely the piecemeal adoption of paternalistic and coercive measures that led towards the extermination of Indians by peaceful rather than military means. These factors were reinforced, in turn, by the increasing influence of scientific and pseudo-scientific theories that appeared to explain the slow rate at which the Indians adopted Euro-Canadian ways while legitimizing the application of increasing degrees of compulsion.

Unfortunately, this pattern would be replicated in all its ugly detail in the west when Canada asserted its control of the Hudson's Bay Company lands. The year 1869 was not just the year of another, yet more coercive, Indian Enfranchisement Act; it was also when the dominion was to assume title to Rupert's Land. Canada's new written constitution, the British North America Act, said that 'Indians and lands reserved for Indians' were the responsibility of the federal government and parliament. The Indians of the Province of Canada knew by now what could be expected from that quarter. How would the Indian and native populations of the lands west and north of Lake Superior respond when they came face to face with this new authority?

7

The commercial frontier on the western plains

West of the Province of Canada a belated version of the same pattern that had been established in eastern British North America was developing. In the east, Indians and Europeans had cooperated for separate, though complementary, reasons from the sixteenth to the late eighteenth centuries in mutually beneficial relationships. The frontier on which indigenous people and newcomers had met was one of navigation, commerce, faith, and military alliance. Until these sorts of arenas for interaction were supplanted in the early nineteenth century by an expanding agricultural frontier, relations between the two peoples had been fairly harmonious and without traumatic effect on either party. Though there had been borrowings in each direction, little directed cultural change had occurred before the Victorian era. In the western interior much of this pattern was replicated. Europeans and western Indians met and interacted for most of the same reasons, though the military aspect here was minor, with much the same results. But in western Canada relations began later and passed through the various phases of cooperation to the age of the Indian's irrelevance in a much shorter space of time.

Contact began in the west because of the familiar commercial motive that led seventeenth-century Englishmen to emulate the French in their search for furs. In fact, it was renegade French traders, Pierre-Esprit Radisson and Médard Chouart, sieur des Groseilliers, who defected to the English in the 1660s, taking their knowledge of North American fur-trade routes with them. Their familiarity with the waterways and native peoples of New France combined with a growing interest among commercial elements in England to produce the Company of Adventurers of England trading into Hudson Bay in 1670. The Hudson's Bay Company, as the firm was usually known, received a charter from the English crown that purported to bestow on it a monopoly of commerce in all lands drained by the rivers flowing into Hudson and James bays. By an audacious stroke of the pen, in other words, Charles II of England presumed to grant trading rights to a vast region encompassing parts of present-day northern Quebec and Ontario, Manitoba, Saskatchewan, Alberta, and portions of the Northwest Territories. And, though the significance of the act seemed not to cross the minds of king or traders, they were pretending to dictate to the many Indian nations in that huge empire with whom they would trade.

The lands that King Charles assigned to the Hudson's Bay Company embraced a large number of Indian tribes of Algonkian, Athapaskan, and Siouan language stocks. In the east there were the Cree of northern Quebec and Ontario, as well as the Ojibwa in the region between Lake Superior and Lake Winnipeg, a people who would later generally be known as Saulteaux in western Canada.[1] There were also Cree north and west of the Ojibwa, as well as the Siouan Assiniboine to the south. Like the Blackfoot Confederacy to the west of them, the Assiniboine relied on a Plains culture that centred around the magnificent bison, a larder and clothier on the hoof. In the north the principal Indian tribe was the Chipewyan, for whom the caribou was nearly as important as the buffalo was to southerly nations. The Ojibwa depended on a mixed economy of hunting, fishing, and horticulture, in particular the gathering of the wild rice that grew in many of their region's lakes. The Cree were principally hunter-gatherers who relied on hunting, fishing, and the collecting of naturally occurring food products such as berries and nuts. As Friesen has aptly observed, the 'cultures of the western interior of Canada were successful adaptations to the environment.'[2] The rugged terrain and harsh climate of the western interior probably supported between 15,000 and 50,000 Indians in the middle of the seventeenth century.

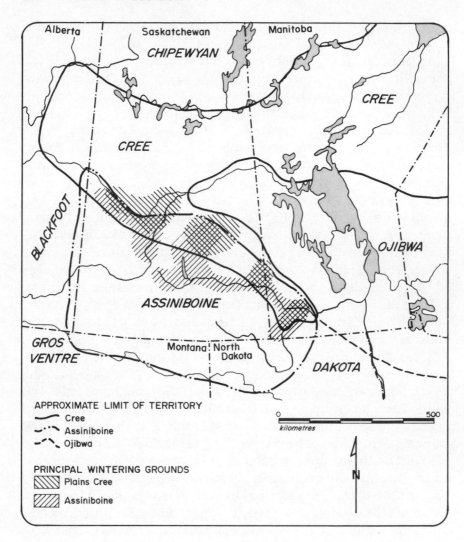

Location of western nations, 1821

Although there were wide variations among the western and
northern Indian peoples, there were also some important similarities. It would be as foolish to generalize about the social structures
and everyday life of such dispersed and different nations as it
would be to suggest that a seventeenth-century Muscovite and a
contemporary Londoner followed the same social routines. But, as
among the Indians of eastern Canada, there were some shared
characteristics, just as there were among the different nationalities
of Western Europe. Indians of the western interior, like those to
the east, had developed various forms of animistic religion that
emphasized the presence of spirits and gods in objects both
animate and inanimate. They felt a close sense of kinship with flora
and fauna, and they had developed elaborate rituals and taboos to
ward off evil and to placate offended spirits. Not surprisingly in a
region of dry climate and much sunshine, more especially on the
southern plains, the spirit of the sun occupied a special place in
native religion.

Western Indians also shared with their eastern counterparts the
fact that they had developed trade among themselves long before
Europeans appeared bearing trade goods. Northerly Indians
exchanged hides for corn from agricultural Indians far to the south,
in present-day United States. And commerce in wild rice, furs, and
various handicrafts was fairly common. Western Indians also had
well-developed traditions of warfare, which was usually motivated by vengeance, commercial calculations, or the need to perform
rites of passage. Among western males the need to prove bravery
in raids and battles was an especially strong stimulus to embark on
war. A young man simply could not establish himself in his tribe
without proving his manhood by martial acts against another tribe.
But, again, as in the east, pre-contact warfare tended not to be very
destructive. Until firearms were used, Indian warfare did not
result in extensive loss of life.

In western Canada, then, the onset of fur trading brought
together two different ways of life, the European and the indigenous North American. And, as in the east, the fact that contact led
to cooperation rather than repulse was explicable largely in terms
of the mutual advantage that could be derived from interaction.
For the English who began to undertake their regular voyages to
the edge of James Bay and Hudson Bay in the 1670s, obviously, the

benefit lay in the furs that they obtained in these northerly latitudes, furs that were lush because of the climate and plentiful because of the limited demand that previously had existed in the region. For the Indians of the west, the motive for trading with the foreigners was access to products of European technology. In particular, cloth and blankets, tools and implements, weapons and rum were prized items of the western commerce that began slowly after 1670 and continued fitfully for a century. It used to be thought that the Bay's traders had a particular advantage over French rivals because their trade goods were cheaper and of higher quality, but recent research has raised serious doubts about this assessment.[3] What is clear is that the English were much readier to trade firearms and rum than were the French, until competitive pressure from the English on both the Hudson River and Hudson Bay impelled them to in the eighteenth century. And, again, what needs to be stressed about contact in the fur-trade era of western Canadian history is that without Indian tolerance of and cooperation with the English, these traders could not initially have maintained their presence at the edge, and later penetrated the interior.

Part of the explanation of the Bay's greater willingness to employ alcohol in the western trade lies in the fact that the English commercial penetration was not accompanied by a missionary presence. The French fur traders had not much wanted to transport and support Jesuits in eastern Canada either, but they had been compelled to do so by the French crown that was responding with Counter-Reformation zeal to convert the world to Catholicism. French traders had also recognized that the presence of Jesuit missionaries in Huronia or among the migratory bands of Algonkians served to cement the commercial link, making missionaries a necessary evil in the trade. Such influences did not come into play in the west in the first century and a half of the Bay's activities. The English king and parliament saw no reason to insist on commercial support of evangelical efforts among the aboriginal peoples of North America. Furthermore, the manner in which the Bay men conducted their trade for the better part of a century largely removed the necessity to station Europeans – even clergymen if necessary – among the groups with whom they traded. The Bay encouraged the Indians to bring their furs to their posts at the mouths of the rivers, such as the Nelson and the Churchill, that emptied into the northern waters. And while it is not true that for a century the English traders 'slept by the frozen sea' as used to be said of them, their largely sedentary manner of conducting a fur trade removed the compulsion to probe the interior and to station Europeans among the native people there. Lacking a need to exchange personnel to hold the commercial alliance, English traders had one less reason to tolerate the presence of missionaries in their vast patrimony.

Although Hudson's Bay Company men did over the decades undertake some exploration of the western interior with the aid of Indian guides, by and large they relied on the Indians to come to them to trade. This manner of conducting the trade meant that, in western Canada, particularly well-situated groups of Indians emerged as middlemen in the commerce. The Ojibwa had experience in this role, having transported furs to the French and Canadians and returned European products for consumption and further trade with groups such as the Cree and Assiniboine that were more remote from the zone of commercial transactions. After the English established themselves on the bay, some Ojibwa moved northwest to take advantage of the commercial opportunities that presented themselves. Gradually, however, it was the Cree and Assiniboine who became dominant as intermediaries in the western trade. The Cree moved westward around the turn of the eighteenth century and joined with the Assiniboine in playing the middleman role. Large numbers of Indians, in other words, responded to the economic opportunities created by the emergence of a commercial frontier by migrating and modifying pre-contact trading networks so as to maximize the benefits of trade for themselves. In so doing they spread the effects of European presence broadly throughout the western interior.

The coming of the fur trade meant diffusion of European technology, but not dramatic alterations in native societies at first. Perhaps the most visible change was the shift in territories of the various Indian nations. Similarly, the volume of commerce among the Indians themselves increased dramatically, as the middleman tribes developed a broad and lucrative trade. In some instances the intermediaries used goods they obtained from the French for one or two seasons and then sold them to the Blackfoot for triple the price they had paid for them at York Factory.[4] But such behaviour does not mean that the Indians had adopted a capitalistic ethos as a result of trading. Much as the Huron had used their new-found wealth in traditional ways, natives in the west generally used the European items in ways compatible with established values in the early decades of the commerce.

One manifestation of this traditionalism was what Bay men regarded as the Indians' perverse response to market incentives. In the emerging capitalist society that was England, it was believed that a rise in the price of a product stimulated an increase in supply. If the price of furs rose substantially, according to the market theory that Adam Smith would codify in the eighteenth century, Indians should bring more furs to trade, and should keep doing so until the increased supply caused a decline in price. But western Indians did not react this way; they did not respond as 'economic men.' The Indian's demand for European goods was 'inelastic'; once a fixed level of individual needs and desires was satisfied, exchange ceased.[5] One estimate was that an individual required a total of 100 Made Beaver (MB), the unit of exchange in the fur trade, consisting of seventy MB for subsistence items and thirty for luxuries and amusements. If fur prices rose, the Indians simply acquired the goods they desired for fewer furs. They did not respond to higher prices by increasing supply. (Another, more typical, market response might be that more individual Indians would be drawn into the fur-trade commercial nexus, producing a larger volume of furs.) This non-market behaviour demonstrates that Indians remained traditional, or pre-capitalist, in attitude and ethos while participating in the trade. Commerce reinforced and enriched traditional practices in the west; it did not supplant them. The contact of European traders with western Canadian Indians at first resulted only in non-directed cultural change.

The manifestations of that non-disruptive change were many and obvious. The expansion and multiplying of commercial patterns was one, as the Cree and Assiniboine replaced the Ojibwa as middlemen and expanded their networks. The emergence of a group of Indians, known as the Home Guard Cree, who moved in close to the posts and came to look to the traders rather than the resources of the country as their provisioner, was another. On occasion these groups, some Assiniboine or the Home Guard Cree,

could be reduced to hardship and deprivation if the supply of
European goods was disrupted by warfare in Europe or North
America between the French and the English. It is probable that the
dependence of groups further from the posts was much less,
although all western Indians sooner or later were affected by the
Europeans' introduction of firearms. In the first century of the
trade from the bay, it was principally the Assiniboine and
Woodland Cree (especially Home Guard) who adopted muskets,
but other groups were affected if only as victims of these more
destructive implements of war. Early in the eighteenth century,
firearms coming from the north met the horse coming from the
south in the Canadian prairies. This meeting was to help substantially to fashion the unique Plains Indian culture that distinguished
western Canada. Nations such as the Plains Cree and the Blackfoot
were to create a complete way of life based on Spanish horses,
English muskets, and the North American bison.

The introduction of European goods, whether firearms or
horses, did bring about adaptations in Indian society. Obviously,
the muskets made warfare more destructive. Indian raiding parties
would continue to swoop down for revenge or to prove virility by
stealing horses, but if resisted now could often do greater damage
to each other. However, western Indians did not immediately
suffer large-scale losses as a result of alliance. Although there were
attempts by rival fur-trading groups to draw Indians into alliance,
on the whole western Indians were exempted from the territorial
strategies of the European powers. Early in the eighteenth century
French traders in the west enjoyed some success in getting the
Dakota Sioux to worry the flanks of English traders. One consequence of this commercial-military strategy was a shift of the
Assiniboine northwest away from danger.[6]

But western Indians were spared the larger European territorial
quarrels that had so marked the military history of the eastern half
of North America in the eighteenth century. What rivalry and
conflict occurred in the western interior was between rival British
and French or *Canadien* traders, rather than European armies and
their colonial and forest allies. The French strategy of encirclement
that was employed from 1700 to the 1750s applied only to the area
east of the Mississippi; there was no point in attempting such
tactics in the west. Moreover, since French rule ended everywhere

but the French Shore of Newfoundland and Louisiana in the 1760s, there was no reason for the extension of European quarrels and military alignments into western Canada in the second century of the Bay's existence. What warfare the Europeans encouraged in the west was largely commercial in nature. In this, of course, western Indians fought in their own interest or abstained for the same reason.

More devastating was a consequence of contact that western Indians shared with other aboriginal peoples: disease. Here the indigenous populations' lack of exposure and resistance to European ailments such as smallpox and tuberculosis proved as destructive as it had in the east. In particular, two massive smallpox epidemics of 1780–1 and 1837–8 decimated the lodges. In some cases the Bay's employees were able to employ a crude form of vaccination in the second visitation, ensuring that the consequences in that case would be uneven. The Assiniboine were drastically reduced, but the Cree whose proximity to traders made them candidates for a preventive program were largely unscathed.[7] The Assiniboine might have been reduced to approximately a thousand souls by this second, devastating epidemic.

Other consequences of the contact that took place in the trade were happier. Certainly this was the case for the Europeans. From the Indians they acquired geographical knowledge and guidance on trips of exploration and mapping. They also became acquainted with native food sources such as caribou and waterfowl, gaining knowledge that was invaluable for survival. They also adopted some of the clothing styles and the guerilla tactics of Indian warfare. It is probable that the influence of western Indians on English attitudes was less intense than that on the *Canadiens* of the St Lawrence, since prolonged contact between Indians and English was minimized by the way in which they conducted their trade for the first century after 1670. But informal interaction there was.

The mingling of Indians and Europeans in the western fur trade had an extremely important social result. Miscegenation produced a new native people who emerged as a distinctive group. Sexual contact between the races had also occurred earlier in other parts of Canada, of course, but in western Canada the resulting mixed-blood community was more extensive and had longer lasting social and political results. Officially, the employees of the Hudson's Bay

Company were not supposed to have close relations with the female native population. Company policy forbade such behaviour. But given the isolation of bay posts and the loneliness that inevitably troubled the miserable males stationed at them, it was hardly surprising that such prohibitions were more often honoured in the breach than in the observance. There were cases in which senior officers of the company, while flouting the rules themselves, attempted to enforce the regulations among subordinates, usually with unhappy results for the officers. Gradually the rules were conveniently forgotten, at least in North America, and liaisons between European traders and Indian women became frequent.

The presence of *Canadien* traders in the west from the 1770s onward considerably hastened the process of *métissage*. These traders from Montreal became more common in the west after the Quebec Act reopened the hinterland in 1774 and Jay's Treaty of 1794 forced them out of the American northwest. To prosecute the distant western trade the Montreal men formed a succession of parnerships between 1779 and 1804 that were known as the North West Company. Nor'Westers faced no prohibitions on associating with Indian women, and they clearly understood the commercial value of forming unions with them. As a result of what Montrealers called *mariage à la façon du pays* (marriage according to the custom of the country), commercial links could be established and maintained with the Indians. An Indian wife's family would have a special relationship to their new, Euro-Canadian family member. Unlike European and Euro-Canadian societies, Indian societies did not draw a distinction between public and private spheres, and did not treat women according to an idealized stereotype of weak and helpless femininity. Marriage entailed obligations between the parties, and women were expected to do considerable work alongside their husbands.[8] An Indian wife knew the transportation routes and was expert at taking or trading for skins. Although such marriages were often dissolved when the white man left the country, the wife usually returning to her own people without any fuss or difficulty, many were stable and enduring relationships. What was involved was marriage and economic partnership, not casual sexual gratification and exploitation.

The development of the unique institution of *mariage à la façon du pays* itself indicates that Indians adapted to, rather than being fundamentally altered by, their fur-trade contacts with Europeans. It was the few and amorous Europeans who had to conform to Indian usages, not the much more numerous Indians who adjusted to the newcomers. Indians insisted that the traders pay the customary bride price or gift to the woman's family before the marriage could take place. And the union was often accompanied by traditional Indian rituals such as feasting and gift-giving, smoking of a symbolic pipe, and other familiar practices that varied from nation to nation. Fur-trade marriages further demonstrated that the trade was a relationship in which the natives dominated and from which they benefited.

Although the *Canadiens* may have entered into relationships with Indian women with fewer difficulties than the Hudson's Bay Company employees, both took Indian wives and produced many large and healthy children. In many cases, the offspring of these unions were themselves incorporated into the fur trade as employees of the commercial companies. In the early nineteenth century growing numbers of these mixed-blood people began to locate in the valleys of the Red and Assiniboine rivers in what is now Manitoba. During the first half of the century they would develop as two distinguishable, though in many ways similar, peoples. The Métis were the offspring of the French Canadians in the North West Company and Indian wives; the country born were the descendants of English or Scottish and Indian marriages. (Both groups were and are sometimes referred to as Métis, a blending of terms that somewhat confuses historical references to the two groups.) Both engaged in casual employment for the Hudson's Bay Company, dabbled in illegal trading with men not connected to the company, and occupied a provisioning role in the trade that grew very important as the Bay extended its network inland in response to competition from the Nor'Westers between the 1780s and the early nineteenth century. The Métis were also particularly noteworthy for the way in which they took to the buffalo hunt and made it part of their annual cycle. A distinctive way of life was developing in the narrow, river-front strip farms that stretched back from the Red River in the neighbourhood of Fort Garry.

One of the factors encouraging the emergence of a distinctive mixed-blood community and of that community's sense of its own identity and purpose was the competition and conflict that worsened between rival fur-trade companies in the late eighteenth and early nineteenth centuries. After the abandonment of the posts in the American northwest in the 1790s, the Montreal-based fur traders swung their attentions increasingly to the northwest, to Rupert's Land. Ultimately they extended their trading networks well to the northwest, reaching the watershed that flowed by the Mackenzie River into the Arctic Ocean. The response of the fur trade to competition and the expense of operating over vast distances had always been concentration and monopoly. So, the Montrealers after the revolutionary war fashioned the North West Company, an amalgamation that combined the leadership and capital of a group of Scottish-Canadians with the brawn and daring of largely *Canadien* voyageurs and trip men. The North West Company simply ignored the Bay's claims to monopoly rights in the Hudson Bay watershed and set the Bay's protests aside by their actions, including violence on occasion. This conflict encouraged the growth of Métis nationhood.

Although the emergence of a sense of cultural identity among the Métis was probably only a matter of time and the right circumstances, a decision by a Scottish noble accelerated it. Lord Selkirk's determination to establish an agricultural colony in the Red River area posed an immediate threat to the North West Company and a longer-term danger to those, such as the Indians and the mixed-blood community, who relied on the resources of the country. Colonists meant farms; agriculture meant conflict with commerce. The proposed Selkirk settlement lay athwart the routes used by the Nor'westers in particular, and the prospect of such a colony meant an economic challenge to both Indians and Métis who controlled the provisioning trade. The Montreal men began to point out to the Métis that they were a special people, the New Nation, and that Red River was their territory. The Selkirk settlers were interlopers who had no right to invade their lands and ruin their way of life.

Métis unrest reached a crisis point in 1816. Encouraged by the Nor'westers and led by the able young country-born Cuthbert Grant, the Métis attacked and pillaged Bay posts. As they tried to make their way to meet up with a North West Company brigade, they instead encountered Governor Semple, the leader of the

Selkirk settlement, and a band of farmers at Seven Oaks. When the clash was over, twenty-one settlers and one of Grant's band lay dead. For the Métis the event was the symbolic establishment of nationhood. Seven Oaks was critical to the development of a mixed-blood sense of identity and common purpose.

Seven Oaks was but one of the signs of the change in the western fur trade, an evolution that would have great significance for the Indian peoples. Between the beginning of the trade in earnest in the 1670s and the 1820s there had emerged a large and mutually beneficial trade in furs. The competition had intensifed – driving the commerce further to the north and west, while encouraging amalgamation of at least one of the fur-trade companies – about a century after the Charter of the Company of Adventurers. The arrival of the Nor'westers increased competition, stimulated the use of alcohol in trade, and created incentives to use force to drive the other trader out. Temporarily the Indians were even better positioned to benefit materially from commercial competition. The fur trade was, as already seen, a mutually beneficial trading relationship in which both parties adapted but neither party changed the other fundamentally. Certainly Indians in the fur trade in western Canada during its first century and a half experienced only non-directed cultural change. But the beginning of agricultural settlement at the behest of Selkirk was only the prelude to other important developments. Five years after Seven Oaks, the Montreal-based traders succumbed to competition and distance. Competition with the Bay over such enormous distances was proving too great an economic strain; not even concentration into one company had relieved the pressure for long. In 1821 the Montrealers capitulated to distance and the inner dynamic of the fur-trade frontier: the North West Company and Hudson's Bay Company amalgamated under the title of the latter. The fur trade from the Montreal base ceased; the Bay had defeated the River.

In the half century between the termination of the Montreal-based fur trade and the entrance of Rupert's Land into Confederation major changes occurred in the relationship between Europeans and Indians in what was emerging as the Canadian west. After the amalgamation of 1821, shifts in Hudson's Bay Company policy and in the patterns of western trade depressed the economic condition of the natives and provoked militant reactions. The fur-trade frontier began to be challenged by new forms of the European economic presence. In the Red River district the early stirrings caused by the coming of the agriculturalists, in combination with the arrival of missionaries and the religious institutions of which they were a part, helped to usher in an era of greater prejudice and discrimination by Caucasians against native peoples. By the time the west was integrated politically into the new dominion its native populations were being marginalized by economic change and vanishing resources. They were entering their own age of irrelevance to the needs of the small Euro-Canadian population. At times the changing relations provoked armed resistance, but in most other ways the native inhabitants were unwilling or unable to do much to hold back the changes that were destroying their way of life.

After 1821 the most important factor in the relations between western Indians and the traders was the absence of competition in the fur trade. Having eliminated the North West Company's demand for furs that had driven up prices and encouraged violence and alcohol abuse, the Bay moved to trim its expenses. Many casual employees, particularly Métis and country born in Red River, found themselves without work; and most Indians found the prices that they could get for their pelts dropping. The economies that Governor George Simpson effected had their greatest impact in the northern departments of the Bay's vast territory, but to one degree or another these changes reached almost all the Indians in the lands in which the Bay traded.

Not all the changes were intended to benefit the company at the expense of westerners. Simpson's 'reforms' included attempts to curb the widespread use of alcohol, a measure that no doubt was beneficial to the Indians. Unfortunately, whatever good effects flowed from this change were more than offset by the continuing problem of disease, in particular the massive 1837–8 epidemics in the western interior. Although the terms of the commercial relationship had turned somewhat against the Indian and mixed-blood populations throughout the west, the essence of the link continued to be that each party harboured a benign attitude towards the other. A minuscule fly in the fur-trade ointment, however, was the increasingly shrill criticism flung by church and humanitarian groups against the Hudson's Bay Company for doing nothing to 'raise their level of civilization.'[9]

The philanthropists were going to make it their business in western Canada, as they had already in Maritime and central Canada, to interest themselves on behalf of the native populations. Their concerns and ministrations were the humanitarian side of the juggernaut of British imperialism and trade. In 1820 John West of the British Church Missionary Society (CMS) arrived in Red River to minister to the anglophone and non-Catholic part of the mixed-blood community.[10] The Roman Catholic Oblates also continued their efforts in the prairie region, the one continuing link between Quebec and the west between 1821 and the 1870s.

This form of missionary presence was different from the early Jesuits and from the commercial and military Europeans who had hitherto dominated the relationship. These missionaries, especially the Anglicans of the CMS, had a program of assimilation of the Indians. Unlike the Jesuits in New France, whose sophistication and worldwide experience had led them to reject the notion that it was necessary to turn the Indians into Europeans before they could be made into Christians, the nineteenth-century evangelists were convinced that assimilation had to precede or at least accompany religious conversion if conversion was to be thorough and lasting. In part this difference was attributable to the lesser degree of familiarity with cross-cultural relationships that the missionaries of the nineteenth century had. But it was also based on an increasingly racist attitude towards indigenous peoples in the British Empire that was infecting and affecting British policy towards native peoples. Thus, British humanitarianism was the soft core of a drive to bring about directed cultural change whose hard outer shell was racism. That 'science' was increasingly 'proving' that notions of superiority towards native peoples were justified merely made that shell all the tougher.

In western Canada after the 1820s an attempt to bring about directed change was visible in and around the small outposts of European settlement, as at the forks of the Red and Assiniboine rivers in Rupert's Land. John West was fairly typical. Unwilling or unable to master the Indian languages, his approach was to teach English so as to impart the Word in his own language to his country-born children who often spoke Cree. Schools thus made their appearance in Red River, not as agencies of social control so much as institutions of culture change. Both day schools and a residential school were used. The desire to educate was frustrated, however, by the nomadism of the pupils' families; hence teaching agricultural methods as well as basic academic subjects was required to lead the people from a wandering way of life to sedentary agriculture. In the tiny Anglican experiment at Red River in the 1820s were found the principal elements of the later drive to assimilate Indians throughout many parts of Canada: schooling, religion, and agriculture. With the missionaries came the 'policy of "the Bible and the plough."'[11]

White-skinned women were another disturbing presence in the west. There had always been women in close relationship to the Europeans, because the fur trade encouraged unions between male traders and female Indians. Over time observers noted that fur traders began to turn more and more towards the mixed-blood daughters of these earlier marriages. Apparently, Métis and country-born women had all the skills and advantages of their Indian mothers, but found it easier to adapt to life with Europeans. The final stage of this process was commented on by a Hudson's Bay trader in 1840: 'There is a strange revolution in the manners of the country; Indian wives were at one time the vogue, the half-breed supplanted these, and now we have the lovely tender exotic torn from its parent bed to pine and languish in the desert.'[12] The fur trader expressed poetically an ugly social reality. White men preferred white women when Caucasian females were available and the economic usefulness of native women had declined. This racial preference was encouraged by the attitudes and practices of senior company men such as George Simpson. In the 1820s in Red River, Simpson began to shun and ostracize socially the Indian and mixed-blood wives of company men, and he soon replaced the succession of native companions he himself had had with a British wife. The racist tendency to look down on native women – and, by extension, on natives in general – was greatly strengthened by the presence of an increasing number of European women. Such attitudes were generally encouraged by the missionaries, who regarded *mariage à la façon du pays* as no marriage at all.

These attitudes began to drive a wedge between the previously close-knit Europeans and mixed-blood people in the western interior. There is also some evidence that these developments encouraged a rift between the Métis and the country born, though this is not absolutely proven.[13] However, it is certainly true that, in some cases, members of the country-born community associated themselves with the British Caucasians and with the small trickle of 'Canadians' who began to arrive at mid-century because of the social advancement they believed such connections would bring. The growth of a white female population and a clique of white missionaries in Red River in the decades after 1821 began to jeopardize the racial harmony of the community. This was a gloomy local example of what was happening to Indian-white relations generally in British North America.

But in other practical ways the mixed-blood community in Rupert's Land was growing in confidence and comfort at the time. If it were true that the serpent of racism had entered the garden, it was still a pretty lush and comfortable arbour in which to reside. If Simpson's economies had reduced employment and lowered prices for furs and provisions, and if the Métis and country born had now to compete with the Indians for the revenues of the provisioning trade, there were also compensations. In particular the growth in demand for buffalo robes in the United States in the first half of the century was creating an economic alternative for both Indians and mixed-blood groups. The annual buffalo hunt of the Métis, with its quasi-political organization and socially integrating rituals, became a force for strengthening the Métis sense of collective identity that had emerged at the battle at Seven Oaks. Unfortunately, the increasing demand for buffalo hides to which the Métis responded encouraged a great expansion of the hunting of these animals.

The development of an alternative commercial market, in this case for buffalo robes, also raised the old question of the Métis community's relations with the Hudson's Bay Company. The Bay, after all, claimed to have a licence to all the trade of the region, and it would resist efforts to exploit the advantages of trade in the south. The Métis, with Seven Oaks still a memory and with their growing sense of unity, were not likely to acquiesce easily in company attempts to curb their commercial ambitions. The clash, in some ways a non-violent version of Seven Oaks, came in 1849 in the Sayer case. Guillaume Sayer was a Métis trader whom the company prosecuted for trading with the Americans in breach of their monopoly. Sayer's countrymen, with the senior Louis Riel among their leaders, organized a local version of the buffalo hunt they used on the plains and overawed the court. Court and company found a sensible way out: the jury convicted but recommended mercy; the Bay's chief factor claimed to be satisfied and dropped charges against other Métis freebooters. The armed men who surrounded the courthouse understood the significance of what had happened. They discharged their weapons in celebration and shouted, 'Vive la liberté! La commerce est libre!'[14]

For the Indians of the western interior there was less reason to celebrate in these years of transition away from commercial relations with the Europeans. One sign of impending change was the initiation of treaty-making in the west – a sure indication that more white men wanted to come, and to come not just to trade but to remake the region. Even before the amalgamation of the fur trade, Lord Selkirk had arranged in 1817 for a treaty with the Indians of the Red and Assiniboine rivers area in preparation for the agricultural settlement he planned to sponsor and direct. With representatives of Ojibwa and Cree, he had bargained an annual payment of tobacco worth £100 to each tribe in return for a 'tract of land adjacent to Red River and Assiniboine River' that extended 'in breadth to the distance of two English statute miles back from the banks of the river.' When the Indians asked what constituted two statute miles, they were informed 'that it was the greatest distance, at which a horse on the level prairie could be seen, or daylight seen under his belly between his legs.'[15] The agreement was an interesting blend of tradition and innovation. It paralleled what was happening in Upper Canada by using modest annual payments rather than a large one-time financial settlement, and it adopted a distinctively western Canadian definition of the extent of the ceded lands. The closest approximation to this in previous treaties had been the 'gunshot treaty' in Upper Canada.

Other aspects of the new era after 1821 were more problematic for the western Indians than the treaty of 1817. After the amalgamation of 1821 the dramatic increase in demand for the products of the bison affected some of them seriously. In central

Manitoba, for example, the Ojibwa found themselves increasingly dependent on the Hudson's Bay Company for foodstuffs by the 1860s, as the land's ability to provide adequate supplies of game and fish declined. The Ojibwa became virtual employees of the company, but without security of real employment. If the Bay's needs changed, the Ojibwa would find themselves abandoned.

The effects of shifting trade patterns had more immediate and more negative effects on the nations of the southern plains in the 1850s and 1860s. The leading groups were the Sioux, many of whom were based in the United States, the Blackfoot Confederacy of present-day southern Alberta, and the Cree and Assiniboine who began to gravitate to the southwest in pursuit of the bison herds that yielded such profitable products. These groups resented the expanding Métis buffalo hunt. In 1857 the Cree announced that they would try to prevent the mixed-blood bands from hunting in their territories or traversing them for any commercial purposes. The Indian-Métis confrontations over access to the bison resource produced many conflicts. One of the major encounters, part of Métis legend, took place between them and the Sioux at the Grand Coteau, the escarpment that separates the Missouri and Assiniboine river systems in the northern United States and southern Canadian plains, in June of 1851. A youthful Gabriel Dumont was a member of the party that fought off the Sioux from inside a circle of carts reinforced with sacks of food and other materials. These encounters became all too frequent in the middle decades of the century, as the resources of the plains came under increasing pressure from Indians, Métis, and whites.

The decade of the 1860s was one of increasing warfare between the Cree and the Blackfoot as a consequence of the Cree invasion of Blackfoot traditional hunting territories. Such conflicts between Blackfoot and Cree and their Assiniboine neighbours were not new; there was a well-established tradition of raiding and small-scale skirmishing. In the past these incidents had usually been the consequence of a desire on one side or the other to steal horses. Such exploits were demonstrations of manliness, rites of passage into adult society among the Plains Indians. Horse-stealing, like counting *coup* (usually a non-violent exploit such as sneaking into a foe's camp and touching one of the sleeping enemies, but occasionally also the taking of the scalp of a fallen rival), was a means of winning full acceptance into adult society. In the 1860s, however, the conflicts became increasingly serious and destructive, for they were motivated by a desire to restrict access to a diminishing resource by the various Indian nations. Indian diplomats tried repeatedly but futilely to restore peace towards the end of the 1860s, but the general rule remained enmity and bloodshed between the Cree-Assiniboine and Blackfoot forces.[16]

These developments among Métis and western Indians reflected the increasing pressure that the innovations brought by Europeans were applying to traditional ways. Although the years from the 1820s to the 1860s would later be regarded by the Métis as a golden age in which they prospered and refined their cultural practices and institutions, the period was in fact part of a transition towards a new, less glittering age. The Indians, who first were affected by the changes, and who attempted to resist the negative effects by protecting their hunting territory and principal resource, would be even more seriously disrupted by these alterations. They knew, as the Métis appeared not to, that the coming of Euro-Canadians spelt, directly or indirectly, trouble for the indigenous populations. For those among the Métis and Indian community in the western interior who did not appreciate the threat, rumours that the Province of Canada wanted to acquire the entire region from the Hudson's Bay Company began to bring the danger into focus.

8

Contact, commerce, and Christianity on the Pacific

Between approximately 1770 and 1870 the Indian peoples north and west of the plains area went through a similar experience to that of their prairie neighbours. The Subarctic, Cordillera, and northwest coast regions contained a bewildering array of indigenous peoples, but almost all of them found that history subjected them to the common experience of contact and commercial intercourse with European newcomers. The effects of this interaction were uneven. The northern Athapaskans, isolated as they were by distance and climate, probably experienced the least disruption of their traditional ways. The tribes of the British Columbian interior felt the impact of European commerce later than most other native peoples in Canada, but they went through the same phases in a compressed period of time. The coastal nations of the Pacific province profited immensely, in both material and cultural terms, from the fur trade in their region. But after 1770 all three groups – northern Athapaskans, Indians of the Cordillera and British Columbian interior, and natives of the northwest coast – became familiar with the impact of, first, European commerce and, later, European evangelization.

The Athapaskan-speaking groups of the area north and west of the plains comprised a number of separate peoples. From north to south, from Alaska to the prairie provinces, they numbered the

Kutchin, Nahani, Hare, Dogrib, Yellowknife, Slave, Chipewyan, Beaver, and Sekani. (The Sekani, Beaver, and Slave actually resided in the northern part of present-day British Columbia, but are usually classified with the other Athapaskans as part of the Subarctic Indian cultural area.)[1] In many ways they resembled the Algonkians, though the Chipewyan were inveterate enemies of the Cree. Theirs was principally a nomadic hunting, fishing, and gathering economy, and their social structure was based on the small hunting groups that were also found among many Algonkians. During the brief summers, larger concentrations of up to 100 people would assemble at commonly known sites that were good for fishing and hunting. Given the harsh land in which they lived and their nomadic way of life, Athapaskans' population concentration and political organization were at a rudimentary level. One of the distinguishing features of their culture, however, was its rich artistic accomplishments. Decorated clothing, adorned carrying bags for infants, and other colourful items of everday use displayed an astonishing richness.[2] With hide, quills, hair, and sinew, Athapaskans produced parkas and footwear that were as attractive as they were useful. It was almost as if the small Athapaskan bands, unable to accumulate many material goods, poured their creativity and pride into artistic expression.

Prior to the twentieth century most of the Athapaskans had only restricted contact with Euro-Canadian society. From about the 1770s onwards the commerce in furs began to impinge on their homeland, introducing the varied influences and adaptations that have been noticed elsewhere. On the whole it was the more southerly groups such as the Chipewyan, Slave, and Beaver who were most in contact and most influenced. However, since the fur trade, especially after the amalgamation of 1821, was a fairly restricted presence, its impact was less among Athapaskans than it was on the Cree, Saulteaux, and Assiniboine to the south. The greatest negative effect of contact was disease; the most positive the acquisition of tools and weapons.

The Indian peoples of the British Columbian interior came into contact with European strangers later than the Athapaskans and felt a greater impact. These groups included, from north to south, the Carrier, Chilcotin, Interior Salish, and Kootenay, and each of these groupings in turn contained a number of smaller subgroups.[3]

Indian nations of British Columbia

The Interior Salish, for example, numbered the Thompson, Lillooet, Okanagan, and Shuswap among their nation. The Carrier broke down into Upper Carrier, Lower Carrier, and Babine. The classification of these various peoples was based upon their languages, and each major linguistic group contained within it several dialects. In general, the Cordilleran Indians of British Columbia depended on hunting, fishing, and gathering of natural foods for their survival. Their degree of nomadism and population concentration depended greatly on the topography, climate, and resources of the region in which they dwelt. As will be seen, the interior Indians briefly became part of the fur trade in the nineteenth century, but prior to their involvement there was an important maritime phase of the fur trade on the Pacific.

In a cultural sense, the northwest Pacific coast, where the maritime fur trade began late in the eighteenth century, was one of the wonders of the world. In the many fiords of the mainland and of the large island to which Captain George Vancouver would give his name dwelt a bewildering array of Indian nations. Although they had many similarities, especially in their dependence on the sea and lush vegetation of the region, these peoples are classified into a large number of ethnic divisions by anthropologists, their separate existences in the isolated portions of the coastal areas having produced sufficient distinctiveness to justify such treatment. Running from north to south down the coast were found the Tlingit, Tsimshian, Bella Coola, Kwakiutl, and Coast Salish; the Haida were concentrated in the Queen Charlotte Islands, while the Nootka resided on the west coast of Vancouver Island. Within an ethnic division (such as the Tsimshian) there might be language subdivisions (Tsetsaut, Tsimshian), not to mention several major dialects (Gitksan, Nishga, and Tsimshian). There were also groupings into tribes and bands based on their social and political organization that were more meaningful than dialect, language, or ethnicity. The Pacific Indians were a diverse and distinctive human community.

The Haida, Nootka, Kwakiutl, Tsimshian, Bella Coola, and Coast Salish were characterized by three features. The first was their Maritime orientation, which in pre-contact times gave them a level of affluence and comfort largely unknown by other Indians in the future Canada. No fewer than five species of Pacific salmon sent millions of their kind to the rivers to spawn each season, and herring and smelt were there, too, in great profusion. The eulachon, or candlefish, which provided coastal Indians with a valuable oil, also spawned in the rivers, while clams and crabs were easily available in many centres. Sea mammals such as whales, seals, and porpoises and the sea otter added to the rich supply, and on the mainland many freshwater fish, such as trout, could be taken easily. The maritime resources of the area permitted a rich and secure life for the Indian peoples of the northwest Pacific coast.

Second, affluence combined with a prolonged rainy winter season to encourage the development of a spectacular art. The vast moisture-laden clouds that were generated by the warm Japan Current emptied their water on the land and produced immense forests of fir, spruce, hemlock, and cedar. Affluence, precipitation, and easily available timber created both a need for substantial houses and the means to build them. Many of the coastal peoples dwelt in relatively large population concentrations in massive wooden houses. Affluence and a sedentary existence also made it possible for these coastal Indians to develop their art to heights unreached by other peoples in North America. The Haida in particular were noted for their elaborate art, including baskets and the tall totem poles and house fronts that graphically recorded their history and identity. The same factors also produced complex and sophisticated social and political structures. One measure of the impact of affluence on the Northwest Coast Indians was the hierarchical nature of their social structure: their villages consisted of nobles, commoners, and slaves, the latter usually the unfortunate victims of war.

A third distinguishing characteristic among some of these peoples that was also an offshoot of their material wealth and leisure was an extensive and time-consuming ceremonial life that passed the long, rainy winters while, at the same time, filling certain social needs. The most famous of these practices, one that was most pronounced among the Kwakiutl, was the potlatch. This important feasting ritual had several social purposes. It was employed as a rite of passage, as in a young person's coming of age and taking a name. It was used to reinforce status or to challenge the higher status of another, and to overawe neighbouring villages. The means in each case was the same: distribution of vast quantities of food and gifts at monumental feasts. It was for use at these potlatches that many of the beautiful coastal works of art and utility – such as bent-corner boxes, copper escutcheons, and highly decorated eating utensils – were created. The potlatch was deservedly called a form of 'fighting with property'; but it also was an ingenious method for registering important events, reordering status relationships within a group, and redistributing material wealth.[4] The potlatch and the totem pole were merely two of many distinctive features of Pacific Indian societies that had emerged prior to the coming of the European.

Although it was Spaniards who came at first to the Pacific coast, they were quickly followed and then supplanted by Englishmen and Americans.[5] The Spaniard Juan Pérez encountered the Haida in July 1774, in the first meeting whose record has survived, and traded for furs with them. Four years later the British captain James Cook spent weeks in Nootka Sound and discovered the availability of sea-otter furs. By the 1790s the maritime fur trade was well established, American vessels having joined the British and Spanish. This form of commerce dominated until the second decade of the nineteenth century, when a land-based trade that involved coastal and interior tribes such as the Interior Salish, Kootenay, and others developed. The pattern of relations that emerged between the Europeans and natives bore striking resemblances to the commercial encounters that had begun earlier in the Hudson Bay watershed, the Shield region of New France, and the Atlantic littoral.

The commercial relations on the Pacific 'were part of a mutually beneficial trading relationship.'[6] Bloody incidents between traders and natives, even in the maritime phase, did occur. But generally relations were harmonious as newcomers and indigenous peoples participated in a commerce for furs, especially that of the sea otter, that rewarded both parties. Indians traded because commerce meant access to European goods, and the coastal Indians were both demanding and selective. The Nootka spurned glass beads that were so obviously inferior for decorative purposes to their own metalwork and wood products; the chief prizes that Indians of the Pacific sought were iron products. The Haida called the Europeans 'Yets-Haida,' which meant 'iron men.'[7] The Indians on the Pacific quickly learned to barter skilfully in order to exact the highest prices, and as early as the 1780s one Spaniard lamented that the truly profitable days of the trade were over. Exactly as the French on the St Lawrence had discovered, the Indians on the Pacific learned to await the arrival of numerous vessels before trading. During the land-based phase of the commerce, the additional demand for furs from Russians and Americans as well as the 'King George men,' as Pacific Indians called the English, enabled them to profit substantially. The other principal trade item in both the maritime and land-based exchange was the blanket, which served not just as clothing for the Indians who obtained them from the Europeans but also as a form of currency that they could use in the potlatch and in trade with more remote tribes. As the interest in blankets partly indicated, coastal Indians soon made use of their access to Europeans to forge for themselves a role as middlemen.

The early trade in British Columbia, especially its maritime phase, brought about harmonious relations and non-directed cultural change. Traders on occasional visits by means of vessels had neither reason nor opportunity to interfere with the Indians' way of doing things. There was no incentive to attack the more numerous and well-organized Indians. The dominance of the Indian partner in the commerce was signalled on the west coast by the language of business. A dialect called 'trade Chinook,' based on Indian languages, developed as the common tongue of business people in the Pacific fur trade. But the familiar patterns of losses to disease and the adverse effects of alcohol abuse could also be seen on the Pacific in the first few decades of both the maritime and land-based fur trade there. Although the maritime trade did not, for obvious reasons, encourage marriage between Europeans and Indians, some liaisons did occur, and during the land-based period of commerce more enduring relationships developed alongside the temporary unions that had typified the maritime phase. The emergence of Home Guards near some of the forts was also observable in the land-based phase, though the relative proportions of Indians and mixed-blood people are not at all clear.

Finally, the Pacific fur trade enriched the material life of the

Indian peoples. But here, too, European goods meant principally cultural efflorescence rather than substantial change: European tools made producing the art – especially wood carving – easier, and affluence allowed for more elaborate ceremonial. 'There is little doubt that the fur trade produced an increase in the number and size of potlatches among the coastal Indians.'[8] Greater wealth also allowed the Kwakiutl to use potlatching, rather than traditional warfare, to humble enemies and rivals. An elderly Kwakiutl said in 1895, 'the white men came and stopped up that stream of blood with wealth. Now we fight with our wealth.'[9]

The Pacific fur-trade relationship between the 1770s and 1820s, in other words, was a 'mutually beneficial economic symbiosis' that brought about non-directed cultural change.[10] The essence of the relationship was identified by a trader who pointed out that his kind 'are desirous of gain' and asked, 'Is it not self-evident we will manage our business with more economy by being on good terms with the Indians than if at variance'?[11] Mutually beneficial interaction and non-directed change added up to harmony and profit for both sides in the early decades of the relationship in British Columbia. In this respect the Pacific coast was like Rupert's Land before the amalgamation of the rival companies, or the eastern woodlands before farmers began to encroach in the early nineteenth century on the forest.

Between the amalgamation of the fur-trade companies in 1821 and the union of British Columbia with Canada in 1871, a pattern that was similar to that on the plains, though less traumatic, emerged on the Pacific. The period from 1821 until the 1850s was one in which a land-based fur trade supplanted the old maritime commerce. But, although the locus of trade shifted from the decks of ships to posts beside rivers, the nature of the commercial relationship between Indians and Europeans did not change. The economies instituted by Governor Simpson of the Hudson's Bay Company might have meant serious loss of income for the Indians had not continuing competition from both Russians in the north and Americans to the south forced the Bay to keep its cost-cutting there to a minimum. Over the decades the Bay would gradually eliminate most of this competition, but by the time this was accomplished the fur trade was declining in importance on the Pacific anyway.

Many features of the commercial relationship of Indians and white men on the Pacific were reminiscent of developments that had occurred earlier on the plains, in the eastern woodlands, and by the Atlantic. Indian bands that were providentially well situated exploited their position by preventing access to the traders by other groups, carving for themselves a lucrative role as middlemen in the trade. In most cases the commerce between these middlemen and less fortunately situated groups was built on a network of trading relationships that had existed before the Europeans arrived with their iron goods and alcohol. In some cases a 'Home Guard' of Indians emerged in close proximity to the fur-trade posts, and sometimes these Indians became dependent on the posts for subsistence. A particularly noteworthy example of this development were the Songhees who moved from the Cadboro Bay area in the 1840s to be close to Fort Victoria. Indian women played an important role in the land-based fur trade in British Columbia as they had in the western interior because of their skills and knowledge, their role in cementing commercial alliance, and because of the mutual attractions that developed in many cases between the native women and the strangers. And, finally, Indians to a great extent continued to determine how, or even if, trade would be conducted. In this respect, the case of the interior Chilcotin was particularly instructive. They rebuffed all company blandishments and steadfastly refused to be drawn into the commercial network.[12]

Throughout the land-based era the fur trade in the Pacific region nurtured relations between Indians and Europeans that were mutually beneficial. Although exposure to alcohol and to prostitution around the posts was demoralizing to some Indians, most other aspects of the trade were advantageous. As had been noticeable with the Huron in the seventeenth century, the coastal Indians in particular benefited from the trade by accumulating great amounts of material wealth that were used to enrich their existing ceremonial practices. The infusion of European goods enriched this process of redistribution and contention for status without disrupting it during the fur-trade period. Similarly, coastal art experienced its most significant growth. The totem pole, in particular, enjoyed great popularity in this affluent era.

The 1850s and 1860s were a transitional period in the Pacific region as they were in the western interior. The dates 1849 and 1857–8 marked key points in the evolution that was under way: in 1849 Britain created the colony of Vancouver Island under company jurisdiction; in 1857 William Duncan, one of the most famous missionaries in Canadian history, came to the coast; and in 1858 a horde of gold-seeking adventurers descended on the mainland. With the arrival of the prospectors the frontier of settlement was born. Although the gold-mining phase seemed painful while it was going on, it would turn out to be trifling compared to the disruptive impact of government administrators, missionaries, and settlers on the Indians of the Pacific.

If all the administrators had been like the second governor of Vancouver Island, these changes might not have been so negative for the Indians. James Douglas, the governor of Vancouver Island from 1851 to 1864, and then of both the island and the mainland colony of British Columbia, brought long experience in the fur trade to his dealings with the Indians.[13] Douglas followed a policy of treating complaints against Indians by the small but growing number of whites in the colony scrupulously: individual malefactors were pursued and punished, but bands were not held accountable for the misdemeanours of individuals. This did not always satisfy settlers who claimed the Indians had engaged in unprovoked incursions on their lands or property, but it did preserve the peace.

Douglas also negotiated some fourteen treaties with Indians in Victoria, Nanaimo, and Fort Rupert, securing access to the region for settlers in exchange for modest lump-sum payments from company stores. Because the governor's sole purpose was to secure title in order to permit settlement, the areas for which he bargained were few and limited in extent. For example, when the Cowichan Indians on Vancouver Island indicated that they would like to negotiate a treaty as the Songhees in the Fort Victoria area had done, they were turned down because there was no interest in settling that far north on the island. What the Indians understood the treaties to mean, and what their motives for negotiating were is less clear. That they understood that they were agreeing to total and exclusive ownership – alienation, to use the English legal term – of land by the European power seems unlikely. In any event, the pattern of treaty-making came to a halt as Douglas's access to company supplies from which to make payment was terminated in the 1860s when the governor had to share power with an elected assembly. The emerging settler society did not agree with Douglas that the best policy was to satisfy Indian interests in advance of settlement.

Douglas also followed a policy of laying out tracts reserved for Indians, regardless of whether or not there was treaty with them, as the incursions of whites increased in the 1850s and 1860s. The governor's instructions to commissioners were to give the Indians what they wanted, both in terms of location of reserves and their extent. Near Kamloops, for example, the reserve that was set aside stretched some six miles along the North Thompson River, twelve miles on the South Thompson, and ran back to the mountains. If Indians subsequently decided that they needed more land, Douglas wanted his officials to oblige them. And in marked contrast to what had occurred in the Maritimes and in central British North America, under Douglas squatters on Indian lands in the Pacific were informed that they had to decamp. While Douglas was not without his prejudices and desires to 'improve' Indians by education and other means, his administration stands out as singularly intelligent in comparison with others elsewhere on the continent and with those who came after him. The fact that he was a former fur trader and had a mixed-blood wife explained much of his sensible approach to dealing with the Indians; the same fact went far to explain the settlers' increasing hostility towards him in the 1860s.

Among the greatest problems that Douglas and the Indians had to face was the gold rush that occurred in 1858. The sort of men who came up the Fraser in search of gold were not likely to worry much about Indians or Indian rights. They were largely single adventurers without roots or commitment to the country, and those among them who came to British territory from the rush in California unfortunately brought with them American attitudes towards Indians. But too much should not be made of national differences, because underlying the conflicts between Indians and prospectors or miners were irreconcilable desires for land. Indian groups often tried to stop the ingress of prospectors, either to monopolize control of the gold resource or to secure compensation for use of lands they considered theirs. Once the white miners became established, there were the usual incidents about missing equipment, or attacks on Indian men or their spouses. It was only with the greatest of difficulty that order was kept in the gold-mining districts during what was a brief but intense encounter. The Fraser rush was largely confined to 1858; the craze in the Cariboo occurred mainly in the early 1860s; and more remote valleys were the sites of strikes and rushes a decade later. What came after the prospectors and miners would be much worse.

What came after were large numbers of settlers and missionaries. Again, it is important to keep the proportions of the change in some perspective. What would become the province of British Columbia in 1871 remained predominantly Indian in population until the 1880s. Not until the arrival of the railway and significant immigration in the 1880s would the white population surpass the native. But even a minority of settlers proved troublesome in the 1860s. The fundamental reason was that settlers on Vancouver Island and in the valleys of the interior wanted exclusive access to lands that Indians regarded as theirs. The Indians, as they had with the gold seekers, sometimes tried to resist the invasion. In 1860, at Alberni on the island, Indians informed a large party that arrived on armed vessels that they wanted no part of their proposed purchase of lands on which to erect a sawmill. Their spokesman pointedly told the whites 'we do not want the white man. He steals what we have. We wish to live as we are.'[14] But the Indians were as realistic about the white man's power as they were about the white man; these Indians understood the threat of the ships' cannon and reluctantly removed themselves from the spot after concluding terms for the land in the area. Other forms of resistance could be more forceful if the size of the parties were different from those at Alberni. In 1864, for instance, thirteen of a party of road builders were killed by Indians in the Homathco valley in the northern interior.[15] How many Indian bands responded to these incursions by tactics of withdrawal is unknown.

The Indians' problems were compounded by a change in the attitude of government administrators and the arrival of missionaries. After 1864 Douglas was no longer in charge of relations with the Indians, and his successor, Joseph Trutch, lacked his sympathy with and understanding of Indians and their ways. Trutch not only refused to apportion lands to Indians in reserves; he and his agents worked steadily to despoil those Indians who had taken reserves of much of their land in response to settler demands that they be allowed access to property they regarded as standing unused. Government and settlers undertook these actions with a combination of legalistic justification and economic ambition to persuade themselves of the legitimacy of their actions. Tiresomely familiar doctrines about ownership of land being acquired only by the addition of labour in horticulture and husbandry were borrowed and articulated by the squeamish. Notions of the importance of rapid development and racist stereotypes of Indian shiftlessness and improvidence were bandied about by those, like Trutch, who were less concerned with moralizing than with economic growth.

Whatever the rationalization used, the Indians paid the price. They were in many cases forced off parts or all of lands they had been guaranteed. The most infamous instance was the Songhees reserve in what was now the growing settlement of Victoria. Indians there were moved in response to the demands of people who had their eye on real estate; the dislocation was justified with preachings about removing them from the degradation brought by alcohol and commercial sex. The fact that Victoria was becoming a summer haunt for northern bands in search of trade and recreation simply made the settlers all the more uneasy. The coerced removal of the Songhees was a metaphor for the dispossession of thousands of British Columbian Indians in the era of settlement and under Trutch's ministrations.

The era of transition was also marked by the arrival of more concerted missionary action. The Oblates began their work in the lower mainland of the future British Columbia in the 1840s, and over the next five decades spread their missions up the Fraser, into the Cariboo district, and even into the remote country of the Carrier in the northern interior. Their most notable contribution to the history of missions to the Indians was the 'Durieu System' that was developed by the Oblate bishop for whom it was named. The system had two phases, one of repression of faults and another of character formation. Wherever possible, as at Mission City on the Fraser, the Oblates gathered their Indian followers in settlements of their own, the better to protect them from contact with European vices. For purposes of detecting and repressing faults, Durieu and his Oblate followers appointed chiefs, captains, and watchmen, who also meted out punishments. Especially controversial were the whippings that were part of the public penance in which these missionaries believed. A more positive aspect of the system was an emphasis on symbolism and religious spectacle. The Oblates gave chiefs in whom they had confidence flags with the order's motto – 'Religion, temperance, civilization' – emblazoned on them, and they promoted and produced elaborate passion plays which, for the natives, became important spectacles and feasts.[16]

The other major evangelical presence on the Pacific was the Anglicans' Church Missionary Society. The Anglicans had ministered there in the 1840s, but from the later 1850s on their work became more extensive and better organized. In particular, the arrival of William Duncan of the CMS at Port Simpson in 1857 inaugurated an important new phase in Indian-European relations along the frontier of faith. Duncan's efforts among the Tsimshian were merely a local example of an extensive missionary effort by British Christians in such places as Africa, New Zealand, and Australia.[17] The CMS advocated a program that would lead to the indigenization of the Christian church by training natives to become not just parishioners but also clergy of their own communities of worship. In British Columbia, Duncan's experiment would deviate from this pattern. European leadership would degenerate into control; and, partly in consequence, natives would not assume leadership of the new institution.

In 1862 Duncan and a band of Tsimshian moved from Port Simpson to Metlakatla to get away from the corrupting influence of whites and Indian unbelievers. At Metlakatla they established a type of commune that practised Christianity and also transferred education, industrial training, and Europeanized amusements. The Indians were encouraged or coerced to become European in everything but the colour of their skin: their clothing, houses, decorum, and their adoption of that quintessentially English of amusements – the brass band – testified to the complete cultural change that Duncan was trying to effect. But Duncan found that even among adherents and supporters, compulsion remained a necessity. Not only was he preacher and teacher, but as magistrate he also directed the native constables who enforced the community's laws.

Duncan's experiment was but a tiny island in the sea of relations at this time, and too much should not be made of it or its significance. Only part of one major ethnic group, the Tsimshian, was affected, and even among those in Metlakatla there were disruptions. A nativistic movement challenged the dominance of Christian beliefs at one time,[18] and Duncan had to remove from Metlakatla to New Metlakatla in Alaska because of conflict with his supervisors in England. Moreover, there were signs at Metlakatla and other missionary establishments that Indians in the far west tended, if left to their own devices, merely to appropriate the Christian god and incorporate it in their pantheon of spirits and ghosts. But what is significant is the way that Duncan and his experiment, like Bishop Durieu and his 'system,' were lionized both in Britain and the Dominion of Canada. Clearly, many so-called humanitarians thought that the near-totalitarian control and directed cultural change that Mission City and Metlakatla represented were what was best for, and worked most effectively with, the aboriginal inhabitants in an era of settlement and missions.

From the mid-nineteenth century onward, Duncan and the Anglicans would labour among the Indians of the Pacific in the company of other Christian groups. The Catholics, represented by the Sisters of St Ann and the Oblates, competed with them both in coastal and interior locations. Anglicans and Oblates were joined in the latter part of the Victorian era by Methodist missionaries, the best known of whom was Thomas Crosby. All such efforts were manifestations of the increasing interest in evangelism in Britain and in British North America, a growing interest that would lead in the last decades of the century to massive overseas efforts and extensive endeavours within Canada to convert the people that missionaries termed 'the heathen.' However well-intentioned their efforts were – and there can be no doubt that their motives, judged by their assumptions, were benign – the results would often be harmful to the Indians who were already suffering the corrosive effects of the immigration of European and Euro-Canadian agricultural settlers.

Thus, in the Pacific region, the era that stretched from the fur trade to the entry of this vast territory into the Dominion of Canada in 1871 was one of dramatic shifts. In the north, in the lands of the

Athapaskan peoples, the mutually beneficial fur trade had become well established after the 1770s, and changes in the organizational structure of the fur trade in 1821 did not have a profound effect. (Indeed, it would not be until almost the twentieth century that the Euro-Canadian presence had a heavy impact on the northern peoples.) On the Pacific coast and in the Cordillera the same pattern that had established itself in the plains region emerged after 1774. The fur trade, which had begun its maritime phase in that year, moved inland early in the nineteenth century and pretty well ran its course save in the northern interior in the half century after 1821. The land-based fur trade gave way to the mining and settlement frontiers in the 1850s and 1860s, much as the maritime fur trade had been supplanted earlier in the century by the commerce centred on the posts. Experiments in treaty-making, reserve allocation, and the directed cultural change of the mission-aries all took place both on Vancouver Island and the mainland. At the time of British Columbia's union with Canada, Indians were still numerically dominant in the new province, but those of them who had come into contact with settlers, missionaries, or Joseph Trutch's employees understood all too well that their future was far from bright.

9

Resistance in Red River and the numbered treaties

Canada's acquisition of Rupert's Land would create the need for a new Indian policy. Since the later 1850s agrarian and business expansionists in the future province of Ontario had futilely been demanding the acquisition of the Hudson's Bay Company lands and their annexation to the Province of Canada. After the union of the Province of Canada was dissolved and its constituent elements merged into a general union of British North American colonies in 1867, Canada intended to acquire and absorb the Hudson's Bay Company lands to appease the commercial ambitions of Toronto and the land hunger of farmers in Ontario's southwestern peninsula. The acquisition of the northwest, which would be attempted in 1869, was fraught with problems and challenges. And it would make clear the need for a new native policy in western Canada.

The old Province of Canada and the new Dominion of Canada between them took several steps that largely shaped the policies that would be applied to western Indians in the 1870s and 1880s. The first event of this critical phase, Canada's Gradual Civilization Act of 1857, defined who was an Indian, provided for the acquisition of full citizenship by educated Indians, and promised such enfranchised individuals a land grant from reserve lands. In 1867 the British North America Act assigned jurisdiction for 'Indians and lands reserved for Indians' to the federal government and parliament of the Dominion of Canada. The new dominion's 1869 Gradual Enfranchisement Act repeated the provisions of 1857 for enfranchisement and conversion of parcels of reserve land into freehold tenure, but it added an attack on Indian self-government. Recognizing that the obstacle to enfranchisement was Indian resistance that expressed itself through political organizations, the new act empowered Indian Affairs officials to remove elected leaders 'for dishonesty, intemperance or immorality.' The interpretation and application of these vague terms was conveniently left to bureaucrats in Ottawa. The 1869 act also restricted the jurisdiction of band councils to matters of municipal government. And, finally, the same measure established a governmental veto of Indian legislation by making all band measures 'subject to confirmation by the Governor in Council.'[1]

Although the Gradual Enfranchisement Act of 1869 was designed specifically for central Canadian Indians who had long been in close contact with a Euro-Canadian population, its tactics of interference and coercion would be carried over later to western Canada when policy was developed for those regions. The young dominion put the best face possible on this policy when, in 1871, it described its purpose as being 'to lead the Indian people by degrees to mingle with the white race in the ordinary avocations of life.'[2]

In the same formative period important preparatory events took place in western Canada as well. One development that proved to be crucial to the future of both the Indians and mixed-blood populations was the continued overhunting of the bison in response to high demand for buffalo robes and the decline of alternative economic activities for both the Indians and Métis. The emergence of the repeating rifle and the coming of the American transcontinental railroad in the late 1860s also made hunters' depredations on the herds all the more severe. Other people came, too, and their coming was noticed with disapproval by some of the native population in the west. In the late 1850s and 1860s a trickle of Ontarian settlers, mainly homesteaders but also including some townspeople, began to make its way to the valleys of the Red and Assiniboine rivers. They were the human manifestation of an Ontarian sense of manifest destiny, but unfortunately they brought with them the assumptions that the acquisition of the west was a foregone conclusion and that it would be for the best of all, both westerners and Ontarians. Such attitudes, as well as the assumptions of racial superiority that some of these newcomers displayed in their dealings with the Métis and country born, caused irritation. Unbeknownst to Canadians, an antipathy towards their acquisition of the west developed.

The actions taken to unite the Hudson's Bay Company lands and the dominion greatly aggravated these fears and suspicions. Canada's acquisition of the lands was carried out like a gargantuan real-estate transaction. Canada, with Britain's help and pressure, succeeded in obtaining the lands for the trifling sum of £300,000 and one-twentieth of the land. The Bay, which would take its 5 per cent of the land in many cases adjacent to its posts, was disgruntled by Canadian parsimony and British pressure. That dissatisfaction was nothing, however, in comparison to that of the population of some 12,000 mixed-blood people in the region when they learned what had transpired. Their homeland was being sold for a song, and they were not being consulted about it.

The high-handedness and insensitivity of London and Ottawa, though explicable, were to prove disastrous. The inhabitants of Rupert's Land were not consulted partly because of Canada's anxiety to annex the lands before the Americans to the south could interfere and arrange events so that the territory would fall to them as had Oregon, California, Texas, Florida, and other regions the Americans had coveted in the past. But the failure to consult was also partly attributable to a belief that there was no one in the region to consult; Indians and people of mixed Indian and European ancestry simply did not figure in any political equation that Victorian politicians and bureaucrats attempted to solve. The dominion was so unconcerned about local feelings that even before transfer from the Hudson's Bay Company was arranged it took two other measures that were to offend the inhabitants. In 1869 Canada sent a party into the region to begin surveying the lands in preparation for immigration. And in the same year it appointed a governor for the region, William McDougall, and equipped him with an act for the temporary government of Rupert's Land. Both initiatives were added to the list of complaints that the people in Red River were compiling.

These grievances were both specific and general. They objected to the lack of consultation, and they feared McDougall's appointment presaged a form of rule that would continue Canadian insensitivity and high-handedness. McDougall was a former Clear Grit, and as such was identified as an enemy of Catholicism and the francophone community. The fact that he was to govern the new territory with a council appointed by Ottawa simply made his selection all the more ominous. Under an apparently unsympathetic governor, the Métis and country born were not to be given any form of representative government with which to make their views known or to resist unfriendly acts by Ottawa and its appointee.

The Métis regarded the dispatch of a survey team to the district as an even greater threat. Both mixed-blood communities had developed a distinctive land-holding system, but it was a system that might be jeopardized by the coming of Canadian rule. In the French parishes that stretched up the Red River from Fort Garry (Winnipeg) and also in the English parishes along the Assiniboine, the farms ran back from the water in narrow strips. The occupants' title to their holdings was customary rather than formal. In the past the only authority in the region had been the Council of Assiniboia, a creation of the Hudson's Bay Company that had never seen the need to establish a land registry. Though there were rudimentary judicial and legislative institutions under the Bay's rule, there were no survey, land titles office, or paper deeds. Such instruments were unnecessary in a region where settled population was sparse, where agriculture was an incidental economic activity, and where everyone knew one another and one another's rights and property.

The Métis recognized that the coming of Canadian authority and Canadian homesteaders could be threats to the security of their land title. The Canadian provinces in the east had formal systems of land tenure and land registry. If Canada chose to disregard customary title and treat the lands as being legally unoccupied, where would that leave the mixed-blood population and their river lots? The fact that a Canadian survey party in 1869 laid out their surveying lines in such a way as to cut across and disregard existing lot boundaries excited a fear that Canadian authority meant spoliation of the resident population. And for the Métis, in particular, there were related fears. Would the coming of Canadian authority, especially in the form of a Grit governor and his appointed council, mean an attack on their traditional institutions of culture, the schools and the church? It was concerns such as these that impelled the Métis and the young Louis Riel to interfere with the surveyors and challenge the new governor in the summer and autumn of 1869.

Louis Riel, junior, emerged naturally as the leader of what would become known as the Red River Resistance. His family was prominent in the Métis community: his father had been one of the leaders of the challenge to the Hudson's Bay Company commercial monopoly in the Sayer case of 1849. Louis, junior, had gone east in 1858 as one of a party of young Métis who had been selected by the Catholic priests for education in Quebec. In Montreal Riel had experienced the currents that surged through French-Canadian society as well as a series of personal traumas. Nationalistic opposition among some francophones to the terms of Confederation and the intensely Catholic and nationalistic Ultramontane faction within the Catholic church in Quebec were two intellecutal fashions that influenced Riel. At the same time he suffered a series of personal blows: his father died in Red River in 1864, and Louis felt powerless to do anything for the family left behind; he abandoned what he had thought was a priestly vocation and unsuccessfully sought alternative employment; and, finally, he fell in love with a young French-Canadian girl, but was rejected by her family at least in part because of racial prejudice. Riel was only one-eighth native, but this was considered reason enough to reject him. By the time he returned to Red River in 1868 he was a troubled, if prominent and well-educated, young man.

On 11 October 1869, several Métis challenged the Canadian survey party headed by J.S. Dennis at André Nault's farm near St Vital. When the locals informed the surveyors that they were trespassing, the Dennis party sensibly withdrew. This assertion of the local community's rights proved to be the prologue of a major drama. Within a fortnight the Métis had organized themselves into a National Committee and barred the road south in an effort to prevent the would-be governor from entering and asserting Canadian authority. After McDougall was turned back, Riel and the others increased the pressure their actions had put on Canada to negotiate the terms for the transfer of the territory. On the same day another party seized control of Fort Garry, the centre of authority in Red River. And, finally, Riel attempted to unite the people of the region so as to present Canada with a solid front. He and his Métis guards called on the parishes of the region to send delegates to a convention on 16 November that was to establish a provisional government. Riel and his followers defended their actions on the grounds that there was no legitimate authority in the region and that they, under the law of nations, had the right to establish their own government. This assertion was a latter-day demonstration of the Métis sense of themselves as 'the New Nation' that had grown out of the conflicts with the Selkirk settlers, the annual buffalo hunt, and the Sayer case.

Canada eventually did negotiate with the resistors in Red River, but not before tragic events intervened. The dominion appointed individual emissaries to go west to discuss the situation with the inhabitants, and later it negotiated in Ottawa with three representatives that Riel's provisional government and a convention of inhabitants dispatched to treat with Canada. However, Canadian representatives and champions closer to the scene of resistance took steps that were to cause serious problems. Although Ottawa had served notice on the Hudson's Bay Company that the transfer would not take place as scheduled on 1 December because peaceful title could not be assured, McDougall acted in ignorance of this prudent move. He entered British territory and proclaimed his authority. He also authorized a rising against the Métis forces by the Canadian party in the colony. Riel's troops captured the Canadians' supplies and took a number of the Canadians into custody. The following day, 8 December, Riel declared his provisional government. One of the Canadian prisoners, a young Ontario Orangeman named Thomas Scott who clashed with his guards, was executed by the Métis in March for being insubordinate and abusing the guards. Riel's motivation was revealed by something he said at the time: 'We must make Canada respect us.'[3]

By the time negotiations occurred in Ottawa in the spring of 1870, then, drastic events in Red River had overtaken the diplomatic efforts of the Métis. In February an attempt by the Canadian party in Red River to rescue their fellow countrymen who were in custody was defeated by the Métis. J.C. Schultz, one of the Canadian party, escaped to Toronto where he fanned the glowing embers of Ontarian resentment at the resistance into a conflagration. The death of Scott intensified Ontario feeling. Somewhat surprisingly, given this background, negotiations between Riel's representatives and the dominion government produced agreement largely on the basis of demands that the convention in Red River had formulated and that Riel and his clerical advisers had revised.

Under the Manitoba Act that came into effect in the summer of 1870, Manitoba entered the dominion as a province, as Riel wanted, rather than a territory ruled from Ottawa, as Macdonald had desired. However, the extent of the new province was so small that provincial status was rendered almost meaningless. Similarly, the fact that the dominion retained jurisdiction over crown lands and natural resources in Manitoba, whereas control of these matters was provincial in the original four provinces, also reduced the significance of Manitoba's creation as a province. The legislature of the new province was to have two houses, like Quebec's, rather than being unicameral, as Ontario's legislature was. Either the French or English language could be used officially in the legislature and courts of Manitoba. And the denominational schools, Catholic and Protestant, were protected by Section 22 of the Manitoba Act, which limited provincial jurisdiction over education by guaranteeing the educational rights that religious groups enjoyed 'by law or practice' in the region at the time of union. In these respects, too, Manitoba was established on the model of Quebec rather than Ontario. Quebec had dual, confessional schools; and Quebec had official protection of both languages in its courts and legislature. This was unacceptable to many Ontarians, who were already incensed by Métis resistance and what they thought the priests' and politicians' connivance in it.

Ontario's wrath drove Ottawa to take actions that were to cause lingering resentments not just in central Canada but also in Manitoba. First, Macdonald and his cabinet decided that it was necessary to dispatch an expeditionary force to Red River, more for political and strategic reasons than because of military necessity. Ottawa was worried about American intentions towards the unsettled west, and it thought that sending British troops to Fort Garry would make it clear that the dominion was asserting its control over the region. Second, sending a force to deal with the 'rebels' would assuage somewhat Ontario's anger. The fact that all was now tranquil in Red River was overlooked in the interests of pursuing broad strategic and narrow partisan objects. In addition, the federal politicians reneged on a pact they had secretly made with the Roman Catholic prelate of St Boniface, Bishop Taché, to grant an amnesty to Riel and his followers. Once Scott's death began to inflame Ontario opinion, the politicians refused to carry out their promise to grant amnesty to the leaders of the resistance.

The final, critical element of the terms of the Manitoba Act was the provision concerning land. Security of title to individual holdings along the waterways was granted to those in possession of them when union occurred. The act also set aside 1.4 million acres so that the lieutenant-governor could make land grants of 240 acres to 'the children of the half-breed heads of families residing in the province at the time of the said transfer to Canada ...' These provisions satisfied the most immediate and specific concerns about land rights, but they did not provide a secure, long-term land base for the mixed-blood population. Riel and his clerical advisers had wanted to get a large tract of land set aside as a resource for the community and as a barrier against the direct effects of immigration and settlement, but Ottawa was unwilling to make such a provision. A program to provide land grants to future generations by the federal government from crown lands was the best that the Provisional Government could negotiate. But if the land grant itself was not satisfactory, the language in which it was described was to prove extremely important to the Métis later on. The Manitoba Act explained that the grant was made 'towards the extinguishment of the Indian Title to the lands in the Province,' and Prime Minister Macdonald defended the provision in the Commons as necessary 'for the purpose of extinguishing the Indian title.' The 'half-breeds had a strong claim to the lands, in consequence of their extraction, as well as from being settlers.'[4]

The aftermath of the resistance and the Manitoba Act was largely damaging to the native population. In the first place, the expeditionary force that arrived in Red River in August 1870 contained elements of the Ontario militia that were intent on wreaking vengeance. Forewarned, Riel escaped before the troops arrived, but the Métis community suffered violence at the hands of the undisciplined forces. At least one innocent Métis died before military administration gave way to a civil government. In the longer term, many of the mixed-blood community discovered that the land-grant provisions in the Manitoba Act for their young remained a nullity. Ottawa improperly altered the terms of the grant to the disadvantage of the Métis; surveys proceeded slowly; government land offices proved unable to redeem the land scrip (or promissory paper) that the Métis were issued for real estate; and land was diverted to white speculators.[5] Many of the natives, abused by the triumphant Canadians and exploited by a bureaucracy apparently unable to honour the promises of the Manitoba Act, gave up and removed to the Saskatchewan country. They hoped to re-establish their traditional way of life in new settlements such as St Laurent and Batoche along the South Saskatchewan River, but relocation merely postponed a confrontation with the edge of Euro-Canadian immigration and settlement.

The Indians' fear of, as well as the government's hope for, the arrival of that agricultural host in the former Hudson's Bay Company lands led to a series of initiatives by Ottawa in the 1870s. The Northwest Territories acts of 1875 and 1877 established rudimentary institutions of civil government, while the creation of the North-West Mounted Police (NWMP) in 1873 both prepared for agricultural settlement and protected the Indian population in the meantime. Originally, before the troubles in 1869, Ottawa had intended that half of the force would consist of Métis, whose knowledge and experience had seemed to make them ideal for the purpose. However, when the law marched west in 1874, the force consisted of eastern Canadian and British men, many of them with impeccably Tory political credentials.

The government was anxious to get the police into the west in large part because of menaces from the south. The presence of a Canadian police force would strengthen the Canadian claim to the west, and the constabulary would expel the American whiskey traders who were debauching some of the Indian bands of the southern plains from a series of 'whiskey forts.' The depths to which relations could descend in these settings were plumbed in the winter of 1872–3 in the Cypress Hills massacre. A group of American wolf hunters tangled with a party of Assiniboine who were camped in the area to rest and consume alcohol. The upshot of the encounter was the death of a score of Indian men and the capture and rape of five Indian women. Such events, though neither frequent nor typical, occurred often enough in the troubled years of the 1870s to convince authorities in Ottawa that the police should be sent west quickly. The Plains Indians recognized the beneficial aspects of the police presence. 'If the police had not come to the country, where would we all be now?' asked Crowfoot, head chief of the Blackfoot. 'Bad men and whiskey were killing us so fast that very few, indeed, of us would have been left today. The police have protected us as the feathers of the bird protect it from the frosts of the winter.'[6]

Negotiating a series of treaties with the Indians of the western interior between 1871 and 1877 was part of the process of preparing for western development and protecting the Indians, too. However, it is also important to note that initiation of the treaty-making process was at least as much the work of Indians resisting Euro-Canadian incursions as it was the prescient preparations of the government. Because the Ojibwa near the Lake of the Woods objected to the progress of surveyors and troops through their territory, the government began talks with them as soon as the Red River resistance had been dealt with. Similarly, the Saulteaux in Manitoba 'warned' settlers near Portage la Prairie 'not to cut wood or otherwise take possession of the lands upon which they were squatting,' and some Plains Cree interfered with the work of the Geological Survey and construction of the telegraph line in 1875. Such actions maintained the pressure on the government to negotiate.[7]

At the same time, it is also important to recognize that Ottawa's decision to precede immigration and settlement of the western plains with the negotiation of treaties with the Indians was merely a continuation of a century-old policy. The Royal Proclamation of 1763 had assigned the right to treat for access and title to Indian lands exclusively to the crown, now operating through the machinery of the Dominion of Canada. This was the approach that had been followed when it was deemed necessary to make provision for Indian Loyalists who had fought alongside Britain in the American Revolutionary War and for Indian allies who had joined the British and Upper Canadians in resisting the American invaders in the War of 1812. The practice had been continued after the War of 1812 in Upper Canada, where land cessions were negotiated. The final precedent had been the Robinson treaties of 1850 that secured from the Indians north of Lakes Huron and Superior a large tract of land and permission for British Americans to occupy and to use it. When Ottawa instructed its officials to begin negotiations with the western tribes, it was following a tradition that began with the Royal Proclamation.

But there was more to the motivations of the Canadian government than fidelity to a British-Canadian tradition. Negotiation in advance of settlement was also cheap. The alternative American way was very costly. The republic followed a *laisser faire* approach that allowed small bands of settlers to invade Indian territory, often leading to bloody repulses that precipitated the dispatch of militia by indignant assemblies. Besides being destructive of life and deterring development, such a policy was beyond Canada's financial means. In the 1870s, when the United States was spending $20 million a year on Indian wars, Ottawa's entire budget was only $19 million.[8] How would the dominion bankroll a railway across the prairies if all its money was being spent on battling the Indians of the region? The Mackenzie government's defence of its expenditures on treaty-making in 1877 was revealing:

My Commissioners have made further treaty arrangements with certain of the Indian tribes of the North-West Territories, by which their title is extinguished to a very large portion of the territories west of Treaty No. 4; and, although some of the provisions of this treaty are of a somewhat onerous and exceptional character, I have thought it nonetheless advisable on the whole to ratify it ... The expenditure incurred by the Indian Treaties is undoubtedly large, but the Canadian policy is nevertheless the cheapest, ultimately, if we compare the results with those of other countries; and it is above all a humane, just and Christian policy. Notwithstanding the deplorable war waged between the Indian tribes in the United States territories, and the Government of that country, during the last year, no difficulty has arisen with the Canadian tribes living in the immediate vicinity of the scene of hostilities.[9]

The speech nicely captured both the frugality of the Mackenzie government and Canadians' smugness about their Indian policy.

Besides being financially wasteful, the application of force meant political problems and a departure from well-established Canadian tradition. Any government that imitated the Americans would immediately find itself under attack from church and other humanitarian groups that took a lively, if condescending, interest in aboriginal peoples. Moreover, in the Canadian experience it was unthinkable to say what an American general had in 1869: 'The only good Indian is a dead Indian.'[10] Until at least the second third of the nineteenth century, the indigenous population had been partners with, not opponents of, the newcomers and their various activities. In Canada, historically, Indians had been prerequisites to the success of the European traders and generals, not opponents of their efforts. At the same time, because of the problems of vast distances and sparse population, the state had played a much more active role in economic development than was the case in the United States. When Canadians began sorting out how to develop the resources of the western interior, they turned naturally to the federal state to ease the way, knowing that Indians were not ferocious and implacable enemies but cooperative people with whom it was possible to do business.

But what accounts for the Indians' cooperation in the endeavour during the 1870s? First, it is essential to note that not all Indian leaders favoured making treaty. For example, the Cree chief Big Bear was extremely suspicious of government negotiators and reluctant to sign a pact.[11] Second, some Indian groups were influenced towards making treaty by missionaries whom they had come to trust. Men such as the Methodist George McDougall and the Oblate Father Scollen supported the Indians' entering treaty because they believed an agricultural life was essential both for the Indians' survival and for their successful conversion. Nonetheless, the treaty-making process was one in which two active parties, government representatives and Indian leaders, played roles; it was not a procedure in which one side consisting of bureaucrat and cleric dictated terms to the other. The Indians were as much agents as the government, though not actors with as much bargaining power as the federal commissioners.

Indians' awareness of events in the United States and of the dwindling of the bison resource meant that they approached the negotiations anxiously. They could say, as Sweet Grass did to Lieutenant-Governor Adams Archibald in 1871, 'We heard our lands were sold and we did not like it, we don't want to sell our lands; it is our property, and no one has a right to sell them.' But they also knew that they needed 'cattle, tools, agricultural implements, and assistance in everything when we come to settle – our country is no longer able to support us.'[12] The rapid depletion and impending disappearance of the bison was a force that the Plains Indians recognized and feared. George McDougall explained to an eastern friend in 1875 what the collapse of the buffalo economy meant to the Plains Indians:

Just suppose that all supplies were cut off from Montreal: all factories closed because there was nothing to manufacture; the markets forsaken because there was nothing to sell; in addition to this neither building material nor fuel to be obtained; how sad would be the condition of the tens of thousands of your great city! Now, the situation of these prairie tribes is exactly analogous to this state. For ages they have lived upon the buffalo; with its pelt they make their wigwams; wrapped in the robe of the buffalo they feared not the cold; from the flesh of this wild ox they made their pemmican and dried meat; while they possessed his sinews they needed no stronger thread; from its ribs they manufactured sleighs ... The manure of the buffalo is all the fuel they had – in a word they were totally dependent on the buffalo ...[13]

Behind the eagerness of some Indian leaders to negotiate lay a recognition that their way of life was collapsing.

What was the nature of the seven numbered treaties that were negotiated between 1871 and 1877? In large part because the two sides approached the negotiations with different purposes and assumptions, their understanding of them was different at the time and has remained unhappily so to this day. The government, though it did not recognize that Indians possessed title to the lands in the way that a Euro-Canadian could possess title in a system of freehold tenure, pragmatically faced up to the fact that Indians had some sort of claim to occupancy and use of the land. Unlike the French, the British had never denied aboriginal interest in the lands. The British-Canadian position was that Indians possessed what the courts in the later 1880s would define as a 'usufructuary right,' or a right of usage. To the government, then, the numbered treaties were land surrender agreements in which the Indians conceded whatever claims they had to occupancy and use in return for gifts and annual payments.

The Indians' understanding was different. Though they agreed with Sweet Grass that the territory was theirs and that no one could sell it out from under them, they did not hold to a concept of absolute property right in a European legal sense. The land and its resources were the creation of the Great Spirit, and the Indian was but one inhabitant of the world with obligations to use its resources prudently and pass them on to succeeding generations undiminished. They could not negotiate surrender of title because they did not possess it. What the Indians sought in the negotiations of the 1870s was the establishment of a relationship with the Dominion of Canada that would offer them assurances for the future, while agreeing to permit entry and some settlement of the region. To them the treaties were intended to be pacts of friendship, peace, and mutual support; they did not constitute the abandonment of their rights and interests.

The differing purposes and assumptions of the two parties manifested themselves frequently both in the bargaining process and in the final product of the negotiations. Government representatives came with instructions to secure Indian surrender of claim to the land cheaply, in return for initial sums and annual payments. Because they also recognized the need to assist the Indians to provide for alternative economic pursuits, they were prepared as well to negotiate limited areas in which the Indians could adapt to the sedentary agriculture that must replace the nomadic economy that was based on the disappearing bison. The Indians, in negotiation after negotiation, pressed not just for larger payments but also for more extensive tracts of land and promises of continuing assistance. The result was usually an agreement, mainly but not always totally embodied in the text of a treaty, that achieved at least a modicum of what both parties sought.

The divergent approaches of the two parties were best expressed in what each proposed by way of reserves and aid. The Indians, envisaging the reserves as extensive homelands in which they might carry on their traditional practices as long as possible, pressed for larger allotments for reserves than the commissioners were inclined to grant, and hammered steadily away to gain promises of aid in times of distress and financial help in making a

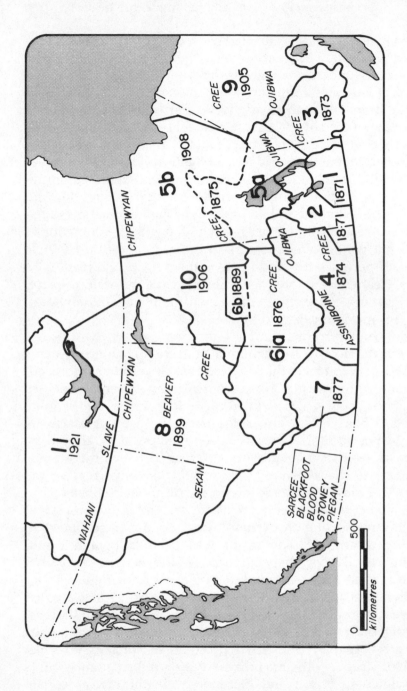

The numbered treaties, 1871–1921

transition to agriculture. Negotiation of the easternmost of the numbered treaties, Treaty 3, was protracted and difficult primarily because the Ojibwa of the Fort Frances district insisted that the government emissaries must specify what areas Canada wanted for roads and other purposes. They clearly intended that they would retain control of the vast bulk of the lands. A similar gambit was employed by the Indians of the Red River area in 1871 in the negotiation of what became Treaty 1.[14] The assumption on which the Indians were operating was put most graphically by Pound-maker in the 1876 negotiation of Treaty 6: 'The government mentions how much land is to be given us. He says 640 acres one mile square for each band. He will give us, he says ...' and in a loud voice, he shouted, 'This is our land, it isn't a piece of pemmican to be cut off and given in little pieces back to us. It is ours and we will take what we want.'[15]

But when the government negotiators insisted on restricted areas as reserves, some Indians, so anxious were they for a treaty, sooner or later capitulated. Their concession to the government was made somewhat easier by the answers they got to their expressions of concern that they not be interfered with in the practice of their traditional hunting and fishing pursuits. Commis-sioner Morris told the Indians at the negotiations of Treaty 3, the North-West Angle Treaty, 'It may be a long time before the other lands are wanted, and in the meantime you will be permitted to fish and hunt over them.'[16] The government's commissioners usually attempted to keep the reserve lands small, and they were reluctant to make extensive promises of aid in distress and assistance with adjustment.[17]

Because the Indians saw the treaties as establishing a relation-ship that would guarantee them assistance in adjusting to the new order in the west, it was they who were mainly responsible for the inclusion of many of the terms that promised continuing assis-tance. It was the Indian negotiators who suggested the treaty obligations to supply farm stock, implements, and supplies.[18] It was the Indians' clear perceptions of their needs and determina-tion to secure as much of them as they could before agreeing to treaty that lengthened the negotiations and led the commissioners to complain of the Indians' stubbornness and outrageous de-mands. That was a governmental perception of a determined effort by the Indians to obtain what they thought they needed: agreement that traditional pursuits could be carried on; an alternative land base; assistance in both instruction and equipment to make a transition to a different economy; and promises of aid in times of crisis such as famine and epidemic.

The terms of the treaties included a neat blend of what government and Indians wanted. The seven treaties of the 1870s that covered an area from the Lake of the Woods to the Rocky Mountains, and from the forty-ninth parallel in the south to the middle of the three future provinces on the north, promised 'reserves for farming lands,' annual payments in compensation for the lands surrendered, livestock, seed, ammunition, twine, promises of assistance, and even, in some cases, the maintenance of a medicine chest in the house of the agent. In return, the Indians, according to the treaties' text, agreed to 'cede, release, surrender and yield up to the Government ... all their rights, titles and privileges whatsoever, to the lands' covered by the treaties. And the Indians 'do hereby solemnly promise and engage to strictly observe this treaty, and also to conduct and behave themselves as good and loyal subjects of Her Majesty the Queen.'[19]

The two parties' fundamentally different purposes in making treaty were even embodied in the text of the agreements. Treaty 6, for example, clearly expressed the government's intent to secure the surrender of whatever claim or interest the Indians had to the lands: 'it is the desire of Her Majesty to open up for settlement, immigration and such other purposes as to Her Majesty may seem meet, a tract of country, bounded and described as hereinafter mentioned, and to obtain the consent thereto of her Indian subjects inhabiting the said tract, and to make a treaty and arrange with them ...' But the very same paragraph – indeed, the same sentence – went on to say that another purpose of Treaty 6 was to ensure 'that there may be peace and good will between them and Her Majesty, and that they may know and be assured of what allowance they are to count upon and receive from Her Majesty's bounty and benevolence.'[20] Given that sort of wording, it was not surprising that officials and Indian leaders emerged from the negotiations with different understandings of what had transpired. Indians thought that they had concluded treaties of friendship and mutual assistance, while agreeing to the entry into their lands at some future date of agricultural settlement. The government in Ottawa believed that the treaties secured the Indians' surrender of whatever claim they had to the vast lands of western Canada.[21] These differences were to cause much difficulty in the future.

In the two decades leading up to Treaty 7 of 1877, important changes occurred in the relationship between Euro-Canadians' government and the native peoples of western Canada. Canada was established in 1867 and its borders extended westward between 1869 and 1877. This process sparked a major native resistance to the assertion of Canadian authority in Red River in 1869, thereby frightening the government and spurring it to establish its control of the region after this setback was overcome by negotiation and compromise. Ottawa moved into the west in advance of settlers with institutions of government, an agency for policing, and a treaty-making process that it thought extinguished whatever rights to absolute possession of the territory that Indians had. For the Indians, the coming of civil administration was largely irrelevant, the arrival of the NWMP welcome, and the making of treaty somewhat confusing though apparently satisfactory in its results. To them it appeared that they had negotiated a relationship with the white man's government that would ensure that they could continue for some time to enjoy their traditional avocations, that they would be protected and assisted in times of crisis, and that they would be provided with lands and other means to make a successful transition from a hunting to an agricultural economy. The most troubling aspect of the events of the 1870s was not the entry of the policeman or the coming of the treaty commissioner; what worried the natives was the disappearance of the bison.

10

The Northwest Rebellion of 1885

The rebellion that broke out in the spring of 1885 has been the subject of a great deal of misunderstanding and myth-making. Among the many distorted views of that event, none is more ingrained than the notion that rebellion was the consequence of the meeting of two distinct ways of life.[1] According to this view, both the Red River Resistance of 1869 and the trouble in the Saskatchewan country in 1885 are best understood as the lamentable consequences of the encounter between a sophisticated society and a more primitive people. Both represented futile attempts by technologically backward peoples to resist the march of more advanced societies. In Saskatchewan in 1885 the Métis and Indians used force to defend a fading way of life against the expansion of commerce and agriculture. Led by Louis Riel, the Métis precipitated a rebellion in which some of the Indian nations joined, both groups being motivated by a desire to repel the advance of agriculture. Such an interpretation, while seductive in its simplicity, fails to appreciate the complexity of the events and the variety of the motives of the actors in the Northwest Rebellion.

A proper understanding of these events requires careful consideration of at least three distinct elements. These are the Indians, the Métis communities of the Saskatchewan, and Louis Riel. The behaviour of each was quite distinguishable from that of the others, particularly in the preliminary stages of the armed struggle.

And, in the case of the Indians, there were important differences among the various nations: the use of force was confined to the more northerly bands. It is impossible to understand why some Cree killed people, while others remained quiet, without analysing the situation in which the Indians of the Western interior found themselves between the signing of Treaty 7 in 1877 and the outbreak of violence in 1885. And it is impossible to appreciate why a peaceful Métis struggle for redress of grievances culminated in rebellion without careful examination of both the people who had grievances and the individual whose leadership they sought. Such an analysis will demonstrate that there was no Indian rebellion in the Northwest in 1885; there were only sporadic and isolated reprisals by small groups from some bands. It will also illustrate that Louis Riel was the spark that caused the mixture of Métis and government to explode.

If any people in the North-West Territories had reason to rebel in the 1880s it was the Indians. They saw the basis of their economy shattered in the 1870s, and then watched in the 1880s as the new relationship with the Dominion of Canada that they had negotiated in the 1870s failed to provide them with the relief and assistance on which they had counted. Moreover, they watched as Ottawa deliberately and systematically violated its treaty promises in order to coerce the Indians into adopting the government's plans for settlement rather than following their own. Finally, they endured great hardship as Ottawa implemented policies of retrenchment that bore savagely on them. The underlying cause of the Indians' problems was the disappearance of the bison. It had come under greater pressure after the 1820s, as the Métis increasingly shifted into the provisioning trade for the Hudson's Bay Company and attempted to satisfy the expanding market for buffalo robes. Other factors that accounted for the depletion of the herds included the arrival of modern weapons, such as the repeating rifle, and the completion of the transcontinental railway in the United States that brought to the plains the 'sports' hunter whose only interest was the acquisition of a trophy. Buffalo hides were also in demand in eastern factories for use in the belts that drove machinery.

One final factor was American policy towards the Indians south of the forty-ninth parallel. In the 1860s and 1870s the United States was still engaged in military campaigns against various Indian nations. Among the most spectacular was the ill-fated foray of General G.A. Custer and the Seventh Cavalry that resulted in their annihilation at the hands of Sitting Bull, Crazy Horse, and their warriors on the Little Big Horn River in 1877. In the aftermath, Sitting Bull and hundreds of his followers fled across the 'medicine line,' as the international boundary was called by Indians who recognized its importance in demarcating a land of refuge from a territory in which they could be hunted. Sitting Bull's presence in what is today southwestern Saskatchewan added to the strain on the food resources of the region and encouraged the American military to undertake operations designed to compel him to stay in Canada or starve him into submission in the United States.[2] At times in the late 1870s American forces burned the prairies in an effort to prevent the southern bison herd from trekking into Canada where it might help to sustain the fugitive Sioux.

The result of this combination of factors was the near-extinction of the bison by the 1880s. Of the herds that had impeded travellers on the prairies and parkland for days at a time in the 1840s, mere hundreds were known to exist by the end of the 1870s. In 1879 a Hudson's Bay Company man wrote in shock of 'the total disappearance of buffalo from British territory this season.' By 1884 only 300 buffalo hides were sold at St Paul, and by 1888 an American game report said that 'only six animals were then known to be in existence!'[3] The horror of starvation, never totally absent from Indian societies, now became all too familiar in the lodges of both Plains and Woodlands bands.

The devastating hardships that the Indians faced as a result of the disappearance of the bison were compounded by the government's response. As the Indians, especially the Cree, moved southward into the Cypress Hills in search of game and a base from which to pursue the bison herds, the Canadian authorities became increasingly alarmed. When the Cree, led by Piapot, Little Pine, and Big Bear in particular, began to press for contiguous reserves in the region of the Hills, Ottawa's man on the spot became determined to prevent such a concentration. The fact that all three of these Cree leaders had refused to adhere to Treaty 6 when it was signed in 1876, and that Big Bear in particular had expressly rejected the concept of submission to Canadian law that was part of the treaty, made their actions a source of concern to uneasy officials.[4] The disappearance of the bison and the consequent hardships provided North-West Territories Lieutenant-Governor Edgar Dewdney with his opportunity.

Dewdney, who was also commissioner of Indian affairs for the Territories after 1879, could use the Indians' plight to defeat their diplomatic campaign for the creation of an Indian territory and to disperse them into other parts of the Territories where they might be more easily controlled.[5] In deliberate violation of treaty provisions that covered at least Piapot and Little Pine, Indian Affairs officials refused them the reserves they requested in the south. At the same time the government used denial of food aid to the starving bands as a weapon to drive them out of the Cypress Hills. In 1882 they were informed that they would get no more rations in the Cypress Hills, and in 1883 the Mounted Police post, Fort Walsh, was closed. The bands were forced to make their way north to lands in the Saskatchewan country. One by one the recalcitrants accepted reserves; even Big Bear entered treaty in 1882 and in 1884 accepted a reserve well away from Little Pine and Poundmaker in the Battleford district in order to secure assistance for his starving people. But his retreat was merely a strategic withdrawal, not a surrender.

Over the next few years the Cree chieftains tried to unite the Plains Indians so as to force a revision of the treaties. Piapot in the south and Big Bear and Little Pine in the Saskatchewan district attempted to persuade various bands of Indians – even such traditional enemies as the Blackfoot and Cree – to combine in a united front in their dealings with the federal government. Gradually, through personal appeals and the use of thirst dances that were designed to unite different groups through communal ritual observances, headway was made on this diplomatic offensive. In the summer of 1884 an Indian Council was held at Duck Lake by leaders of twelve bands to protest the snail-like pace with which the government was honouring its treaty promises on agricultural assistance. This was evidence of the success that Big Bear and some others were achieving in their drive to secure reserves in the same areas and other revisions of the treaties. These consummate diplomats were confident that next spring, 1885, would see the triumph of their strategy when the Blackfoot joined them in a council on Little Pine's reserve. Progress could not come too soon. During the winter of 1884–5, the worst on record, younger Indians were becoming very restive.

Indian Affairs officials such as Edgar Dewdney had not been sitting idly by while the Cree attempted again what they had tried but failed to do in the Cypress Hills in the late 1870s. Dewdney used a policy of 'no work, no rations' to try to force the Indians into adopting agriculture speedily and to assert the government's control. At the same time, his officials and the Mounted Police did whatever they could to interfere with the movements of Indian diplomats. Where possible they prevented chiefs from travelling to councils or disrupted council meetings. They also instructed their agents and farm instructors to use rations to force a speedy transition to agriculture. In the south some chiefs were taken by the new railway to visit Regina and Winnipeg so that they would become acquainted with the numbers and power of the white population.

This tendency towards coercion was made all the more painful for the Indians by Ottawa's decision after 1883 to implement a policy of retrenchment that would necessitate a reduction in assistance to Indians. A combination of renewed recession and mounting demands on the government treasury for the completion of the Canadian Pacific Railway created a strain on the federal budget that led to cuts in many government departments, including Indian Affairs. Officials on the spot warned the department that such measures were false economy, but Macdonald's deputy minister was convinced by a quick tour of the region he made in 1883 that such reductions were possible. And the prime minister was too busy with other matters and too little informed about western affairs to overrule his senior bureaucrat. Such parsimony was as unwise as it was inhumane, given the situation that prevailed among the Indians of the western interior in 1883 and 1884.

Ironically, these economies were ordered at the same time as the Indian Affairs department began to divert an increasing share of its budget to education. Prior to the 1880s nothing that could be called an Indian educational policy existed. In eastern Canada there were schools that were run by representatives of missionary organizations, and in Ontario there were even a few boarding schools for

Indians. On the prairies and in British Columbia that same chaotic approach to Indian education had been allowed to develop. Missionary societies on their own initiative had set up schools associated with their mission stations. Many of these rudimentary efforts were day schools presided over by ill-trained and worse paid missionaries who had far too many other duties to worry unduly about the abysmal attendance and poor academic showing of their students. A few missionaries had also begun to experiment with boarding schools in the west. By the 1880s a hodgepodge of schools had developed in the region west of Ontario: there were day schools to which the government sometimes made small grants that paid much of the teachers' stipends; and less frequently there were also boarding schools to which the government rarely contributed anything. Between 1878 and 1883 the government embarked on an extension of the day schools and the creation of a wholly new system of industrial schools. In 1883–4 costly residential schools that were designed to teach Indians trades and agriculture were opened in Battleford, Qu'Appelle, and High River in the North-West Territories. The financial impact of these schools, which were expensively built and maintained, was significant in an Indian department that was already under financial pressure as a result of the policy of retrenchment.

Commissioner Dewdney had one final weapon that he proposed to use to cow and control the Indians of the plains and Pacific in the mid-1880s. Convinced that the policy of harassing Indian diplomats and applying pressure by restricting the flow of rations was only partially successful, Dewdney urged Macdonald to adopt a policy of 'sheer compulsion' in dealing with the leaders of those Indian bands who refused to behave as the department desired.[6] His efforts to prevent Indian leaders from meeting in 1884 had been thwarted by the small numbers of officials and police and by the absence of legislation enabling them to control Indians' movement. More police would be recruited by 1885, and the Indian Act would be amended to authorize officials to arrest Indians who were on reserves other than their own without department permission and to outlaw the potlatch of the Pacific Indians. Dewdney was confident that, when these amendments came into effect in 1885, he would be equal to the challenge posed by the likes of Big Bear, Piapot, and Little Pine.

While Big Bear had been manoeuvring and Dewdney had been countering, increasing dissatisfaction had arisen within some of the Cree bands, discontent that threatened to overthrow the traditional leadership and to rise up against government authority. Experienced leaders such as Big Bear and Piapot understood the need for a united front and the futility of armed action, but some of their younger followers did not. The less experienced men found it hard to bear the suffering caused by want and the indignities resulting from the actions of overbearing bureaucrats. By 1883 their anger was approaching the boiling point, and in the summer of 1884 there were confrontations on reserves, such as that of Yellow Calf in the Qu'Appelle area, between hungry Indians and out-numbered policemen. In such disputes it was all that cooler, more mature heads could do to prevent the slaughter of the constable or agent. Big Bear complained at the 1884 council in Duck Lake that he was losing control of his band to more militant young men, such as Little Poplar, who advocated an all-out war as an alternative to diplomacy.

Though it did not have to be that way, it was in fact the grievances of the Métis, in combination with the influence of Louis Riel, that brought armed rebellion to the Saskatchewan country in 1885. The mixed-blood population of the region were largely Manitoba Métis who had migrated westward in search of a new home in which they could pursue their customary life of hunting, fishing, casual employment, and some agriculture. In the 1870s, while white settlers were establishing the nearby town of Prince Albert, some 1500 Métis founded villages such as St Laurent and Batoche in the South Saskatchewan valley.

Both the Métis and the Euro-Canadians of the Saskatchewan had grievances with the federal government in the 1880s. The white farmers objected to the slowness of the land registry system, the failure of the transcontinental railway to make its expected way through their region, and the hardships resulting from several bad seasons. They joined the Métis in a campaign to pressure the federal government to deal with their problems. The Métis not only shared in the whites' disgruntlement with government and economic adversity, but had additional concerns of their own as well. As usual, land was at the heart of most of their grievances. As in Manitoba earlier, the Saskatchewan Métis feared that the arrival of a land-registration system from Ottawa might jeopardize their customary title to river-lot farms. They could not get assurances from an ominously silent federal government that their title would be respected. Some of them also believed that they had a claim for compensation for loss of aboriginal title in the Territories. They argued that the dominion had by treaty extinguished the Indians' title to the lands, but not theirs. Before extensive development occurred, Canada should recognize in Saskatchewan as it had in Manitoba that the Métis shared in aboriginal title and should compensate them for their loss of this interest in the land. And, finally, some of the Saskatchewan Métis argued that they or their children had unresolved claims against the dominion for land grants as a result of the promises made to future generations of Métis in the Manitoba Act of 1870.

The problems the Métis experienced in advancing their case in the early 1880s were similar to those that white farmers encountered: Ottawa never seemed to deal with their complaints. In part the problem was that federal politicians were preoccupied with other, to them more important matters. In part the difficulty was simply that the ministers responsible for western matters, David Macpherson and later Sir John A. Macdonald, knew little about western problems. In Macdonald's case the problem was still further compounded by his age. Old Tomorrow was getting on. He was sixty-three when he returned to power in the general election of 1878; he was running out of energy. And he had little sympathy for the Métis. Macdonald mistakenly believed that much of the talk of land compensation from the Métis was nonsense that had been inspired by white land speculators who were stirring up the people of Batoche or St Laurent. So far as a repetition of the Manitoba Act's promise of land to mixed bloods by virtue of their partial Indian ancestry was concerned, Macdonald was having no part of such schemes. The promise of the Manitoba Act had been a disaster to fulfil, not least because the slowness, dishonesty, and incompetence of federal officials delayed the distribution of land so long that many Métis gave up and sold their land scrip for a pittance to speculators. Macdonald was, if possible, even more unsympathetic than he was uninterested in the complaints from the Saskatchewan country.

The response of both Métis and whites to their failure to get the federal government to deal with their grievances was a decision to ask Louis Riel to return to Canada to lead their movement. Both parties were clear that what they wanted was Riel's experience and skill in dealing peacefully with an unresponsive government. To obtain his help with their movement for redress of grievances, they sent a party south to Montana at the beginning of June 1884 to ask him to come to their assistance. Had they thought about his response to their request for any length of time, they might have been troubled about what they were doing. 'God wants you to understand that you have taken the right way,' said Riel when he met the delegates, 'for there are four of you, and you have arrived on the fourth of June.'[7]

What Riel's cryptic response to the invitation imperfectly disguised was the fact that the Louis Riel who accepted the invitation in June 1884 was a very different man from the Riel who had led the resistance fifteen years earlier. Riel had felt himself ill-used by the Canadian government in 1870. Forced to flee, denied the amnesty he had been promised, elected to parliament but unable to take his seat for fear for his life, he was finally banished from the country for five years in 1875. The distressing events of the 1870s had unhinged him mentally. Riel was now convinced that he had a divine mission. Like the poet-king of Israel, David, whose name he adopted, he had been chosen by God. His mission was to prepare the world for the second coming of Christ and the end of the world by transferring the papacy from Italy to the new world, replacing the bishop of Rome with the Ultramontane bishop of Montreal, and ultimately locating the Holy See at St Vital, his home parish in Manitoba. The northwest was to become a new homeland in which the oppressed peoples of Europe could join the Métis and Indians to live in peace during a millennium that would precede the final end of the world.[8]

Like most prophets, Riel found himself without honour in his own land once he began to act on the revelation of his divine mission. He spent two periods of incarceration in asylums for the mentally ill in Quebec in the 1870s, and, when he was released, he was told that his cure would last only if he avoided involvement in matters that excited him. He moved to the United States, married, became an American citizen and participated in American politics, and settled down to the life of a mission schoolteacher in the west. However, he had not forgotten his vocation; he continued to look for a sign that it was time for its fulfilment. When, on 4 June 1884, four delegates from the Métis of Saskatchewan invited him to return with them, he knew that it was the signal he sought.

In the initial months after his return with his wife and children to Canada, Riel played the role he had been asked to rather than the role he knew God ultimately intended for him. He served as an adviser and organizer of legal protests, attending meetings and helping with the preparation of yet more petitions to Ottawa. He was even at Duck Lake at the time of the Indian council in 1884, but there is no record that he sought to incite either the Indians or his own followers to acts of rebellion. It was only gradually during the winter of 1884–5 that his purpose became known to the Oblate priests with whom he was in frequent contact. One of them claimed that Riel said he had personal claims – no doubt based on the terms of the Manitoba Act – that the federal government should redress. The priest informed Ottawa, but the prime minister declined to play the game of bribery, if that was the game that Riel intended.[9] The clerics became convinced that Riel was heretical if not completely deranged, as they became aware of his peculiar religious ideas. They would be the first in the community to turn against him; they would be followed during that winter by the white settlers who set their face against the conversion of the movement from peaceful protest to armed struggle.

It was clearly Riel – not the community at large, not even the Métis as a group – that pushed events in the direction of rebellion in the early weeks of 1885. For many months he had simply advanced the existing agitation; a petition of December 1884 did not include his own exalted claim for a land grant to the Métis by virtue of their sharing in the aboriginal title to the country. By March, Riel was poised to attempt a recreation of the strategy that had worked so well in 1869. His pretext was the lack of response from Ottawa. In fact, in January the federal government decided to appoint a commission to inquire into the grievances of the Métis, and, while they made that decision known to Riel through an intermediary, they did not follow up their actions until two months later when the members of the commission were appointed. By that time Riel had raised the stakes, proclaiming a provisional government, of which he would be the prophet and Gabriel Dumont the adjutant-general. The insurgents demanded the surrender of Fort Carlton and its police detachment.

If Riel thought he was re-enacting the events at Red River in 1869, he miscalculated. The two situations were starkly different. In 1869 he had enjoyed clerical support and the backing of a reasonably united community. In 1885 the priests turned against him and the white settlers' support evaporated. It might have been possible in Rupert's Land in 1869, especially after McDougall's abortive proclamation of Canadian authority, to argue that there was a vacuum of legal authority that justified a provisional government. In 1885 there was little doubt that Canada was the effective government in the North-West Territories. Red River had been distant and vulnerable, partly because Ottawa feared that the Americans had designs upon the region. Batoche in 1885 was geographically more remote, but in actuality more accessible, thanks to the nearly complete Canadian Pacific Railway. If the dominion chose in 1885 to crush Riel rather than negotiate, his rising was doomed. That, of course, was precisely what Canada decided to do.

It was largely a matter of coincidence – certainly not a matter of design – that a series of Indian actions occurred about the same time that Riel and the Métis confronted the police. In the camp of Big Bear, effective power had shifted to the young men in the warrior society by March 1885. Such a transition was by no means unusual in the fluid and subtle political systems of Indian communities. What the shift meant was that the authority of the elderly diplomat, Big Bear, was greatly lessened, while the ability of men such as his son Imasees and the war chiefs Little Poplar and Wandering Spirit to carry the band on their more warlike policy was increased. Irritation had been building up against some of the white men at Frog Lake, where Big Bear's band was established, and, when news arrived of a Métis victory over the police at Duck Lake, some of the young warriors attacked the Hudson's Bay Company storekeeper and the Indian agent. Big Bear attempted to restrain them when he became aware of what was going on, but before he could make peace prevail nine whites lay dead.

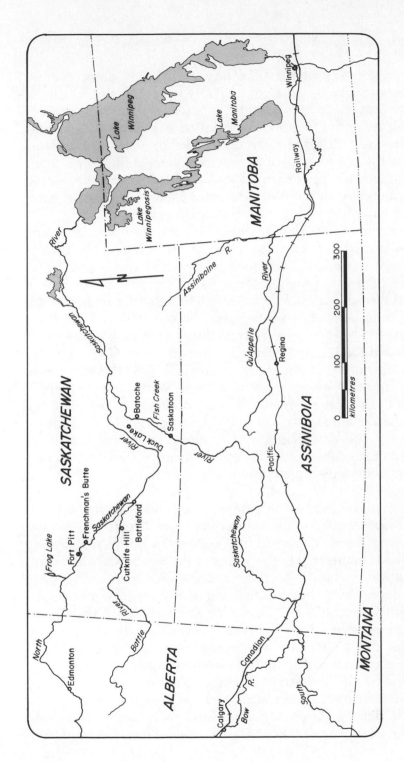

Northwest uprising, 1885

The incident, essentially a bloody act of vengeance against unpopular officials, became unjustifiably known as the Frog Lake Massacre. That it was nothing of the sort was illustrated by the fact that not all the Euro-Canadians were killed; one company man and two white women were spared, thanks in part to Big Bear. Moreover, though these people were prisoners in Big Bear's camp for weeks, they were not harmed at all. If the death of nine people and the humane treatment of three others constitute a massacre, then, and only then, was Frog Lake a massacre.

But the impression that prevailed at the time was that the Indians were rising in response to the Métis initiative. The rout of the police at Duck Lake had been followed by the 'massacre' at Frog Lake. Panic set in, nowhere more obviously than in the Battleford district, where white settlers had fled for refuge to the fort not long after the Duck Lake encounter. Groups from Poundmaker's band who were travelling to the post in search of badly needed food looted some abandoned homesteads near the fort. In the minds of the settlers and the government, these relatively innocent events became a 'siege' of the fort by Poundmaker and the Cree. Again, it was nothing of the sort, as Poundmaker's retreat to his own reserve clearly illustrated. Nonetheless, the Canadian government was convinced, and set about convincing others, that the entire northwest was threatened by a combined Métis-Indian rising.

Canada's military response was devastating and indiscriminate. In all, some 8000 troops, militia, and police were dispatched into the region along three routes: from Qu'Appelle north against the mixed-blood community in the valley of the South Saskatchewan; from Swift Current north to 'relieve' Battleford; and from Calgary north to Edmonton. The only fighting of any consequence occurred at Fish Creek, Batoche, and Cut Knife Hill. At Fish Creek, Dumont persuaded Riel to let him attack the military column from hiding, but then nullified the advantage of surprise by prematurely revealing his position. The final stand came at Batoche, where the Métis dug rifle pits and established fortifications from which they rained a withering fire on their attackers. Unfortunately for the Métis, the defenders quickly exhausted their ammunition and were reduced to using makeshift projectiles. The attacking Canadian forces, troops and militia, greatly outnumbered the few hundred armed Métis. Moreover, they were equipped with ample arms and ammunition, not even counting the Gatling gun that the American military had thoughtfully provided for field testing or the steamer that the commander attempted to use as a diversionary naval force. Finally, the ill-disciplined militiamen, tired of three days of feinting and long-range firing, and fed up with their general's cautious probes of Batoche, ignored their orders and overran the rifle pits.

Louis Riel, who had behaved throughout the encounters at Duck Lake and Batoche as though he was conducting a religious service rather than leading a revolt, surrendered. The truth was that, at least in his own mind, his was a religious cause. He could not fail because he was carrying out God's mission. If the deity had arranged for a defeat, it could only be because Riel was to make his case at a trial after the surrender. Dumont, practical fighter that he was, lit out for the United States.

The other military actions of the Northwest campaign involved Poundmaker and Big Bear. When Colonel Otter's column 're-lieved' Battleford, its leader decided to set off in search of Poundmaker, whom all held responsible for the 'siege' that had never happened. Otter caught up to Poundmaker's people at Cut Knife Hill and attacked. He and his men soon found themselves in trouble as the Cree fired from protected positions at the soldiers who were silhouetted on a hillside. The troops were astounded when they were able to retreat in an orderly fashion without suffering further losses. What they did not know was that Poundmaker had persuaded his men not to pursue and inflict any more damage on Otter's battered soldiers.

Big Bear and his followers spent much of May evading yet another Canadian force led by T.B. Strange in the bush country north of Frog Lake. The aftermath of the 'massacre' had been the restoration of the old leader's authority, and he used his control to follow his traditionally pacific paths. He allowed a frightened contingent of police to vacate Fort Pitt safely, and then he tried to take his people away from all trouble, including advancing troops. Strange caught up to Big Bear once, to his sorrow, near French-man's Butte, in the Fort Pitt area. Strange had to withdraw to Fort Pitt. Eventually, after Big Bear had led the soldiers a merry chase in the northern bush, his forces began to melt away. Finally, Big Bear returned to the Fort Carlton area and surrendered on 2 July. With Riel and Poundmaker already in custody, Big Bear's surrender marked the end of the rebellion.

What was at least as significant as who participated in the rising was who did not. Piapot in the Qu'Appelle area did not take up arms, perhaps because the government quickly stationed troops on his reserve to discourage his men from violence. At Round Lake, near Broadview, Assiniboia, the Presbyterian missionary noted that the Indians became excited and prepared to leave only when they heard that 'the soldiers are comming [sic] & will take us prisoner & we would rather fight & die on the battle field than to go away as a prisoner.' However, when he assured them that if the troops came and took the braves they would have to imprison the missionary as well, 'I was not a little astonished to see them take my advice & remain at home.'[10] In other words, Indians in Assiniboia either chose or were persuaded by the presence of troops not to join in the rising.

Nor did the Blackfoot Confederacy in the southwest take up arms. Part of the explanation lies in how weakened the southern tribes were by hardship, hunger, and disease by 1885. Here, again, the pacific influence of older chiefs such as Crowfoot was part of the explanation. But so, too, was the southern Indians' familiarity with whites and their power. The Blackfoot, four of whose chiefs had earlier travelled by train to Regina and Winnipeg at Dewdney's invitation, appreciated the general significance of the large numbers of Euro-Canadians and the military potential of the railroad.[11] The non-participation of the southern Indians, arguably the people who had suffered most since the making of the treaties and the disappearance of the bison, was further evidence that the events of 1885, whatever Edgar Dewdney said they were, were not an Indian rising.

Nonetheless, Dewdney and the government chose to portray the events as an Indian rebellion and to use that excuse to complete the 'subjugation' of the Plains Cree that they had begun in the late 1870s.[12] Although there was no reliable evidence that Poundmaker was responsible for the 'siege of Battleford' or that Big Bear was the architect of the 'Frog Lake Massacre,' both leaders were prosecuted

and convicted of treason-felony. Their incarceration in a peniten-
tiary in Manitoba, of course, made certain that the movement for
revision of the treaties would not resume. Both were released
before serving all of their three-year sentences; each died within a
year of release. In addition to Big Bear and Poundmaker, forty-two
other Indians were convicted of various offences for actions that
occurred during the insurrection. Students of the trials of the
Indian defendants have concluded that they were much less
carefully handled than those of the Métis and white defendants.[13]
The explanation of the unfairness of the Indian trials lies in a
combination of Dewdney's desire to use the courts to complete the
cowing of the Indian leaders and the prejudice of Euro-Canadian
juries.

It is an interesting comment on the preoccupations of historians
that it has been the trial of the Métis leader that has captured most
attention. It is often claimed that Riel's trial was a travesty of justice.
Critics object that he should not have been charged with high treason because he was an American citizen; that he should not have
been tried before a magistrate because he faced a capital charge; that
he should have been granted a change of venue to Manitoba where
he would have been entitled to some French-speaking jurors rather
than the six English-speaking Protestants who decided his fate
during the tense days of July 1885. And, finally, most observers
have argued that Riel was insane and should, consequently, not
have been found guilty, or, if convicted, should have had the
sentence of death commuted. These criticisms are unfounded.

The charge of treason was valid, as was the venue and
composition of the court. Anyone residing, even temporarily,
within a jurisdiction owes a sort of allegiance and obedience to the
legitimate authority of that territory. Riel owed obedience to the
laws and queen of Canada when he came into the country in
1884.[14] Riel was not entitled under Territorial law to a change of
venue to another province; Regina was a legal, if not entirely
appropriate, site for his trial. Where else in the Territories should
the trial have occurred? Battleford? Prince Albert? And there was
no doubt that Magistrate Richardson was entitled to hear the case,
even if it must be admitted that he did not sparkle on the bench.
There was a precedent for conducting a capital trial before a
territorial magistrate and jury of six.[15]

The most tangled issue surrounding Riel's trial and conviction was his mental health. That he was mentally ill, perhaps even insane, seems indisputable. However, his lawyers' opportunity to argue for a not-guilty verdict on this basis was largely wiped out by Riel's public protestations to the court that he was not insane and by his cogent closing address to the jury. Riel opposed the insanity plea because he believed that he was the instrument of a great cause that deserved its day in court. To have agreed to a plea of insanity would have been to deny the validity and importance of both his and the Métis cause. Riel was mentally ill, but his lawyers were unable to plead effectively that he should be acquitted on grounds of insanity. Accordingly, once the jury found him guilty, the presiding judge had no choice but to impose the ultimate sentence. The only possibility of avoiding execution, given the charge and the verdict, lay in the jury's recommendation of clemency.

Only the federal government could recommend commutation of Riel's sentence to life imprisonment. And within Quebec a demand began to develop for clemency once Ontario extremists began to demand the carrying out of the sentence in terms that were offensive to the French-speaking Catholics of Quebec. It was not that Quebec sympathized with Riel or supported his actions; it was rather that Ontarians had converted him into a symbol of Quebec itself by demanding his blood not as a Métis traitor, but as a French and Catholic rebel.[16] But if Ottawa was to accede to Quebec, on what grounds could it do so?

Many people, then and since, were prepared to come forward with arguments that they thought justified commutation. Some argued that the rebellion had been justified by the federal government's neglect. Obviously, no government – certainly not Sir John Macdonald's – was going to accept such an argument. It is a painful but real fact of life that the only thing that justifies rebellion is success. The successful revolutionary is a statesman, the unsuccessful a criminal. A suggestion that Riel should receive clemency because his offence was a *political* crime received a similarly chilly reception from Ottawa. Such a category of offence did not exist, and no conventional government was interested in creating one. One person's political crime was another's act of treason. That left only the insanity argument.

The insanity issue came in two phases: the trial and the prelude to execution. If Riel had been found legally insane at the trial, he would have been acquitted by reason of insanity. But the nineteenth-century criteria of legal insanity were extremely narrow and rigid. The test boiled down to the question, 'Did the accused know right from wrong when he committed the act?' Doctors who examined Riel found that, though he held strange ideas on political and religious issues, he did know right from wrong. He was not *legally* insane. However, there was an additional point. If Riel had become insane since his conviction, it would not be humane to execute him. The federal government explored this possibility with a medical commission that, though not unanimous, concluded that the condemned prisoner in the Regina jail was not insane. (The federal government misrepresented the views of one of the doctors to strengthen its case, thereby earning the opprobrium of later commentators.)[17]

Advocates were running out of arguments, and Riel out of time. Since there were no medical grounds for commutation, since there were no effective arguments in favour of clemency, and since Ontario was demanding the carrying out of the sentence even more vehemently than Quebec was insisting on commutation, Macdonald and the federal cabinet concluded that the stern course of justice should be followed. The prime minister did not doubt Riel's guilt and the justness of the sentence. Macdonald believed that no matter what his government did it would be damned by some group. If they were damned if they did and damned if they didn't, then he was damned well going to do what he personally believed was right. The federal government announced that it would not interfere. And on 16 November 1885, Louis Riel was hanged.

In a sense Riel never died. Though they took down his body and transported it to St Boniface where a grieving Métis community interred it in the cathedral cemetery, he lived on. Riel became a symbol of many causes in the century after his execution. To the French-speaking people of Quebec he immediately became a token of their own vulnerability in a Confederation dominated by English-speaking Protestants. They reacted by electing a so-called *parti national* government in 1886. In the twentieth century Riel has served as a representative figure for western politicians such as

Saskatchewan's Ross Thatcher who have exploited his tragic life to make their case against an unresponsive federal government. 'Whether we realize it or not, we of 1968 face a situation which is similar in some respects. If Riel could walk the soil of Canada today, I am sure his sense of justice would be outraged as it was in 1885,' intoned the Liberal premier of Saskatchewan.[18] Pierre Trudeau also exploited the Métis martyr by holding him up as a symbol of intolerance towards ethnic and racial minorities. At the unveiling of a monument to Riel in Regina in 1969, Trudeau warned, 'We must never forget that, in the long run, a democracy is judged by the way the majority treats the minority. Louis Riel's battle is not yet won.'[19] And in the 1960s Riel was adopted and patronized by white, middle-class student radicals who found him an acceptable substitute for the Cuban Revolution's Che Guevara. He has been the subject of innumerable stories, plays, and one important opera. Canadians find Riel or, more accurately, their own concerns that they project on Riel endlessly fascinating.

The native communities have had a more difficult time deciding how to handle the historical memory of Riel. For a time the Métis embraced him as the principal symbol of their problems at the hands of an unsympathetic government and community. In the early 1970s the Association of Metis and Non-Status Indians of Saskatchewan even petitioned Ottawa for a pardon for Riel, but later they withdrew their request, arguing that it was not Riel but the federal government that needed a pardon. The equivocal nature of the Métis attitude towards Riel is illustrated by their tendency to exalt his adjutant-general, Gabriel Dumont, as a symbol. Most still admire Louis Riel greatly.

No corresponding fascination has developed with those who lost the most by the Northwest Rebellion – the Indians. One can point to a National Film Board account, *Ballad of Crowfoot*, or a major novel on *The Temptations of Big Bear*, but not to any pattern of utilizing leaders such as Poundmaker or Big Bear as symbols of various causes.[20] It is almost as though a great amnesia descended on Canadians as a result of the crushing of Indian leadership after the rising of 1885. There was no Indian rebellion in the Saskatchewan country in 1885; there were scattered and isolated acts of violence by angry young men who could no longer be restrained by cooler heads. The Indians did not rebel. Yet they have suffered the most.

11

The policy of the Bible and the plough

After the Rebellion of 1885 Ottawa continued to move towards coerced assimilation of natives. To Canadians and their national government, Indians were largely irrelevant. They no longer played a critical role in commerce save in the north, they were not considered vital as military allies, and they were even less useful for purposes of exploration and mapping than previously had been the case. Ottawa thought it obvious that the best Indian policy was one that eliminated Indians, not by violence but by assimilation to a Euro-Canadian pattern. The 'great aim of our legislation,' Sir John Macdonald noted, 'has been to do away with the tribal system and assimilate the Indian people in all respects with the inhabitants of the Dominion, as speedily as they are fit for the change.'[1]

Canadian policy after Confederation became steadily more interfering and coercive as Ottawa became increasingly impatient about the slow pace of Indians' 'civilization' and 'assimilation.' The 1876 Indian Act maintained the elective band councils that the 1869 act had instituted to the annoyance of the eastern Indians, but did so now on a voluntary basis. When the Indians demonstrated their opposition to this interference in their political affairs, the measure was amended in the 1880 revision of the Indian Act to make it possible for the Department of Indian Affairs to impose an elected band council on Indians whether they preferred traditional, non-elected leadership or not. The 1880 act, which formally established the department of Indian Affairs (DIA), applied to all status or registered Indians, that is to all who were recognized by the department. In 1884 the so-called Indian Advancement Act augmented Ottawa's powers yet again by authorizing the superintendent general to depose chiefs whom he considered unfit or unable to discharge their duties. Finally, eastern Indians were offered a further inducement to take up the opportunities of citizenship in the 1885 Franchise Act, which extended the right to vote in federal elections to the Indians east of Lake Superior. These provisions were designed to undermine traditional forms of self-government and to permit Ottawa to intervene actively in band matters.

The Indians resisted these attempts at interference in their political affairs. Between 1857 and 1920 only 250 individuals opted for full citizenship and loss of Indian status by means of enfranchisement.[2] It was the very fact that eastern Indians refused to take up the elected councils under the 1880 act, or, if they did, proceeded to elect their hereditary leaders, that prompted the reintroduction of compulsion in subsequent amendments. And on the Six Nations reserve near Brantford, Ontario, a conflict between elected and hereditary leaders developed that was to divide the Indian community, lead to endless political agitation and litigation, and culminate in the Indians' unsuccessful appeal to the Assembly of the League of Nations at this meddling in their internal affairs.[3] Similarly, few eastern Indians used the ballot the Franchise Act of 1885 offered them, and in 1898 it was withdrawn.

Next to political control, Ottawa was most interested in reshaping Indian attitudes towards land and land ownership. As had already become apparent in the contests in Upper Canada before Confederation, the Indians regarded communal land-holding as essential to the preservation of their identity. The location ticket, the means by which reserve lands held in common would disappear as individual Indians were enfranchised, reappeared in the 1876 act. An eastern Indian who had demonstrated that he lived as a Euro-Canadian could receive a ticket for an individual plot and, after three years' probation, be enfranchised and receive absolute title to the land. An analogous program of encouraging western Indians to hold their lands 'in severalty' rather than in common was introduced in the 1880s. 'The policy of destroying the tribal or communist system is assailed in every possible way,' explained Indian Commissioner Reed, 'and every effort made to implant a spirit of individual responsibility instead.'[4] The department soon learned that the Indians opposed the subdivision of reserves for fear 'that the Government will deprive them of the residue of their lands, should there be any, after the location titles have issued for the lots allocated to individual Indians, and that the latter will become subject to taxation, as are the lands of white people in municipalities.'[5] This assault on Indian land-holding never succeeded to the extent that officials desired.

Not all government initiatives aimed at interference and coercion; some were protective in inspiration. The protective approach was a logical outgrowth of the Euro-Canadians' view that Indians were retarded in their development and required protection from rapacious members of the newly dominant society. As Sir Hector Langevin put it during the debate on the 1876 act, 'Indians were not in the same position as white men. As a rule they had no education, and they were like children to a very great extent. They, therefore, required a great deal more protection that [sic] white men.'[6] This attitude explained why the Indian Act relegated the Indian to the legal status of 'ward,' with the DIA playing the role of surrogate parent.

The act forbade liquor sales to Indians, barred people who were not members of a band from its reserve after nightfall, and prohibited the presence of Indian women in bars. Such limitations were intended to protect Indian women from unscrupulous white men who sought their sexual services, and they were an indirect acknowledgment of the growing problem of the prostitution of Indian women, particularly in the towns of western Canada. Indian reserve lands had to be protected, as the Royal Proclamation of 1763 had also figured, from crooked whites and venal Indians by making it impossible to sell or mortgage them. Indians who adapted to agriculture had to be protected from unscrupulous whites who might try to cheat them when buying their foodstuffs by requiring a permit from the agent to sell their produce.

The protective impulse, as the pass system so graphically showed, usually gave way to coercion. The use of passes in western Canada was instituted, at least in part, to control the movements of Indians during the tense summer of 1885. Under the pass system, Indians were prohibited from travelling off their reserves without written authorization of their agent, who would usually issue a pass only on the recommendation of the farm instructor. The pass system was used to protect the Indian people whom the department thought should be kept away from corrupting whites and to thwart the movement of Indian politicians among the reserves. It was also used to discourage parental visits to boarding schools and to promote certain DIA cultural policies.[7]

The pass system, however, was never very effective. It was not often enforced in the 1880s, and by 1893 was virtually a dead letter. The Indians knew, as did the police and the department, that there was no legal basis for interfering with the Indians, and the Mounties dragged their feet in enforcing it. It was often a simple matter for Indians to evade the agent or even to defy him. Reed explained to the minister of the interior that he instructed agents to 'issue passes to Indians who they know will leave in any case, and so preserve an appearance at least of control, and a knowledge of their movements.'[8] Although passes were still in occasional use in parts of the west during the Great War, the system was never generally, or effectively, applied.[9] Police prudence and Indian defiance prevented it.

Measures to control the availability of alcohol and to protect Indian women from prostitution contributed to the strengthening of the powers of the Indian agent. Like the North-West Mounted Police officer, the agent was given the powers of a magistrate, making him investigator, prosecutor, and judge in his dealings with alleged miscreants. The opportunities for abuse of power were simply too great to be resisted. And the fact that Indians, especially those in western Canada, were not accommodating themselves to the government's desire that they be assimilated made it all the more tempting to apply coercion. Protection of peoples relegated to child-like status in the eyes of the government led inescapably to compulsion.

The quintessential manifestation of the paternalistic mindset, and the clear proof of Indian resistance, was found in 1884 changes to the Indian Act. The amendments, which came into effect in 1885, attempted to control Indian movement and curtail such cultural practices as the Sun Dance and Thirst Dance of the southern prairies by prohibiting Indians from being on a reserve other than their own without department approval. These festivities were at one and the same time important elements of Plains Indians' political and religious life, for these bands drew no distinction between the realms of the sacred and the secular. However, missionaries objected to the practices, and successfully pressed for their prohibition.

Similar treatment was meted out in the 1884 amendments to the Pacific coastal Indians. The amendment threatened anyone 'who engages or assists in celebrating the Indian festival known as the "Potlach" or in the Indian dance known as the "Tamanawas"' with a jail term.[10] The immediate cause of the potlatch ban was a request by Indian converts, but behind it also lay missionary antipathy.[11] Clerics intuited, if they did not comprehend, the importance of the potlatch to the coastal tribes. Its ethos was the antithesis of the individualism and competitive accumulation that underlay Euro-Canadian society, as well as an important part of an alternative religious and social system. As the missionary William Duncan observed, the 'potlatch was "by far the most formidable of all obstacles in the way of the Indians becoming Christian, or even civilized."'[12]

It was one thing to legislate; another to enforce. From a variety of evidence it is clear that the prohibitions against both the prairie dances and the coastal potlatch were largely unenforceable. Even with the pass system and agents who had the powers of magistrates, it was often impolitic for a handful of police and agents to try to compel large numbers of Indians to forego practices they considered central to their way of life. When the Indians were determined to dance, as the Blood who followed Red Crow were in 1900, there was nothing an agent could do to stop them. In the chronicles of the Blood people, 1900 was recorded as the year when 'Yellow Buffalo Stone Woman put up the Sun dance by force.'[13] Other times, guile worked as well as 'force.' On the Poundmaker and Little Pine reserves, which were contiguous, the Cree held their dances right on the boundary of the two reserves. Since the Indians were not leaving their reserve for another, the agent and police could not use the Indian Act to deter them.[14] Throughout the west the dancing went on surreptitiously, even among Indians who claimed to have converted to Christianity, for no other reason than such practices were central to Plains Indian culture.[15] In the 1920s the deputy minister of DIA was still inveighing against traditional dancing; the Indians kept on dancing.[16]

A similar pattern of response was found on the Pacific. There was only one conviction under the 1884 potlatch prohibition, and that was immediately quashed by a judge who ruled that the law was excessively vague. A more carefully phrased amendment in 1895 enjoyed occasional enforcement in some parts of British Columbia, but the effectiveness of the prohibition depended more on the zeal of the agent than the force of the law. 'There is no decrease in the number of potlatches held,' an agent reported in 1912, and no potlatcher served a prison sentence for his activities until 1920.[17] There was a brief and unsuccessful attempt by the department to enforce the ban in 1913, and a short-lived crackdown in 1922–3 stopped the festivities for a few years. But by 1927 those Indians who still wanted to potlatch were back at it. It took the economic stress of the Depression and the influence of acculturation to put an end to it in the 1940s.[18] It says a lot about the ineffectiveness of such culturally oppressive policies as the potlatch ban that potlatching died out earlier in Alaska, where there was no American law against the practice, than it did in British Columbia.[19]

The legislation against the potlatch and the prairie dances were merely parts of an extensive attack on Indian cultural practices carried out in the name of protecting them and moulding them to Euro-Canadian ways. Efforts to curb the abuse of women through prostitution were motivated by humanitarian desires, but they could have the effect of interfering with sexual behaviour that differed sharply from the monogamy and continence that the Euro-Canadians preached, if they did not always follow it. Similarly, a ban on polygamy was a well-intentioned attempt to protect the Euro-Canadian's notion of the family unit, even if the familial and social situations in which some Indians found themselves made multiple brides sensible and socially useful. The Indian Act's tracing of Indian descent and identity through the father was the unthinking application of European patrilineal assumptions by a patriarchal society; but it accorded ill with those Indian societies, such as the Iroquoian, in which identity and authority flowed through the female side of the family. All these attempts at cultural remodelling also illustrated how the first step on the path of protection seemed always to lead to the depths of coercion.

Politicians and bureaucrats thought that these coercive policies were but temporary measures that would be needed only until the great social curative in which Victorians believed so fervently could do its work. Education was held to be the universal panacea for all kinds of social and economic problems in the nineteenth century. Prime Minister Macdonald acknowledged this implicitly in his defence of the 1885 grant of the vote to eastern Indians: 'So I say that the Indians living in the older Provinces who have gone to school – and they all go to school – who are educated, who associate with white men, who are acquainted with all the principles of civilization, who carry out all the practices of civilization, who have accumulated round themselves property, who have good houses, and well furnished houses, who educate their children, who contribute to the public treasury in the same way as the whites do, should possess the franchise.'[20] In 1892 the superintendent general said 'that the sacred trust with which Providence has invested the country in the charge of and care for the aborigines committed to it carries with it no more important obligation than the moral, social, literary and industrial training of the Indian youth of both sexes.' Money spent on Indian education was 'well spent,' for it would mean 'not only the emancipation of the subjects thereof from the condition of ignorance and superstitious blindness in which they are, and their parents before them were sunk, but converting them into useful members of society and contributors to, instead of merely consumers of, the wealth of the country.'[21]

Experience in Upper Canada had already demonstrated that the Indians desired access to education for their children and that day schools were not effective. In the treaties of the 1870s many western Indians had been promised that they could have schools on their reserves when they wanted them, and in the years following the making of the numbered treaties some steps were taken to support the schools that missionaries had already established or wished to erect near or in Indian settlements. In the

1880s the educational policy for western Canada and British Columbia shifted from day schools to boarding institutions.

The theory behind residential schooling had not changed since Ryerson's day: it was still an experiment in social engineering. As the DIA 1889 Annual Report put it: 'The boarding school disassociates the Indian child from the deleterious home influences to which he would otherwise be subjected. It reclaims him from the uncivilized state in which he has been brought up. It brings him into contact from day to day with all that tends to effect a change in his views and habits of life. By precept and example he is taught to endeavour to excel in what will be most useful to him.'[22] The underlying purpose of residential schooling was what the Americans called 'aggressive civilization.'[23]

Initially, Indians welcomed offers of education for their young in western Canada as they had in the east. They understood the significance of the coincident arrival of whites and disappearance of bison: they would have to adjust to new ways and to new methods of earning a living. A young Assiniboine who 'at the age of twelve years ... was lasooed, roped and taken to the Government School' later recalled that he had been sent to school to acquire 'the whiteman's magic art of writing, "the talking paper."'[24] But Indians wanted enough schooling to enable them to cope with the new order, not what they got. From 1883 onward the federal government established 'industrial schools' off the reserves at which Indian children would be educated and trained far from parental and band influence. As a federal cabinet minister explained in the Commons: 'If these schools are to succeed, we must not have them too near the bands; in order to educate the children properly we must separate them from their families. Some people may say that this is hard, but if we want to civilize them we must do that.'[25] A parallel system of boarding schools, which were less ambitious and less well financed than the industrial schools, persisted after 1883. Industrial and boarding schools both aimed at the assimilation of the Indian children.

The residential schools were operated in uneasy tandem by government and the missionary societies of the Catholic, Anglican, Methodist, and Presbyterian churches. Part of the unease arose from denominational rivalries among churches in various locations. More stemmed from the tug of war over funds between

Indian Affairs and the missionaries. Although it was originally the department's intention to concentrate its efforts among western Indians in the industrial schools, finances made it impossible to do so. The industrial schools were very expensive, and parliament was forever complaining about the heavy costs of Indian Affairs. In 1892 an attempt was made to control expenses by shifting to a new financing system, but costs continued to spiral well beyond the results that school inspectors could turn up in their annual visits. Moreover, both teachers and officials encountered substantial Indian opposition to residential schooling. In some cases parents complained that their children worked too long in fields and shops, while learning too little in classes. In other cases they objected to the harsh discipline, including corporal punishment, and the poor food. By the early twentieth century the escalating death rates in the schools were becoming a public scandal as well as a reason for both parental and student refusal to cooperate with the residential schooling experiment. Not even the 1894 introduction of compulsory schooling regulations proved sufficient to keep some of the schools full.

The department's response was to contemplate exerting even more control over young Indians. As early as 1892 Indian Affairs considered the establishment of 'colonies' where graduates of the industrial and boarding schools might be sent to keep them longer from the influence of home and reserve. One such farming community was set up in the File Hills area of southern Saskatchewan at the turn of the century, and others were contemplated. Although the File Hills experiment lasted almost to mid-century, it by no means realized the complete assimilation of the 'colonists' that was intended.[26]

Because the industrial schools, though much more expensive, proved little better in educating children than the boarding schools, Ottawa shifted away from the costly experiment. The Liberal government in power after 1896 was particularly unsympathetic to ambitious plans to train children in trades and agriculture in the industrial schools, the minister responsible for them saying flatly that 'the attempt to give a highly civilized education to the Indian child ... was practically a failure. I have no hesitation in saying – we may as well be frank – that the Indian cannot go out from school, making his own way and compete with the white man.'[27] The federal government reduced funding to the schools, looked for ways to close some and move their students to 'new, improved day schools,' and, finally, gave up the distinction between industrial and boarding schools. In 1923 both industrial and boarding schools were amalgamated into a single category known as 'residential schools.' By then the system had grown quite large. Where in 1883 there had been three government-financed industrial schools and an unknown number of boarding establishments run by the churches, by 1907 there were twenty-two industrial and fifty-three boarding schools. The system still reached only a minority of school-age children, however. These schools would persist till the 1960s.

The failure of Indian education in general, and residential schooling in particular, was attributable to government parsimony and Indian resistance. As Ottawa's refusal to continue for even a decade the high level of funding required for industrial schools illustrated, the government was not prepared to pursue assimilation through education if the struggle was going to be lengthy and expensive. From 1892 onward it tried regularly to shift an ever larger share of the cost of running these schools onto the shoulders of the school children and missionary organizations that, for their part, were becoming increasingly disillusioned with Indians, schools, and their government partners. The government preferred, as in the compulsory attendance provisions, to move to coercion rather than to invest in the schools to such an extent that Indians would want to send their children there. But Indians did not want to, because the schools were ineffective, harsh, unsafe, and interfered with the development of the Indian child into a being with a sense of identity and a place in society. Most graduates found there was no work for them; many returned to the reserves and psychological limbo.

The Indians resisted coercive education in a variety of ways. Most simply they refused to surrender their children to the school and Indian Affairs authorities, no matter what policeman or agent said. Those who were still nomadic or semi-nomadic, as was often the case on the west coast, could simply remove themselves from the reach of those who enforced the compulsory attendance provisions. The parents could disrupt the school by making unauthorized visits or by failing to return their children after holiday visits home. On the Blackfoot reserve in 1895 an Indian Affairs employee was killed and the missionary-principal of the school forced to flee in fear for his life.[28] At the Kamloops school the Shuswap chiefs came to the school and drove out an instructor who had abused a girl. When the offender returned the next year in clerical garb, the 'chief came and really raised hell with him, told him "I don't care if you come camouflaged in a priest suit ... we told you to leave. We don't want you back. Get!"'[29] The children were even more effective at resisting. They could – and did – misbehave, violate rules, refuse to learn, defiantly continue to speak their own languages in spite of official prohibitions, run away, and, in the ultimate case, indulge in acts of arson against the property and violence against the staffs of the schools. One particularly ambitious break-out involved 'planning for weeks on end, packing stuff and hiding it outside.' The girls involved in this escape managed to evade capture for some time.[30]

While some students of these residential schools were thoroughly converted by the experience, many more absorbed only enough schooling to resist still more effectively. It would be from the ranks of former residential school pupils that most of the leaders of Indian political movements would come in the twentieth century. Unfortunately, yet another large group – probably more than one-quarter of the pre-1914 students – succumbed to disease during or shortly after their stay at the schools. By any reasonable standard of evaluation, the residential school program from the 1880s to the 1960s failed dismally.

Closely related to schooling was a series of policies designed to encourage Indians, especially those of the western interior, to adopt agriculture. There was little awareness that the government was attempting to modify the economic activity of a distinctive group of people, a process that in Western Europe had taken centuries to accomplish. In an era in which there was little understanding of cross-cultural differences, officials usually assumed that the shift to agriculture, though certainly not easy, could with good will and effort be accomplished in fairly short order. The fact that the period when many of these policies were getting under way, 1885–90, was among the worst climatically in prairie history simply compounded the problem.

The agricultural program for western Indians consisted mainly of instruction on reserves.[31] Farm instructors were supposed to teach both by example, on their own 'home farm' near the reserve, and directly to the Indians, on reserve lands. However, too often Indian Affairs failed to provide instructors who were familiar with western conditions, neglected to furnish implements and seed in time, and became impatient when Indians showed little progress in adverse climatic conditions. The fact that Ottawa cut back the budget for agricultural instruction as well as rations in 1883 did not help the situation, either.

The problem, though not entirely the fault of the department, was greatly compounded by it. Certainly the government devoted considerable attention to providing advice until the 1890s. The number of instructors rose from twenty-four in 1880 to a high of forty-five in 1890 before dropping to thirty-five in 1895. When Euro-Canadian instructors from central Canada encountered problems in dealing with western Indians, Ottawa even hired a number of Métis, including one who joined in the insurrection in 1885.[32] Aside from the climate, the greatest obstacle the program faced was the department's attempt to impose its will on Indians in the west. When Ottawa began in the later 1880s to push for the subdivision of reserve lands into individual lots and to discourage large-scale farming, Indians resisted. They recognized that advocacy of holding land 'in severalty' was part of a plan to extinguish Indian identity and reserves.

At the same time the DIA's insistence on a 'peasant farming' policy simply discouraged Indian initiative. Ottawa claimed that it wanted to prevent Indians from farming on a large scale with labour-saving machinery because eventually Indian farmers would have to work without the aid of instructors who could service complicated implements. 'The general principle is not to allow them machinery to save them work which they should with hands available on Reserves, do by help of such simple implements as are alone likely for long enough, to be within their reach,' explained the Indian commissioner.[33] But the real reason was that department officials in the west did not want Indians to advance to anything beyond subsistence peasant status.[34] The fact that white farmers in the neighbourhood of Indian reserves resented what they regarded as subsidized competition from Indians might well have been a factor in making politicians anxious to limit native production. Western settlers made their objections to competition from the Indians in the small local markets for produce in such places as Battleford and Fort Macleod known to press and politicians.[35] Since the sale of produce required a permit from the agent, and since DIA officials were susceptible to political pressure from members of parliament who voiced settler complaints, it became all too easy for department officials to reject requests from Indians to sell produce to buy machinery. And those Indians who wanted to borrow money for implements, as some eastern Indians did, found that the Indian Act's prohibition on mortgaging reserve lands prevented their acting like the acquisitive capitalists the department claimed it wanted them to become.[36]

The frustrating case of a Sioux band in Manitoba showed the effect of these forces. The Oak River Sioux were successful farmers in the 1880s, but succumbed in the 1890s to obstacles placed in their way by the department. DIA officers often refused permission to buy machines in line with the 'peasant farming' policy. In response the Sioux reduced their operations to what could be farmed without machinery. Since it was no longer economic to grow wheat in such small quantities, they dropped out of market-oriented grain production and became the sort of subsistence farmers, or peasants, that the department apparently wanted. In the process they removed themselves from competition with their white neighbours and consigned themselves to a marginal existence.[37]

Although Indian agricultural production in the west was regularly described in the annual reports of the Department of Indian Affairs as promising, little progress was to be seen a generation after the agricultural policies were instituted. Bands on occasion won prizes at agricultural exhibitions, but their total crop production remained far below that of their white neighbours in the North-West Territories.[38] An exception to the generally depressing picture of economic failure gradually emerged in Treaty 7 in southern Alberta, where the Indians slowly and with considerable difficulty adjusted to the emerging ranching economy. Though these Blackfoot had been among the most desperate in 1879 when the buffalo resource failed, by 1896 they were moving towards prosperity.[39] There were too few such cases.

Sometimes Indians found that their land was literally disappearing as they tried to utilize it for new economic purposes. The underlying problem here was that the title to reserve lands did not belong to the Indian bands but to the crown in the person of the Department of Indian Affairs. And, while the department legally stood in a trustee relationship to its Indian 'wards' and was obligated to administer a band's resources in the best interests of the group, sometimes the officials disposed of land in a manner that was the antithesis of Indian interests. Particularly after 1896, when climatic conditions improved and large numbers of immigrants began to flood the prairie region, demands arose for transfer of Indian lands to homesteaders. It was a tiresomely familiar argument, based in equal parts on Christian notions of stewardship and capitalist desires for acquisition, that Indians were not entitled to lands unless they improved them. Although the official stance of the government was that the Indians owned the lands and could not be dispossessed, in practice DIA often transferred lands suitable for farming and mining from the Indians to white homesteaders and speculators.[40]

These incursions, too, Indians frequently opposed. An elderly chief in Treaty 4 reminded Indian Commissioner David Laird that he had predicted when the treaty was made in the 1870s that the white man would want the land back. 'Did I not tell you a long time ago ... that you would come and ask me to sell you this land back again, but I told you at that time, No.'[41] The Metlakatla Indian converts who followed William Duncan resisted a government surveyor, as did Ojibwa on Manitoulin Island, for fear that survey was merely a prelude to usurpation.[42] And the Blood fought ferociously with officials in 1907 and 1918 to prevent land surrenders.[43] But impecunious band members frequently found the cash that surrenders promised them impossible to resist. In cases where Indian resistance proved formidable, Ottawa was always ready to reach for the tools of compulsion. In 1895 it amended the Indian Act to authorize DIA to rent out reserve lands at the request of an individual band member, without the group's permission. Further amendments in 1911 allowed companies and municipalities empowered by statute to expropriate reserve land for public works, and established mechanisms for the department to remove Indians from reserves adjacent to or within towns of more than 8000 inhabitants. During World War I, under an ill-starred 'Greater Production' scheme, Indian Affairs was given the power to help themselves to both Indian land and Indian funds to carry out farming projects designed to increase crop production for the war effort. After the war further assaults on reserves were made in the interest of providing agricultural lands for the Soldier Settlement Board.[44]

The erosion of Indian resources with the connivance of the department was extensive in the period of rapid western Canadian development. By one estimate one-quarter million acres, about half of the reserves in the southern Saskatchewan portion of Treaty 4, were sold in the thirty years after heavy immigration began, some of it in conditions that bordered on fraud.[45] In the 1980s efforts would be made to restore some of the lands, successfully in the case of the White Bear reserve in southeastern Saskatchewan. Ontario Indians who refused to sell off valuable timber lands were pressured by the department to drop their sense of responsibility to future generations and grab the cash in the present. When two new transcontinental railways were under construction through western Canada during the first generation of the twentieth century, several Indian bands found their lands coveted for townsites, and some of them agreed to sell.[46] Somewhat more positive was the experience of the Blackfoot in the Calgary area, who sold almost half their reserve for more than $1 million and used the funds to finance their own social security, health care, housing, and economic development programs.[47] Few of the bands who surrendered land enjoyed even the temporary prosperity that the Blackfoot did.

Another area in which there was little progress after the 1880s was treaty-making. That Indians who had made treaty in the 1870s rejected the department view that their lands had been alienated was public knowledge. Piapot, for example, made a point of telling missionaries in 1895, 'Jamais je n'ai consenti à vendre nos terres aux blancs.'[48] But Indian remonstrances were ignored when Ottawa began to consider new treaties for more northerly regions. Once again, although the Indians in the north sometimes indicated a desire to be taken into treaty, it was not until white economic activity encroached on the region that government took steps to conclude agreements. It was the gold strike in the Klondike in the later 1890s, and fear that natives 'were liable to give trouble to isolated parties of miners or traders who might be regarded by the Indians as interfering with what they considered their vested rights,' that led in 1899–1900 to Treaty 8, which covered northern Alberta and Saskatchewan, northeastern British Columbia, and part of the North-West Territories.[49] After the turn of the century, economic conditions among the Indians of the far north would have justified the institution of treaties and government programs of economic development, and Ottawa was lobbied to make treaty with the tribes on the Mackenzie. But it was not until '1920, when oil gushed forth from Indian land at Fort Norman,' that Ottawa acted.[50] In 1921 Treaty 11 was signed to establish Canadian title to the more northerly portion of the Northwest Territories. Treaty 9 (1905) covered northern Ontario, while Treaty 10 (1906) dealt with those portions of northern Saskatchewan that were not included in Treaties 6 and 8.

The northern treaties differed little from the numbered treaties of the south. The annuities were larger, but the formula for alienation and promises of continued use of the land and its resources in a traditional mode were included. Treaty 8 differed somewhat from the earlier treaties in its provision that individuals or individual families as well as bands could take advantage of the allocation of one square mile for a family of five or 160 acres for an individual, and individuals were explicitly promised that they could have their plots elsewhere than on or contiguous to the reserve.[51] Negotiators also, apparently, promised 'non-interference with the religion of the Indians' who feared the assimilative efforts of residential schools would be applied to them after they entered treaty.[52] Few of these oral promises were honoured in later years. Of course, the northern Indians, who believed the treaties established a relationship of friendship and mutual assistance with the government, were shocked by the treatment they received.

The policies pursued in the north by an aloof and insensitive government were depressingly reminiscent of those that had failed in the south. Although there was not, for obvious reasons, a major effort at agricultural instruction, there was extension of the residential school system to the region. In the north, many of the schools in the early period were merely expansions of existing boarding schools, and that approach may have mitigated somewhat the impact of the educational program. But as the twentieth century wore on, more numerous and more elaborate schools were established in cooperation with the Oblates and Anglicans.

Nor were the promises to respect Indians' pursuit of the traditional economy honoured. The native people were brought willy-nilly under federal, provincial, and territorial game regulations, including well-intentioned efforts in the 1920s to conserve the few remaining bison that included the establishment of Wood Buffalo Park as a preserve for the shaggy beasts. As the hunting and fur-gathering economy of the Mackenzie District went into serious decline in the 1920s, the Indians had to starve while the bison multiplied in what had been their hunting territory. To the chief of a band near the park it was puzzling: 'I'm hungry and my children too and I come upon one of the Government buffalo. One or the other has to die because I don't want myself or my children to starve to death simply because this Government buffalo mustn't disappear from the region. Which of us is to disappear first? I would like an answer, is it me or the buffalo?' The government's implicit answer to that question was found in its consideration of a proposal to issue hunting permits to 'big game hunters with wealth' who would 'possibly pay a thousand dollars for the privilege of shooting a buffalo in order to secure a good head.'[53]

The government's theory about how the northern Indians would survive without hunting the bison and other game was that natives would find places in the developing resource economy of the north. About all the government did to facilitate such a transition, however, was to implement its disappointing residential schooling policy. The consequence was that the Indians experienced grave hardship as southern resource companies prospered from the extraction and sale of natural resources. In 1938 'mineral production of the N.W.T. exceeded in value the fur production for the first time,' but there was not yet a single person of native ancestry employed in mining or prospecting.[54]

As the unfortunate Indians of the Northwest Territories learned during the northern resource boom of the 1920s and 1930s, Ottawa experimented with many programs without much success in the period down to World War II. Treaty-making continued, not in any provident way, but in response to immediate needs created by economic development. Although the government often began its relationship with the Indians in a spirit of paternalism, with a desire to protect, it usually ended up employing coercive methods with results that severely harmed the interests of the Indians. The obscenity of protecting bison in Wood Buffalo Park while nearby Indians starved was merely a latter-day manifestation of an attitude that had led to interference with Indian self-government and Indian plans for their own economic development in the south.

As protection slid into interference, persuasion was dropped for aggressive efforts to redirect cultural practices through schooling or prohibitions of traditional rituals such as the potlatch. It is doubtful that these attempts at social engineering produced lasting cultural change, though they contributed to the demoralization of Indian societies. An equally graphic example of the slide towards coercion was the evolution of provisions for enfranchisement of Indians. The theory was that as Indians were educated, they would opt for full citizenship status, gaining the franchise and taking their share of reserve land with them as an individual freehold. But Indians refused to apply for full citizenship; theirs was a response of passive resistance. Under an amendment introduced in 1920, any Indian over the age of twenty-one whom the superintendent general thought fit for enfranchisement could, with two years' notice, be stripped of his (and his wife's and children's) status by the federal cabinet. Once again, Indians protested this gross political interference; once again they were ignored, until a change of government brought about repeal of the compulsion in 1922. However, when the Tories returned to power under R.B. Bennett, they reintroduced compulsory enfranchisement in an 1933 amendment, although this time with recognition of treaty rights in the form of a statement that enfranchisement could not be imposed on any Indian in violation of treaty promises. Such actions were as revealing of the drift of government policy and Indian resistance to directed cultural change as the potlatch laws or the attempts to 'detribalize' western Indians by subdividing their reserve lands.

These compulsory enfranchisement provisions showed that Ottawa still aimed at the peaceful elimination of Indians as a legal and social fact. The department's deputy minister, D.C. Scott, explained in 1920 that

I want to get rid of the Indian problem. I do not think as a matter of fact, that this country ought to continuously protect a class of people who are able to stand alone ... But after one hundred years, after being in close contact with civilization it is enervating to the individual or to a band to continue in that state of tutelage, when he or they are able to take their position as British citizens or Canadian citizens, to support themselves, and stand alone. That has been the whole purpose of Indian education and advancement since the earliest times ...

... Our object is to continue until there is not a single Indian in Canada that has not been absorbed into the body politic, and there is no Indian question, and no Indian Department.[55]

Official thinking had not moved very far from the early nineteenth-century belief that complete assimilation was 'the only possible euthenasia of savage communities.'

Champlain's encounter with the Iroquois in 1609
represented the integration of the European and his firearms
into North American rivalries.

The Maliseet, like the Micmac, were among the first to encounter European newcomers in the Atlantic area.

The great Mohawk soldier and politician Joseph Brant (1742–1807) was an example of the eighteenth-century emphasis on military alliance. William Berczy, *Portrait of Joseph Brant*, c 1807

As Walking Buffalo's (George McLean's) garb and tipi illustrate,
the bison was central to the cultural and artistic life,
as well as the economy, of the Plains Indian.

The bison was as important to the Plains Indian as corn was to the Iroquoians or salmon to the Northwest Coast Indian peoples.

The shaman, in this case a woman, was the major adversary of the Christian missionary in many parts of the country.

The shaman was a healer as well as a leader of religious rites: here he tries to dislodge the sickness of a young boy.

This Kwakiutl soul catcher was used by a shaman.

The fur trade was the foundation of Indian-European relations in the west until the late nineteenth century. Big Bear was trading furs at Fort Pitt not long before the outbreak of the Northwest Rebellion.

The *Canadian Illustrated News* version of the parleys at the Stone Fort in 1871 captured something of the formality of the treaty negotiations of the 1870s in western Canada.

Relations were good between North-West Mounted Police and Plains Indians in the early years of contact.

Northwest Coast art expressed itself in many forms, such as the house front of a Kwakiutl chief at Alert Bay in 1884.

The interiors of the massive cedar dwellings of Pacific chiefs were as impressive as their exteriors. The dwellings were often called 'ranch houses,' and a settlement of them a 'rancherie.'

Europeans' fascination with North American Indians created a market for travelling entertainers. This group of Bella Coola, who went to Germany in 1885, were part of a long tradition of Indian visitors, not all of whom went willingly.

The mining frontier in British Columbia usually displaced the Indians, although these Indians on the Thompson River in the 1880s were trying to extract gold from the river with the pan located on the right of the picture.

Indian Commissioner Edgar Dewdney, here proudly photographed with Chief Piapot and some of his band, shrewdly stationed armed forces on the reserve to discourage participation in the Northwest Rebellion.

The religious flag that Oblate missionaries gave to converted chiefs in British Columbia contained symbols for the Scriptures, the papacy, and European technology, along with 'Temperance' and 'Civilization.'

Oblate missionary Albert Lacombe and translator Jean L'Heureux accompanied Blackfoot chiefs who did not participate in the Northwest Rebellion to the prime minister's residence in Ottawa in 1886.

The Blackfoot chief Old Sun, accompanied by his wife in more traditional dress, sports his triennial chief's uniform and treaty medals.

OPPOSITE

The 'policy of the Bible and the plough' included the encouragement of agriculture, in this instance on a reserve in western Canada.

The contrast between a Plains Indian father and his children, who were students at the Qu'Appelle Indian Industrial School around 1900, was viewed by missionaries as evidence of the schools' successful inculcation of Euro-Canadian ways in the young.

The expedition led by Chief Joe Capilano (near centre, with robe over his arm) to London in 1906 marked an important point in both the land question and the emergence of native political organizations in British Columbia.

This 1913 potlatch at Quamichan, probably a naming ceremony for the young people, was one of many pieces of evidence that efforts to suppress the potlatch proved unavailing.

After the young men of the File Hills Indian Colony enlisted in the 68th Regiment during the Great War, some of their fathers went to town to see them off.

The Hall family was a group of assimilated Tsimshian converts of whom
Methodist missionary Thomas Crosby was especially proud.

As the southern economy expanded its influence northward, it usually did not benefit native peoples. This scene at Fort George, Quebec, in 1973 is a sad comment on the process.

Canada's newly developed welfare state entered the north during and after the Second World War. At the Hudson's Bay Company store at Read Island, NWT, in 1950, a family receives its family allowance.

The nineteenth and twentieth centuries usually meant the economic marginalization of Indian peoples. Here Maliseet boys sell baskets in Fredericton.

Sarcee Chief Gordon Crowchild opens a new 700-acre snowmobile area at Bragg Creek, Alberta.

Assembly of First Nations press conference, 9 March 1984. *Left to right*: Lou Demerais (media liaison), Georges Erasmus (national chief); Rob Robinson (BC region), and Harold Cardinal (vice-chief, prairie region).

PART THREE

CONFRONTATION

12

The beginnings of political organization

By the second third of the twentieth century changes in Canadian Indian policy were inevitable. Missionary organizations and Ottawa bureaucrats had come to recognize that directed change and economic development were not occurring as they wanted. Moreover, by the Depression decade the decline in Indian population that had been an unacknowledged factor in many of the policies had reversed. As Indian numbers began to increase, schools that did not succeed and reserves shrunken by land transfers proved inadequate. The failure of the nineteenth-century policies and a rise in the numbers of Indians made attempts to redefine Indian policy unavoidable. And, as that process began on the governmental side of the relationship, coincidentally among the native population there was a growing restlessness and a desire to control their own affairs.

The people responsible for the 'policy of the Bible and the plough' began to have doubts even before the Great War. To some of the church groups it was obvious, in the words of the Presbyterian who directed his church's schools, that 'instead of gaining ground for the last twenty-five years, we have been losing.' The layman in charge of the Church of England's missionary efforts in Canada in 1908 described the industrial schools as 'a very expensive farce' because of their dismal pedagogical showing.[1] On the government side, both politicians and bureaucrats were sceptical that reserves, missions, and Christian schools were having their desired effect. A senior official noted in 1898, 'Experience does not favour the view that the [reserve] system makes for the advancement of the Indians.' And deputy superintendent general of Indian Affairs Frank Pedley defended a decision in 1908 not to allocate more federal money to residential schools by saying, 'it is clear that the present system with its large expenditure has not operated as was expected towards the civilization of the aborigines.'[2]

A compounding factor was the attitude of Euro-Canadians in an era of advancing agricultural settlement. Such people increasingly regarded the presence of the Indians as simply an obstacle to their realization of dreams of material wealth. As a member of the Alberta attorney general's office put it, Albertans 'with whom I have spoken are not, I would gather, very much in sympathy with the Indian, nor with the efforts to better his condition. They look upon him as a sort of a pest which should be exterminated.'[3] In Sydney, Nova Scotia, in 1916 the Micmac band's reserve was relocated against their will from a downtown location because of attitudes that differed little from those of the Albertans. Such hostility also helped to propel the search for a new policy in the twentieth century.

The fact that Canada's Indians were declining in numbers counteracted the pressure for policy reform that stemmed from disillusionment and racial hostility. The combination of undermining the economy of the western Indians, encroaching upon the land base of many bands that had reserves, and the forced switch in both housing and dietary styles from the traditional to a poor version of the Euro-Canadian's had the effect of continuing the decimation of the Indians. As had always been the case, the single greatest destroyer of the Indian population was disease. And the most destructive disease was tuberculosis, to which Indians still largely did not have an acquired immunity.[4]

Diseases were probably worst in the overcrowded dormitories of the residential schools, most of which were tighty sealed to conserve energy. The fondness of school administrators for brass bands also contributed to the efficiency with which these schools disseminated diseases of the pulmonary system. A great deal of publicity was given this problem by the investigations and writings of a federal medical officer, Dr P.H. Bryce, who revealed the scandalous health conditions in the boarding and industrial schools. As the deputy minister of the department was to concede on the eve of the Great War, 'It is quite within the mark to say that fifty per cent of the children who passed through these schools did not live to benefit from the education which they had received therein.'[5] Because of health problems, poor diet, inadequate housing, and low incomes, the Indian population continued to dwindle through the late nineteenth and early twentieth centuries. This demographic pattern probably explained much of the delay in shifting to new policies. For example, although there was a serious attempt to phase out residential schools in favour of 'new, improved' day schools in the first decade partly because of health considerations, denominational opposition prevented the change. And so the dismal pattern of poor schooling and declining Indian numbers continued for the first three decades of the century.

At the end of the 1920s or beginning of the 1930s, the decline was reversed and Canada's recorded Indian population began to increase. A census taken in the early 1930s showed that, apparently for the first time since Confederation, the population of registered, or status, Indians had increased.[6] During the Depression decade, the Indian population climbed back above the 110,000 level; it would increase slowly till mid-century, when it would accelerate once more. A growing Indian population meant that policies predicated on the eventual disappearance of Indians had become fatuous. Increasing numbers also meant that the department's highly paternalistic programs, such as selling off reserve land and keeping Indian children for prolonged periods in residential institutions, were becoming expensive. The minister responsible for Indian matters said in 1941 that 'the fundamental difficulty which faced the Department in connection with Indian education,' for example, was 'an increase in the Indian population which made an increase in the cost of education, based on the per capita grants to residential schools, a matter of serious moment to the financial programme of the Department.'[7]

The final factor that combined with the churches' doubt and government's fiscal anxiety was the emergence of Indian political protest. In many ways, especially in the sense of long-term effectiveness, this would be the most significant of the factors. As has already been noted, Indian groups throughout the country had not acquiesced in the increasingly paternalistic and authoritarian policies that were put in place from the 1850s onward. But in the twentieth century Indian political movements would become better organized and more effective in bringing their grievances to the attention of government and the Canadian public. Although the bureaucrats and politicians continued to act until the 1960s or 1970s as though Indians were child-like and incapable of influencing policy for the better, the Indians eventually forced an unresponsive Ottawa to pay them heed.

Political confrontation did not begin with the largest group of natives to have come recently into close contact with Euro-Canadians, the Indians and Métis of the west. The Indians of the western interior certainly had as many grievances and problems after the 1880s as did the tribes of the Pacific coast, but for a long time they were demoralized by the aftermath of the Rebellion of 1885. Both the western Indians and the Métis were adversely affected by heavy agricultural settlement after 1895, becoming steadily more impoverished and marginalized. There were occasional attempts by government and church to resettle Métis groups in new locations in which they might have a chance to start anew, but for the most part these experiments had little success. Both Métis and prairie Indians would be a long time in recovering sufficiently from the traumas of the late nineteenth century to mount an effective political challenge.

Because of their particular problems it was the Indians of British Columbia who led the political movements of the early twentieth century. Those special circumstances could be summarized in one word: land. The land issue in British Columbia came in two parts. First, there was a long-running dispute over the allocation of reserves to the province's Indians after British Columbia joined Confederation in 1871. Second, Indians of the coastal province had a claim based on aboriginal title. Very little of the province had been covered by treaties in colonial days, because the legislature after 1864 had refused to make treaty and provide reserves. After 1871 the situation was left largely unchanged, in part because Ottawa was preoccupied with its relations with Indians elsewhere and in part because British Columbia proved uncooperative in disposing of both types of land-related problems. The Pacific province maintained that Indians did not have any title to the lands. A clear statement by the dominion in 1877 that 'Indian rights to soil in British Columbia have never been extinguished' did not move the stubborn settler society.[8] Not even the 1888 decision of the highest court in the empire, the Judicial Committee of the Privy Council (JCPC), in the St Catharine's Milling Case that recognized and partially defined an aboriginal usufructuary right to the lands that Indians inhabited could make British Columbia change its mind.

The long-running dispute over laying out reserves was rooted in British Columbia's refusal to grant reserves on the scale that the dominion had in the prairies. The province held that BC Indians had little need of land, and it insisted upon the inclusion in any grant of a reserve of a 'reversionary interest' to the benefit of the province. What this meant was that British Columbia was prepared to grant public lands for reserves only to a limited extent, and only on the condition that if a band gave up a reserve, ownership would revert to the province. This was profoundly different from the legal arrangement elsewhere, by which the dominion held title to reserve lands on behalf of the Indians. A joint committee was appointed in 1876 to lay out reserves, without a formula for area being established and subject to the province's 'reversionary interest.' This commission, in various guises and formats, continued in existence until 1908. British Columbia continued to make as small grants as possible for reserves. In 1912 Ottawa and Victoria set up another body, a royal commission of five, to settle the reserve issue, in most cases without application of a provincial reversionary interest. Although some bands refused to cooperate with this commission, in three years' work it confirmed existing reserves, added some 43,000 hectares of new reserves, and eliminated 23,000 hectares of old ones. Its 1916 report was finally ratified in 1924.[9]

The second aspect of the BC land question, aboriginal title, was even more fundamental and longer lasting. What was at stake here was the fact that with very few exceptions, Indians in British Columbia had never surrendered their lands to the crown. As the chiefs and principal men of the Port Simpson Tsimshian put it, 'This country was our world and from time immemorial our forefathers taught us by legend and tradition and actual possession that the land was ours.'[10] Since they had never been defeated militarily and since they had never surrendered their land by treaty, they believed that they still owned the lands that they inhabited. BC Indians would not sit still for being told, as one elderly man told the Northwest Coast Commission that was set up to hear the views of Nishga and Tsimshian petitioners in 1887, 'that it is not our fathers' land. Who is the chief that gave this land to the Queen? Give us his name. We have never heard it.'[11] The honest answer was that there was no such person. The Indians of the Nass valley told the same commission that the authorities 'have never bought it from us or our forefathers. They have never fought and conquered our people and taken the land that way, and yet they say now that they will give us so much land – our own land.'[12] The Nass chiefs asked for a treaty that would recognize their title and compensate them for the surrendered part of their land, but the 1887 commission had no authority to grant such a request.

When the BC Indians began to organize to pursue their claims early in the twentieth century, a pattern that was to become very familiar developed. In 1906 Joe Capilano, a chief of the Squamish people whose territory was threatened by the growing city of Vancouver, carried the protests of his people against encroachment to the throne itself. Although this attempt produced no change in the attitudes of governments in Canada, it did help to galvanize BC Indians into political organization.[13] In 1909 twenty tribes petitioned the monarch and formed a body called the Indian Tribes of the Province of British Columbia. The Nishga of the Nass River valley established the Nishga Land Committee and in 1913 forwarded to Ottawa the 'Nishga Petition' outlining their claim and asking for its adjudication by the Judicial Committee. However, since the JCPC was an appeal body and the northern Indians refused to submit their case to a Canadian court in the first instance, a lengthy stalemate ensued. In 1916 the Nass Indians joined with southern bands and the Interior Salish to found the Allied Tribes of British Columbia under the leadership of Peter Kelly and Andrew Paull. Paull, from a Squamish reserve, had been educated by the Oblates and was a strong lay defender of the Catholic church as well as his own people. Kelly, a Haida who had become an ordained Methodist clergyman, was a missionary to the coastal Indian peoples. The Allied Tribes pressed the federal government for settlement of both land questions for a decade. In

1924 Ottawa refused to bargain further on the issue of reserve allotments and decided to implement the Reserve Commission's report of 1916. In 1927 the dominion set up a Special Joint Parliamentary Committee to consider BC claims. This body, which heard Paull and Kelly speak on behalf of the Allied Tribes, concluded that BC's Indians 'have not established any claim to the lands of British Columbia based on aboriginal or other title' and decided that the matter was ended.[14] The Indians' political efforts must have had an impact on the Department of Indian Affairs nonetheless. The Indian Act was amended to make 'raising a fund or providing money for the prosecution of any claim' without the permission of Indian Affairs a crime.[15] The prohibition was in effect until 1951.

In the interwar period, Indians in other regions joined British Columbia in organizing to exert political pressure on the government. They included an Ontario Mohawk leader, Lieutenant F.O. Loft, who held the first congress of a League of Indians of Canada at Sault Ste Marie in the autumn of 1919. Loft, a veteran of the Great War, was an example of the considerable contribution that Indians from all parts of the country had made to the dominion war effort, as well as a manifestation of their understandable tendency afterwards to claim a right to be heard. Traditional arguments that Indians had no grounds for complaint because they had made no recent contribution to the development of the country could hardly be sustained in the face of the military record of some 4000 of them. As Loft said in a letter that he sent to Indian leaders in the central and prairie provinces, 'As peaceable and law-abiding citizens in the past, and even in the late war, we have performed dutiful service to our King, Country and Empire, and we have the right to claim and demand more justice and fair play as a recompense.' Loft also demonstrated that Indians outside British Columbia understood the importance of land issues. His letter argued that Indians should seek 'absolute control in retaining possession or disposition of our lands.'[16]

Gradually in the 1920s the league became dominated by western Indians.[17] Meetings in 1920 and 1922 protested against the restrictions of the pass system and demanded programs to assist the Indians in their development. Although the western movement's first leaders were Christian converts from the residential schools such as the Blood Mike Mountain Horse and the Cree clergyman

Edward Ahenakew who gave it a moderate cast, the western protest began to shift towards a more forceful assertion of traditional rights and demands for assistance. By the 1930s the prairie Indians were pressing for better schooling and agricultural assistance, while asserting their right to follow traditional rituals: 'Resolved that as Canada has freedom of religious worship we Indians would earnestly petition you to grant our request to worship in our own way and according to our past customs the Most High God that created the world and all the beasts thereof and everything that pertaineth thereof, especially as we do not see anything according to our past customs, and especially that we should not be prohibited from holding our ancient Sun Dance, which should be called the Thirsty Dance and the Hungry Dance; a religious ceremony which has been dear to us for centuries and is still dear to us.'[18] These sentiments were reminiscent of what Bull Shield, a member of a Blood sacred society, told a policeman: 'the Horn Society is as good as the Bible.'[19]

There is evidence that Ottawa's continuing attempts to discourage the observance of rituals that distracted Indians from immediate economic needs and deterred their assimilation were often unsuccessful. When the Indians of Poundmaker reserve in Saskatchewan built a meeting hall, they constructed it 'across the creek and out of sight of government health officials. Periodically, big feasts and dances were held there by the community.'[20] On the Pacific coast, potlatching went on in spite of a brief crackdown by Ottawa in the early 1920s.[21] As an Ojibwa had told a Jesuit in the mid-nineteenth century: 'As there are many species of plants, birds, fishes and animals, each one with its own peculiarities, so there are different kinds of men, each one with its own blessings from the Great Spirit. We are not fools. We have our wisdom given to our Ancients by the Great Spirit, and we shall cling to it.'[22] In the twentieth century, Indians across the country were making such views heard anew by means of political organization.

The western Indians' tendency to organize and resist culminated at the time of World War II in the formation of new bodies, the Indian Association of Alberta in 1939 and the Federation of Saskatchewan Indians in 1944. Once again, key figures in these advances toward political expression were products of the residential schools, men such as the clergyman Eugene Steinhauer in

Alberta and the Cree John Tootoosis in Saskatchewan. The two bodies that these men helped to create in their home provinces would be important to Indian political struggles of the later twentieth century.

Developments in British Columbia in the 1930s and 1940s paralleled those in the western interior. There, too, the leading spirits in the spreading Indian political movement were products of the Christian schools. Andrew Paull and Peter Kelly, for example, were both very active in the Allied Tribes of British Columbia until it collapsed after failing to persuade the parliamentary committee of the validity of their aboriginal title in 1927. Neither the 1927 Indian Act prohibition on fund raising or the stresses of Depression and world war stopped BC Indians from organizing. In 1931 the Native Brotherhood of British Columbia (NBBC) was established, and during the rest of the 1930s it spread southward down the coast from its northern centres of strength, eventually establishing itself in the southern interior as well. In 1942, thanks largely to Paull, a Kwakiutl-dominated economic organization called the Pacific Coast Native Fisherman's Association (1936) amalgamated with the NBBC. Soon afterward Paull spearheaded the formation of the North American Indian Brotherhood (NAIB), which, in spite of its name, was principally an effort to forge a national Indian political organization. In the 1940s he reached out to the young movements in the prairie region, but did not succeed for the time being in persuading them to support a national, united front for dealing with Ottawa. In the name of the NAIB, Paull asserted both land claims and more general issues before the parliamentary committee that sat from 1946 to 1948 to consider changes in the discredited Indian Act.

Other developments that had a dramatic impact on western Indians in particular helped to force a reassessment of policy. Perhaps the most important was the transfer in 1930 of jurisdiction over crown lands and natural resources from Ottawa to the three prairie provinces. The transfer agreements included an important statement that reaffirmed treaty rights to hunting and fishing, albeit it in a more restricted way. The act promised that 'the said Indians shall have the right, which the province hereby assures them, of hunting, trapping and fishing game and fish for food at all seasons of the year on all unoccupied Crown lands and on any other lands to which the said Indians may have a right of access.'[23] While this was an important confirmation of the right to hunt and fish regardless of provincial game laws, it also constituted a diminution of what had been promised in treaties because the transfer agreements limited the exercise of the right to occasions when the Indians hunted or fished 'for food.' The three provinces, unfortunately, sought in a myriad of ways to evade their responsibility, and, often in response to Euro-Canadians' political pressure, attempted to subject prairie Indians to the restrictions of their game and fishing laws. Western Indians consistently rebuffed these attempts, and the result was thousands of prosecutions of Indians for hunting and fishing.[24]

The Depression decade that saw the transfer of crown lands to the western provinces was an interregnum in policy-making between the experiments with coercion in the 1920s and the determination in the later 1940s to work out a new approach. The explanation of the inactivity of the 1930s resides largely in the economic depression that beset the country and distracted its governments. While the province of Alberta proved an exception to the general picture of inactivity by its investigation of Métis complaints and its creation of Métis reserves or settlements at the end of the decade, the federal government and the other provinces left natives to get through the troubled thirties as best they could.[25] Naturally, the programs that supported them were subject to frequent budget cuts, and these reductions served only to discredit existing policies still further by making them less effective and more hated.

World War II seemed for a time to have blown Canadian Indian policy apart as it crushed the Axis powers. There was a link between the two. After all, in the midst of a war against institutionalized racism and barbarity, it was impossible not to notice that the bases of Canadian Indian policy lay in assumptions about the moral and economic inferiority of particular racial groupings. The horrors of the war, in conjunction with the widening influence of the relativism of the social sciences, seriously discomfited Canadians when, on rare occasions, they looked at the way in which they treated the aboriginal peoples of their country. The fact that, once again, natives volunteered in exceptionally large numbers for military service also strengthened Indians' claim to consideration by the majority population. Canada's Indians were beginning to move out of the 'era of irrelevance' in which they had been cast by the majority population in the nineteenth century.

One sign of the Indian's emergence from 'irrelevance' was a search for a workable policy. The upshot of the wartime experiences, coming on top of the mounting disillusionment in government and church circles that had been observable for two generations, was the appointment in 1946 of a special joint committee of the Senate and House of Commons 'to examine and consider the Indian Act ... and amendments thereto and suggest such amendments as they may deem advisable.' An Alberta member of parliament claimed that 'the Canadian people as a whole are interested in the problem of Indians ... they are anxious to remedy our shortcomings. Parliament and the country is [sic] "human rights" conscious.'[26] If the hearings of the special committee from 1946 to 1948 were remarkable for the opportunity they gave the newly organized Indians to express their opinions, the subsequent legislation was notorious for the ways in which it ignored what they had said. Indian organizations from British Columbia, Alberta, Saskatchewan, Manitoba, and Quebec were particularly forceful in their condemnations of department political interference in band affairs, compulsory enfranchisement, inadequate economic assistance, and failure to adhere to the terms of the treaties. On the whole, the Indian representatives sought changes that would enable them to advance economically and to re-establish control of their own affairs, without assimilating and giving up status.

In 1948 the committee recommended a complete revision of the Indian Act to remove many of its coercive methods without altering its assimilative purpose. The committee report assumed that the work of assimilation and integration was well advanced, and that all that was required was a little more time and less bureaucratic intervention in Indian communities. The legislation, which was based both on the committee's recommendations and suggestions from the Department of Indian Affairs, that was finally passed in 1951 adopted the same assumptions and goals. While many of the most obnoxious features, such as compulsory enfranchisement, bans on the potlatch and the Sun Dance, and prohibitions on consumption of alcohol, were deleted, and while the department's ability to interfere politically was reduced somewhat, the general outlines of the policy remained unchanged. The 1951 act assumed that the purpose of Indian policy was the end of Indians, as they became assimilated and chose to integrate themselves into the economic, political, and social life of Canada. As a leading authority has written, the 1951 act merely 'returned to the philosophy of the original [1876] Indian Act: civilization was to be encouraged but not directed or forced on the Indian people.'[27] After all the assurances of concern in 1946, and after the special committee had listened to scores of Indian leaders, little of what they said was incorporated into the resulting legislation.

Through the 1950s Indians had to contend with a perpetuation of the regime that assumed their infantile character and sought their emergence into Euro-Canadian adulthood. Although policy was much better funded in the 1950s, it changed relatively little in its purpose. Education, which was increasingly being carried out in provincial schools as Indian Affairs tried to shift from segregated and residential schooling to integrated education, still attempted to assimilate the Indian child. And it continued to fail. Only a small minority of Indian children graduated from the schools, fewer still from post-secondary institutions; but some of those who did emerged with a burning desire to change the state in which Indians had to live.

During the 1950s and 1960s changes in public attitudes also occurred that helped to bring on another attempt at revision of Indian policy. During the resource-based boom that fuelled much of the prosperity that Canada enjoyed until the recession of 1957, Euro-Canadian enterprises began to penetrate Indian country in a way that they had not since the expansion of agricultural settlement in the late nineteenth century. Exploration for raw materials and energy heightened interest in areas of the country that had hitherto been considered economically marginal. For example, as Canada's crown uranium corporation, Eldorado, expanded its operations in northern Saskatchewan, it encountered large numbers of natives who were still following a traditional economy. Similarly, hydroelectric projects and base-mineral mines in the Precambrian Shield area of northern Manitoba, Ontario, and Quebec caused provincial governments and entrepreneurs to take a much livelier interest in regions of the country that were noted for their native populations. If World War II's horrific revelations had brought Canada's Indians 'out of irrelevance' in a moral sense, then the postwar resource boom did the same thing economically.

For their part, since little had changed in their position, Indians remained disgruntled. Their political organizations continued as occasion and finances permitted to express that disenchantment, but their ability to affect policy formation remained limited. Nonetheless, at least some Euro-Canadians began increasingly to worry about Indian policy. The reason for the majority population's concern had to do with more than the relevance of native peoples to the country's economic expansion. The postwar decolonization movement throughout the world raised questions among thoughtful Canadians about how long Canada could go on treating native communities as internal colonies. The civil rights movement of the 1960s in the United States posed similar riddles, while providing both native and non-native in Canada with object lessons in how to bring about change and what the consequences could be of refusal to change discriminatory policies directed against non-Caucasians.

The Trudeau government that was elected in 1968 under the slogans of 'just society' and 'participatory democracy' was a response to, and was particularly imbued with, the idea that it was time for fairer treatment of a variety of disadvantaged groups. In the same period, surveys by social scientists of the conditions in which Indians lived provided proof that the policies, whether modified in method by the 1951 amendments or not, simply did not work. In particular, the famous Hawthorn Report on Canada's Indians that was released in the mid-1960s made it obvious that change was necessary.[28] The Hawthorn Report also coined a memorable phrase about Indian status. The document pointed out that, in spite of their miserable socio-economic conditions, Indians actually deserved better treatment from Ottawa than did other Canadians. Because of their aboriginal title and treaty rights they should be treated as 'citizens plus.'

As a consequence of Indian disgruntlement, the articulateness of non-white peoples throughout the world, and an increased awareness that existing policy did not work, a new initiative was made in the later 1960s to redefine policy. The Pearson government (1963–8) committed itself in its last months in office to revise the Indian Act after an elaborate series of consultations with Indian organizations.[29] The election of a new Liberal government led to an expansion of the project to a full-blown search for a comprehensive, new policy towards native peoples and to a renewed commitment to consultation. It would turn out, however, that Trudeau's strong liberal values were at one and the same time the most powerful force for policy change and the single greatest influence in favour of a policy that Indians would reject.

Trudeau's genuine commitment to popular participation in the policy-making process ensured that all those involved in the policy review that preoccupied parts of the bureaucracy through the winter of 1968–9 would make at least a show of consulting native groups. But Trudeau's individualism also left him unsympathetic to arguments for group rights, and his obsession with defeating the claims of French-Canadian nationalists for special status for Quebec made him anxious to avoid creating any precedents that recognized racial or ethnic groups in legislative or constitutional ways. Perhaps Trudeau's attitude was best expressed in two of his statements. In one he echoed former American president John F. Kennedy, saying, 'We will be just in our time' in response to historical arguments for redress of natives' grievances.[30] Another Trudeau comment illustrated his opposition to special status and treaties: 'It's inconceivable I think that in a given society, one section of the society have a treaty with the other section of the society. We must all be equal under the laws and we must not sign treaties amongst ourselves ... We can't recognize aboriginal rights because no society can be built on historical "might-have-beens."'[31] In other words, Trudeau was unimpressed by historical arguments that Canadians should make redress for past transgressions, and he perceived the body politic as composed of individuals who related to their governments as atoms or isolated entities rather than as members of ethnic, racial, class, or regional collectivities. These views worked at cross purposes with Trudeau's commitment to consult the Indian organizations. If they were consulted, they would make it clear how much they differed with the new prime minister who was having such an impact on both the bureaucracy and the political community in Ottawa.

But the consultations that went on in the name of participatory democracy were not genuine. The series of meetings that took place in 1968–9 were, to use a 1960s phrase, 'a dialogue of the deaf.'

The Indian organizations had finally succeeded in establishing a truly national body, the National Indian Council (NIC), in 1961 thanks largely to the efforts of prairie Indian leaders. Perhaps even more important was the fact that in the later 1960s Indian groups up to and including the NIC were beginning to receive better funding, and, with their better organization and funding, Indians now found themselves able to present their views in a series of cogent, effective arguments. They stressed that they remained committed to the twin goals of advancement and retention of their identity. A common feature of their presentations was a demand that Ottawa create an Indian claims commission with power to settle the increasing number of claims that native bodies were developing. Their model was an American commission that Washington had set up, and part of their argument for a Canadian version was a recommendation of the Joint Parliamentary Committee of the later 1940s in favour of such a body for Canada. They articulated these views and demands with great clarity and force between the summer of 1968 and the spring of 1969. The final consultation session at the end of April 1969 concluded with an agreement for the government to fund still more 'future consultations.' Though the Indians said they were discouraged by the slow pace of the talks, they also told the Indian Affairs minister, Jean Chrétien: 'We are happy with the recognition of yourself that we in this meeting have entered into what you call a new era. Because for the first time our people as a whole are proposing to work with you on a basis of partnership rather than on a basis of directives from your officials. Our delegation is extremely pleased that this has occurred.'[32] Within two months they would be very displeased.

On 25 June 1969, the first anniversary of the Trudeau government's massive electoral victory, Chrétien rose in the Commons to release the long-awaited White Paper on Indian Policy.* It

*The term 'white paper,' though perhaps unfortunate given the subject matter, had no racial connotation. A white paper was simply a statement of preliminary government policy, issued after a series of consultations and prior to cabinet adoption of a plan for legislation. It was a stage in an elaborate process of review, consultation, and policy formulation that Trudeau had introduced after his election in 1968. It might as easily have been termed a 'position paper' or 'preliminary policy proposal,' or, as was the case several years later with immigration policy, a green paper.

would turn out that it was the assumptions behind as much as the content of the white paper that would cause the government its greatest problems.

The *Statement of the Government of Canada on Indian Policy, 1969,* which claimed to be the product of 'a year's intensive discussions with Indian people,' argued that Canada's Indians were disadvantaged because they enjoyed a unique legal status. The problems of poverty, high rates of incarceration, political impotence, and economic marginality were not attributable to insensitive government policies or generations of racial prejudice. It was not because Indians lacked control of their own affairs or because they had been systematically dispossessed of their lands that they experienced severe economic and social problems. No. The explanation was that the law treated them differently, that they had a special status as Indians. The 'separate legal status of Indians and the policies which have flowed from it have kept the Indian people apart from and behind other Canadians.' Canada and the Indians had erred in travelling 'the road of different status, a road which has led to a blind alley of deprivation and frustration.' The white paper proposed that they change course to 'a road that would lead gradually away from different status to full social, economic and political participation in Canadian life.'

The language of the white paper made it clear that it was a path of the government's, not the Indians', choosing. 'This Government believes in equality,' and 'Only a policy based on this belief can enable the Indian people to realize their needs and aspirations.' To that end it recommended 'that the legislative and constitutional bases of discrimination be removed' by abolishing Indian status, that for Indians 'services come through the same channels and from the same government agencies' as they do for other Canadians, and 'that control of Indian lands be transferred to the Indian people.' It proposed, accordingly, 'that the Indian Act be repealed,' that provinces 'take over the same responsibility for Indians that they have for other citizens,' and that the federal government 'Wind up that part of the Department of Indian Affairs and Northern Development which deals with Indian Affairs.' Indian status would be abolished, Indians would relate to their governments as individuals in precisely the way that other citizens did, and as a collectivity they would function just like French

Canadians or citizens of Ukrainian ancestry. 'Today,' intoned the white paper, Canada 'is made up of many people with many cultures. Each has its own manner of relating to the other; each makes its own adjustments to the larger society.' Indians, as Indians, would disappear; Indians would become just another element in a multicultural Canada. The federal government planned to assist the transition, said the white paper, with generous help, but within five years the Department of Indian Affairs was to disappear. So would Indians as a special group.

The government thought this program was fair, a necessary step towards the 'just society.'[33] If some argued that such a treatment would be a violation of treaty obligations, the government had three answers. First, this policy was supposedly being adopted after consultations with the Indians themselves. Second, the services that Indians were receiving in the 1960s went 'far beyond what could have been foreseen by those who signed the treaties.' And, third, 'once Indian lands are securely within Indian control, the anomaly of treaties between groups within society and the government of that society will require that these treaties be reviewed to see how they can be equitably ended.' If critics argued that these changes would do away with Indian status and Indian claims before they were satisfied, the white paper responded that 'aboriginal claims to land ... are so general and undefined that it is not realistic to think of them as specific claims capable of remedy except through a policy and program that will end injustice to Indians as members of the Canadian community.' It was true that Ottawa 'had intended to introduce legislation to establish an Indian Claims Commission to hear and determine Indian claims. Consideration of the questions raised at the consultations and the review of Indian policy have raised serious doubts as to whether a Claim Commission as proposed to Parliament in 1965 is the right way to deal with the grievances of Indians put forward as claims.'[34]

The white paper adopted government solutions and ignored Indian proposals. Indians had said that they wanted economic and social recovery without losing their identity; the white paper proposed the extinction of their separate status as a step towards dealing with problems that Ottawa said were the consequence of a different status. Indians had made it clear that they intended to hold the federal government to the commitments it had made in treaties, obligations that were embodied – sometimes perversely – in the Indian Act. The white paper proposed to absolve the federal government of its commitments by revoking Indian status, eliminating the Department of Indian Affairs, and transferring responsibility for Indian matters mainly to the provincial governments. Indians had been pressing for two decades for a claims commission that would respond to their argument that aboriginal title justified extensive compensation for the loss of lands and resources; the proposed policy airily dismissed the concept of aboriginal rights and explicitly rejected the establishment of an Indian claims commission. And all of this occurred after a year of supposed consultation; all this was done in the name of equality and justice.

The explanation of this grotesque conclusion to the policy review of 1968–9 is that the policy formulation process became subordinated to the needs of government. To a considerable extent the bureaucrats in Indian Affairs had opposed meaningful change, and throughout the policy review process they had given advice that would have resulted in traditional policies being recommended. The political operatives in the Prime Minister's Office and the Privy Council Office, impatient with and contemptuous of such paternalism and caution, seized control of the review. Since their most immediate constituency was the new prime minister, they shaped the proposals according to Trudeau's notions about individualism, equality, and the inappropriateness of recognising ethnic and racial groups as collectivities. The brutal truth was that the series of consultations that had been carried out with Indian leaders never had any impact on the review of policy. When Indian leaders at the end of April 1969 had been congratulating Chrétien for listening to them and agreeing to continue the dialogue, officials were putting the final touches to a white paper whose assumptions, arguments, and recommendations were the antithesis of what Indians had been saying. 'The policy was a response to values within the policy-making arena, not to the basic problems facing Indians.'[35]

It seemed to Indian leaders that nothing had changed, not even in an age of 'participatory democracy.' When the final stage was reached, the process by which policy proposals were generated in 1969 paid no more heed to Indian opinions and desires than earlier phases. The Joint Parliamentary Committee of 1946–8 had not been very responsive to Indian views, but that earlier rcview had at least been honest. The parliamentarians and officials had made little pretence of being guided by Indians' views. From the Indian standpoint, the twentieth-century quest for a new policy that culminated in the white paper of 1969 seemed to show that nothing had changed in a century. The formulation of the first post-Confederation Indian Act in 1869 had not involved Indians at all; the development of the white paper of 1969 did not involve them in any meaningful way, either.

13

Political relations after the white paper

The Alberta chiefs-led the reaction to the white paper by responding bluntly to its assumptions and arguments. Their 1970 reply referred to the concept that Hawthorn had articulated a few years earlier: Indians were not merely citizens, as Trudeau regarded them, but a distinct category of people within Canada who had special rights. They were 'citizens plus.' Perhaps more important, in the process of responding to the white paper, Indian organizations were politicized to fight the federal government and found for the first time that they were sufficiently united to do so in a disciplined and effective way. The white paper thus initiated two decades of political and constitutional struggle by native peoples. The Alberta chiefs argued that 'the recognition of Indian status is essential for justice.' Ottawa 'must admit its mistakes and recognize that the treaties are historic, moral and legal obligations.' The Alberta chiefs 'are opposed to any system of [land] allotment that would give individuals ownership with rights to sell,' and they 'reject the White Paper proposal that the Indian Act be repealed' and 'this proposal to abolish the Indian Affairs Branch.' 'Freedom depends on having financial and social security first.'[1]

Another spectacular response came from Harold Cardinal, the Cree president of the Indian Association of Alberta, whose *Unjust Society* sarcastically dissected the white paper and the century of Indian policy that stood behind it. It was, said Cardinal, 'a thinly disguised programme of extermination through assimilation' that was reminiscent of American policies of termination and much worse. 'The Americans to the south of us used to have a saying: "The only good Indian is a dead Indian."' The Canadian government says, 'The only good Indian is a non-Indian.' It believes that to survive, the Indian 'must become a good little brown white man.' Moreover, 'Talking and listening have been one-way streets with white men and Indians. Until very recently white men have expected Indians to do all the listening.' Indians were no longer willing to participate in this one-way conversation: 'We want the white man to shut up and listen to us, really listen for a change.' Equally important, they no longer trusted white politicians. Said Cardinal, 'We will not trust the government with our futures any longer. Now they must listen to and learn from us.'[2]

These were only the most eloquent of a series of denunciations that soon forced the federal government to beat a retreat from its white paper. The Union of Ontario Indians called the minister a liar; the Manitoba Indians issued their own 'brown paper' to counter the analysis in the government's white paper; BC Indians weighed in; and gradually newspaper editorialists and academics swung into line by attacking the lack of consultation with Indians and the call for their termination. Although Chrétien and Trudeau started off defending the policy, they soon were pleading that it contained merely proposals for discussion, and in less than a year they recanted. In September Ottawa threw Indians a sop by agreeing, finally, to the financial backing for Indian claims research that the organizations had been seeking for years. When that did little to still the outcry, which was amplified by angry Indian reaction to the government's December 1969 appointment of a single Indian claims commissioner without authority to investigate claims based on aboriginal title, the government began to move away from the policy in the white paper.

The next spring Trudeau said, 'If the White people and the Indian people in Canada don't want the proposed policy, we're not going to force it down their throats.' When he met the Alberta chiefs to receive the 'red paper' in June 1970, the prime minister assured them that the government was prepared to participate in a dialogue for as long as the Indians thought necessary. 'You know, a hundred years has been a long time and if you don't want an answer in another year, we'll take two, three, five, ten, or twenty – the time you people decide to come to grips with this problem. And we won't force any solution on you, because we are not looking for any particular solution.'[3]

The discordant notes of the white paper of 1969 continued to echo through the 1970s and into the 1980s. In the first place, the fraudulent consultations and ill-advised recommendations had planted deep suspicions among Indians. They continued to suspect that Ottawa was attempting to implement, piecemeal, the 1969 policy of termination of status and transfer of responsibility for Indian matters to the provinces. The 1969 statement became a benchmark against which every initiative or proposal was measured, a crude litmus test into which every politician's speech was dunked for an instant reading. This distrust helped to embitter Indian-government relations during the 1970s.

The other legacy of the white paper was the stimulus it gave to Indian politicization and organization. In their uniformly hostile reactions to it, Indian leaders found a basis for a pan-Canadian unity they had long sought but failed to achieve. Moreover, in their first political test – the resistance to the White Paper by the National Indian Brotherhood (NIB) and the various provincial federations – they had seen that unified and militant action worked. The granting of federal funding for claims research and Trudeau's renunciation of the white paper were interpreted as victories for organization. The white paper had given them a common enemy against which to mobilize, and the prime minister's retreat had encouraged their troops. It would not be the Indians' last political victory.

The key to understanding the events during the decade after the white paper fiasco of 1969 is the National Indian Brotherhood. The NIB was a spinoff of the National Indian Council (NIC) that the Federation of Saskatchewan Indians had done much to found. Through most of the 1960s the NIC carried on low-key lobbying efforts and organized student exchanges and celebrations of Indian culture. The NIC's highpoint, perhaps, was the Indian Pavilion at Expo 67, the world's fair in Montreal, that attracted a great deal of international attention. But the NIC was also experiencing problems. It was troubled by tensions between treaty

Indians, principally from the prairie provinces, and Métis and non-status Indians over the strategy to be followed. Indians with treaties preferred to pursue claims on the basis of the treaty promises, but those without Indian treaties (both Indians and Métis) found it more attractive to argue from a basis of aboriginal rights. The latter group had never signed treaties that might be construed as having extinguished their primordial rights. In 1968 the NIC split into the National Indian Brotherhood and Canadian Métis Society.

The NIB found itself propelled into national prominence and leadership of Indian peoples largely as a consequence of the reaction to the white paper of 1969. But in the 1970s, especially during the leadership of George Manuel, a Shuswap from British Columbia, the body adopted a more political strategy in Canada while looking outward for international links and support. The NIB adopted a coherent program to present to the federal government, and also attempted to position the Canadian native movement in the worldwide decolonization movement. Manuel in particular subscribed to the notion that Indians and other natives around the world constituted a Fourth World of dependent peoples, internal colonies in a variety of modern states. Such a conceptual approach equipped the NIB advocates with an ideology to understand and present their case to the public, while providing it with allies around the world.[4] The other reason for the NIB's success in the 1970s was its successful campaign to wrest control of some programs that affected Indian people from the federal government. A significant achievement of Manuel's early years in the NIB presidency was securing stable funding of the organization from Ottawa. Core funding assured financial support for the ongoing work of the NIB, and Department of Indian Affairs and Northern Development (DIAND) funding of research in support of Indian claims provided a stability and impetus that no national native political body previously had enjoyed.

Working from such a solid base, the NIB undertook a series of political initiatives in the 1970s, two of the more significant of which concerned social services and education. Indian distrust of Ottawa combined with well-established disenchantment with existing programs pushed the NIB and provincial Indian organizations, especially in the prairies, to demand that Ottawa turn direction of welfare, child protection, and education programs over to them. These demands rarely met with success, and in some cases what can only be described as deliberate sabotage of Indian-controlled social assistance and counselling programs by the department occurred once management was surrendered.[5] The area of child welfare has been a particularly sensitive one because Indians insist that their familial structures and child-rearing practices are different from those of the mainstream society. They oppose sending Indian and native children out of their communities for adoption, as usually happened when child-rescue and child-protection programs were under government administration. This area continues to be one of continuing confrontation between bureaucracies and Indian political bodies in the 1980s.[6]

The Indian experience in gaining control of the education of their young has been more successful. The abject failure of the government-controlled and church-administered educational system either to assimilate or to impart learning to Indians had become painfully obvious to all by the 1960s. Indian groups were disenchanted, most missionary bodies wanted to retire from the field, and Ottawa was aghast at the rising costs of residential schooling. By the end of the 1960s the residential schools were being phased out, some of them being turned into hostels in which Indian children resided while attending neighbouring public schools. Since the alternative to residential schooling, integrated schooling in public schools, was proving to be neither more successful pedagogically nor more satisfactory to Indian children, government was in a quandary.

Finally, in 1973, the federal government acquiesced to a demand of the NIB to transfer control and funding to Indian bands, endorsing a Brotherhood position paper on 'Indian Control of Indian Education.' While there have been serious problems in beginning the real implementation of the policy and in carrying it through all levels of education, significant advances have been made in the past fifteen years. Particularly in the prairie provinces, progress has been made in redesigning curricula to make them more reflective of and relevant to native children, in finding or developing instructional materials that depict natives as part of the visible world, in establishing special teacher-training programs, and, in some cases, in accelerating the hiring of natives by both native-controlled and regular school boards. While it is too soon to know what the results of this shift in educational policy will be, it seems hard to believe that they could be as dismal as what preceded it.

The political assertiveness of NIB on funding, social programs, and Indian education led to an emphasis in the 1970s on Indian self-government. The evolution was natural in two senses. First, if Indians were going to administer policies that previously had been under government control, they would begin to regard bands and provincial federations as bureaucratic as well as political bodies. Second, the development towards increasing insistence on Indians' right to govern themselves was natural because Indians had never conceded that they surrendered powers of self-government to European powers. A succession of Indian groups and individuals had insisted that they were not conquered peoples but groups who retained their right to decide their own affairs. The Six Nations had sternly pointed out this fact to British officials when the United Kingdom surrendered Iroquois lands to the Americans after the revolution. From the first, attempts in the Province of Canada in the 1850s to empower civil government to interfere in internal band matters had evoked angry reactions from Indians. And the Mohawk of the Brantford area had been locked in a battle over whether their own traditional leaders or Ottawa's elected chieftains were the legitimate rulers of their community from the nineteenth century well into the present one.

Similarly, as Canada extended its control westward after 1869, it was met by Indian groups that insisted that no one – certainly not the Hudson's Bay Company – had the right to sell their lands or waive their right to manage their own affairs. Big Bear's comment at the making of Treaty Six in 1876 that he feared the rope around his neck was a metaphorical way of saying, not that he felt any trepidation about hanging, but that he would not accept the imposition of Canadian law. BC Indians in the 1880s had similarly expressed concern at the prospect of Canada's law being administered in their lands.[7] Throughout Canadian history, Indians had insisted that they were not subjects but allies, and that they retained their rights of self-government even if they agreed to share their lands. When the NIB embarked on a drive for Indian self-government in the 1970s, it was simply expressing a well-established belief among Indians.

Since the early 1970s the case for self-government has been advanced with varying degrees of success.[8] Control over education and some aspects of welfare and child care have certainly been parts of a general thrust towards self-government. And DIAND has always conceded that bands have at least a limited scope for self-regulation on the reserves by Band Council Resolutions, which have a force approximating that of statutes passed by other levels of government. But, for a number of reasons, self-government has largely remained something sought rather than achieved. The first is that there is no unanimity on what constitutes self-government and to whom it applies. Will Indian legislative bodies have jurisdiction over everyone, or only Indians, while on the reserve? Will these bodies have jurisdiction over Indians when they are off Indian lands, for example when residing in urban areas? What will happen if Indian legislators attempt to regulate behaviour, whether of non-Indians in Indian territory or Indians outside Indian-controlled lands, and those people resist? How will disputes between individuals and Indian governments be handled? Can Indian governments be hauled before courts established by other levels of government? Can employees of bands bring their employers before a human rights tribunal or labour relations board if they feel aggrieved?

An illustration that some of these questions are real is the dispute between the Fort Alexander band and its teachers. The teachers appealed to the Canada Labour Relations Board (CLRB) successfully in 1984 against the Manitoba band's dismissal of them for bargaining collectively. At no time in the protracted proceedings did the band acknowledge the legitimacy of the tribunal to which the teachers took the case or their own obligation to Canadian labour relations and human rights legislation. Band leaders were fined and jailed for contempt of the Federal Court of Canada that ordered implementaion of a CLRB ruling. The dispute was finally resolved when the band, which still refused to reinstate the teachers, agreed to pay four of them a total of $226,000 in compensation, and the teachers dropped a demand that they be given back their jobs.[9]

A second difficulty with winning acceptance for Indian self-government is the fact that it runs up against the liberal democratic values of the majority population. Many non-Indians do not understand how sovereign Indian nations within the country can operate in harmony with the existing system. Did Canadians not reject such a notion in the case of Quebec separatism, they ask? Many people, perhaps only at a subconscious level, reject political claims based on racial or ethnic and collective concepts because they understand civil society to be a collection of citizens who relate to government as individuals and are treated equally regardless of their place of residence or race or language. This barrier to the full acceptance of Indian self-government is, in most cases, the product of a fundamental difference of political philosophy. It will take a great deal of effort and understanding to remove the obstacle.

Third, a major problem in advancing towards self-government has been economic. Indians and both levels of government recognize that native self-government without the resources to operate will prove a mockery. Consequently, Indian and Métis organizations have insisted that discussions of increasing Indian self-government be accompanied by the negotiated settlement of claims to land and resources that they have advanced. But few of the land claims have been settled, in part because the provinces have proven reluctant to make crown lands available for concession to native groups. Finally, the campaign for Indian self-government that the NIB began in the 1970s has been sidetracked by protracted wranglings over constitutional renewal in the country at large. Ironically, the interminable arguments over patriation of an amending power and creation of a Charter of Rights, while they deflected the NIB's political campaign, ended up by giving both it and other native groups a new basis from which to continue their struggle for political control over their own lives.

The search for a new constitutional formula was a consequence of Pierre Elliott Trudeau and of the Quebec separatism that he had entered federal politics to fight. Trudeau believed that federalism was the ideal form of government for a vast, heterogeneous country such as Canada. He was equally implacable in his opposition to the modern force of nationalism and to the separatists in his home province. Trudeau believed that the existing constitution, especially its written portion known as the British North America Act, was generally satisfactory. All that it needed was the addition of a formula for amending it within Canada (as a statute of the British parliament, the BNA Act could be amended only by the United Kingdom) and a bill of rights that would protect civil, political, and linguistic rights by moving these areas beyond the reach of the legislatures. Trudeau's answer to separatism was not greater power and autonomy for the French-Canadian homeland of Quebec, but the entrenchment of official bilingualism throughout Canada to make the whole country a congenial patrimony for all French Canadians. Although Trudeau worked consistently throughout his prime ministerial career at achieving his vision, he redoubled his efforts after the election of René Lévesque's Parti Québécois government in the autumn of 1976. A proposal for change in 1977–8 ultimately failed, but not before sparking a debate that engaged the leaders of the native organizations.

The leaders of the NIB recognized that constitutional revision could affect their relationship to the federal government and that the process presented an opportunity to assert their role as another order of government. The NIB demanded that it be represented at forthcoming first ministers' meetings on the constitution, and, when the federal government offered only observer status, it boycotted the meetings in February 1979. In that year the NIB carried out a lobbying effort in Britain, whose parliament would have to put into legislation whatever Canadian politicians decided by way of constitutional changes, and at the same time obtained a commitment from the Liberal government that it would be given some form of limited participation in future constitutional talks scheduled for the autumn of 1979. Trudeau's electoral defeat in May 1979 made no difference to this important advance, for the Clark government announced that it would honour the promise of Indian participation in any talks. However, since the new Conservative government seemed committed to avoiding conflict with the provinces, especially Quebec, the NIB was not likely to get a chance to participate in first ministers' talks.

A renewed opportunity was provided for Indian assertiveness with Trudeau's unexpected return to power and the Quebec referendum campaign in the early months of 1980. The Grits' February victory returned to power a prime minister still determined to renew the constitution, and the federal Liberals' important contribution to the defeat of the anti-federal forces in the May referendum in Quebec emboldened Trudeau's supporters to make one final, determined effort to achieve constitutional change. During the course of the referendum campaign, many politicians from outside Quebec had pledged that defeat of the Lévesque government's proposal would lead to their cooperating in another attempt at constitutional renewal. Trudeau tried to call in those markers by initiating another round of talks on constitutional change in 1980–1.

To the intense disappointment of the NIB and other native groups, the earlier promises of at least limited Indian participation in these talks were not honored. (During the period 1980–2 the NIB reorganized itself into the Assembly of First Nations, a title that reflected Indians' view that their political organization represented 'nations' that had a right to negotiate with other governments on terms of equality.) What was worse was that the western premiers took very firm positions against the inclusion of any protections in a new constitution for either Indian self-government or Indian and native rights. The nadir of the Indian cause seemed to be reached in November 1981, when nine of the ten provinces concluded a late-night agreement with federal representatives on an amending formula and the terms of a Charter of Rights and Freedoms, terms that left out any protection either to women's equality rights or native rights. Prairie premiers' opposition forced Ottawa to drop a bid to recognize aboriginal rights in the revised constitution.

By energetic effort, both women's and native organizations rescued something from the constitutional debacle during the winter of 1981–2. They lobbied ferociously to force the politicians to include protections for women's and aboriginal rights in the Constitution Act, 1982, and eventually both succeeded. In the case of the native cause, lobbying succeeded in getting agreement to insert the sentence, 'The existing aboriginal and treaty rights of the aboriginal peoples of Canada are hereby recognized and affirmed.' And, even more important for the Métis, 'aboriginal peoples' was defined to include 'the Indian, Inuit and Métis peoples of Canada.' Inclusion of the first sentence meant that these rights were placed beyond the reach of parliament and legislatures. What rights Inuit, Indians, and Métis enjoyed in April 1982, when the new constitution was formally adopted, were enshrined in Canada's fundamental law. But there were problems. The first was that the adjective 'existing' was restrictive; it was included so as to prevent resort to the courts in an effort to get a definition of 'aboriginal rights' that was more extensive than politicians might be willing to embrace. The second difficulty was that no one knew what constituted 'existing aboriginal and treaty rights.' Therefore, it was also agreed that a series of conferences would be held with representatives of the aboriginal peoples' organizations to define these 'rights.'

The process of constitutional renewal, then, was both a distraction and a support for the cause of Indian self-government. The bruising battles over constitutional reform in 1978–9 and 1980–2 absorbed the time and money of the National Indian Brotherhood and the Assembly of First Nations. Though these struggles seemed at first to have resulted in a terrible betrayal, they ended up giving protection to natives' 'existing' rights and promising discussions to define what rights existed. This gave the native political bodies a platform from which to advance their cause, and all three groups took full advantage of it to argue in favour of self-government and other political objectives. At constitutional conferences in 1983, 1984, 1985, and 1987, representatives of the Indians, Métis, and Inuit argued that they were entitled to redress of their land claims, respect for their treaties, and the right of self-government.[10] Although Trudeau argued heatedly at his final appearance at these conferences in 1984 that the premiers should accept native self-government in principle, leaving to later the working out of the details of what the concept meant, the western premiers refused to agree. At the 1985 conference the issue remained unsettled; and there was no progress at the conference in the spring of 1987. (Ironically, premiers who could not accept native self-government in principle because they did not understand fully its implications a few months later in 1987 enthusiastically adopted the Meech Lake Accord, which contained commitments of astonishing vagueness.)

However, if the cause of Indian self-government stalled at the first ministers' conferences, it received further impetus elsewhere. In 1983 a Special Committee of the House of Commons on Indian Self-Government (the Penner committee) unexpectedly produced a report that endorsed an expansive version of Indian self-government.[11] Perhaps because Penner's committee contained three non-voting members from native political bodies and held extensive hearings at which many native representatives testified, it produced a report that endorsed expanding the concept of aboriginal right from claims to lands to political self-determination or self-government. The Indian Act had always purported to *confer* on Indian bands the right to establish their own councils with limited powers, but the Penner committee recommended that the right to self-government should be *recognized* by other governments and entrenched in the constitution. 'Indian First Nations' would 'form a distinct order of government in Canada.' Such terminology signalled the adoption of the Indian position that they were sovereign nations still possessing the power to regulate their own affairs. Thus the Penner committee conferred a legitimacy on Indian self-government that it had not hitherto enjoyed in mainstream Canadian society, and not even the setbacks at the first ministers' conferences could diminish the moral and political significance of that advance. The clarity of the Penner report's recommendations also served to highlight the fact that politicians faced a choice between conceding that Indians are sovereign, and therefore not mere citizens of Canada, or insisting that they be treated as regular citizens. The report made it obvious that Indian self-government was different from ordinary Canadian citizenship.

Other consequences of the Indians' involvement in constitution-making have been as mixed as those in the area of Indian self-government. The Charter of Rights and Freedoms also focused a spotlight on the Indian Act's discriminatory provisions. Since the 1850s legislation governing Indians had defined who was an Indian in a way that discriminated against women. Under the Indian Act an Indian woman who married a non-Indian or even a non-status Indian lost her Indian status, and her children lost theirs too. Conversely, an Indian man did not lose his status if he married a non-Indian woman; rather she became an 'Indian.' This gender discrimination had bothered many people for some time, particularly after the Supreme Court in the 1973 Lavell case upheld this discriminatory provision of the Indian Act. In 1975 a Maliseet woman, Sandra Lovelace, had taken her complaint against this gender discrimination to the Human Rights Committee of the

United Nations. The committee decided in 1981 that the Indian Act's provision barring Ms Lovelace from residence on the Tobique reserve was 'an unjustifiable denial of her rights under' the United Nations' Convenant on Civil and Political Rights.[12] The UN decision was of limited practical value because of its unenforceability, but the 1982 adoption of the Charter of Rights and Freedoms, which prohibited discrimination on the basis of sex, made it essential that Ottawa grapple with the problem quickly. The full implementation of the Charter was delayed until 1985 to give governments an opportunity to bring their legislation into line with the equality provisions in the 1982 document.

The federal government concluded that it had no choice but to repeal the portion of the Indian Act that discriminated against Indian women and their descendants, but many Indian organizations were strenuously opposed. It was not so much that they favoured discrimination (though the heavily male character of their leadership caused some observers to wonder even on that point) as that they feared the consequences of making it possible for tens of thousands of people to reclaim Indian status. Some bands, especially in Alberta, were oil-rich and reluctant to share their riches with a potential horde of returnees to the reserves. Others simply feared that they did not have enough land and other resources to cope with larger populations. They failed in their efforts to persuade the federal government to put the financial resources in place to deal with larger band numbers before the discriminatory provision was repealed. Eventually, a compromise was worked out that satisfied the stringency of the Charter, though it did not please the Indian bands. The discriminatory term would be repealed, and both women who had married non-Indians or non-status Indians and their offspring could recover their Indian status. But the question of determining if the portion of these people who had lost their status before 1985 would get band membership and services would be determined according to criteria that bands were invited to develop. It was a compromise that satisfied government but alarmed Indians. Some leaders believed Ottawa had no right to tell them how to manage their internal affairs. Others were concerned about the precedent that the measure created by making a legislative distinction between Indian status and band membership.[13]

The other setback that followed constitutional renewal was a split in 1985 in the ranks of the status Indians of Canada. The conferences leading up to and following from the making of the 1982 constitution made it ever clearer that there was a division of opinion and a clash of interests within the ranks of the national political body called the Assembly of First Nations. All the members of this organization were status Indians, but they differed in another important respect. Some of them, principally from the prairie provinces and parts of the Territories, were descended from Indians who had signed treaties with the Dominion of Canada. They could argue for advances using a case built on either aboriginal rights or treaty rights. But other Indians had not signed treaties that contained guarantees of educational and economic assistance. The only basis from which they could argue was aboriginal rights. After the first ministers' conferences in 1983, 1984, and 1985 demonstrated that a case based strictly on 'existing aboriginal' rights was getting nowhere, some Indians wanted to shift strategy. When they could not persuade the AFN to go along with them, and when their representative, incumbent AFN chief David Ahenakew of Saskatchewan, was defeated by Georges Erasmus of the Northwest Territories, they left the AFN and formed their own body, the Prairie Treaty Nations Alliance.

The difference of interest that underlay the division was real, and the decision of the prairie Indians to strike out on their own understandable, but for the Indian political movement as a whole it was a step backward towards weakness. Their great strides forward in gaining control of programs and towards self-government were largely the consequence of the unity they had been able to establish in 1969–70 in fighting the white paper, a unity that was reinforced through the 1970s by effective leadership. But the struggles over the constitution and the best strategy to pursue in getting a definition of 'existing aboriginal and treaty rights' placed too great a strain on the organization. It was not unreasonable to wonder if this renewed division would bring a return of political impotence.

Another political problem of the 1980s that Indian and native groups faced had nothing directly to do with the constitutional battle or the debate over aboriginal *versus* treaty rights. The change in political fashions that occurred in the 1980s would have as powerful an impact on Indians as on the population at large. These changes resulted in the election of more conservative governments and in a greater concern with deficit reduction. The combined effect of these ideological changes was seen most clearly in the native policies of the Tory government that was elected in September 1984.

The Mulroney government talked as though it were part of the neo-conservative trend that had been noticeable in Western democracies for half a decade, though it behaved in office much as the discredited Trudeau Liberals had. The Conservatives' rhetoric about getting government off the back of business people and taxpayers tended to make Canadians think that they had put into power the Canadian equivalent of Britain's Margaret Thatcher or the United States' Ronald Reagan. The prime minister and his coterie encouraged this belief and sought to curry favour in the business community early in their mandate by appointing the deputy prime minister, Erik Nielsen of the Yukon, to chair a task force to review a broad range of government programs and to report both on their efficiency and the possibility of shrinking them.

The study team on Indian and native programs consisted of six civil servants and three outsiders, all of the latter members of consulting firms that operated in the area of native affairs.[14] It was particularly notable for the lack of Indian Affairs officials in its deliberations and for the fact that it operated in secrecy. Secrecy and isolation were not all that it shared with the process that had produced the white paper of 1969; it also took the approach that it was studying the 'needs' of a 'client' group rather than assessing what native 'rights' were and how government should respond to their demands. Its preliminary report that went to cabinet in April 1985 concluded 'that Native peoples were in a state of socio-economic deprivation, that government programs had failed to alter this state, that government spending on programs was nevertheless escalating, and that some of the spending went far beyond the government's legal responsibilities to Native people.' It also found that DIAND perpetuated the problems by providing global programs to Indians and keeping alive the idea that Ottawa bore sole responsibility for native affairs.

The solutions that were recommended were that DIAND should be dissolved, some programs shifted to other federal departments, and 'then all programs were to be transferred to the provinces for delivery to Native peoples.'[15] The study group also recommended that comprehensive land claims were not to be proceeded with, though specific ones should,[16] and that funding for the native political organizations to support their policy development in all areas but the constitutional talks was to be ended and the funds diverted to the bands. Core funding was also to be cut back. The only observable difference between the 1985 study group recommendations and the 1969 white paper was that the more recent effort recognized that native groups would be opposed. They therefore proposed a media management strategy designed to minimize the public relations damage that they anticipated would occur when the 'clients' became aware of their recommendations.

The reaction to the 1985 Nielsen report on native policy was also reminiscent of the white paper of 1969. Indian organizations denounced the preliminary report when it was leaked in the spring of 1985 as a 'restatement of the 1969 White Paper' and a document that 'singled out Indian people – already on the low rung of the country's economic ladder – as a target group for financial punishment.' The Assembly of First Nations described the proposal to hand some programs over to other parts of the bureaucracy as 'inviting the wolves to tend the sheep,' and mainstream press reaction tended to be hostile, too.[17] The Prime Minister's Office moved swiftly to minimize the damage by stating flatly that the report was not government policy. It repeated the promises to respect Indians' special relationship with government and their aboriginal and treaty rights that Mulroney had made to native leaders at a recent first ministers' conference. The legacy of the unsavoury episode was that native groups now had a new benchmark against which to measure what they considered government perfidy. 'As one AFN official said: "You know around here how everyone used to weigh what the government did against the White Paper? Well, now they weigh what the government does against the Nielsen task force. A new generation of cynicism is born, and with good reason."'[18] The last thing that native-government relations needed in the mid-1980s was another dose of disillusionment and suspicion.

The drift of the Mulroney government's policy in the critical area of Indian self-government hardly dissipated the cynicism of native leaders. Here the standard for comparison was the Penner report of 1983 that had been so supportive of the native case for self-government. The Trudeau government had not committed itself to implementing the report, though it did say that it accepted its 'general thrust.' It had promised to introduce framework legislation for implementing self-government, but failed to do so before its exit from office in 1984. When the Mulroney government began to formulate its policy on self-government in 1985, it appeared to revert to a pre-Penner approach to the subject. From the initiatives that Indian Affairs took it looked as though DIAND had turned the clock back to the 1978 policy of encouraging the adoption of municipal-style self-government at the band level. In 1985 Ottawa reached agreement with the Sechelt band in British Columbia, and at the end of that year concluded an agreement with several Indian organizations in Ontario on self-government.[19]

From the Indian point of view these initiatives were ominous. The style of government that the Sechelt accepted was essentially that of a municipality. It seems likely that similarly restricted Indian governments are intended for Ontario. Most Indian groups regard such municipal-type governments as inadequate and dangerous. They are inadequate because they do not confer jurisdiction over a sufficiently wide range, a broad spectrum that Indians believe they must control if they are to direct economic development and social programs in ways compatible with their values, aspirations, and judgment of what is likely to succeed. Self-government on the municipal model is also dangerous symbolically or as a precedent. In the Canadian constitution municipalities are the legal creatures of, and are answerable to, the provinces. In the long shadow of the white paper and Nielsen task force report, native organizations are understandably suspicious that acceptance of municipal-style self-government might be only the prelude to their being abandoned constitutionally by Ottawa and consigned to the provinces. Consequently most Indians, Inuit, and Métis are resisting the initiative that the Mulroney government undertook between 1984 and 1986.

It also has not been lost upon native leaders that Indian Affairs can defeat their more ambitious plans for province-like native

governments very simply. If Ottawa concludes a series of arrangements with bands that are so impecunious that they are willing to
trade acquiescence in the municipal approach for access to the
funds they badly need, it will drive wedges into native political
organizations. This development would create a rift between
provincial and national leaders who want to hold out for extensive
self-government and poverty-sticken band officers who prefer a
more modest and short-run approach. Such a strategy could even
deprive the organizations of their following. It could erode their
support by conferring limited self-government on bands in a
piecemeal fashion. Once all, or even most, of the 573 bands become
self-governing, what need will they have for a Federation of
Saskatchewan Indian Nations, an Assembly of First Nations, or an
Inuit Tapirisat of Canada?

In the nearly two decades between the Pearson government's
undertaking to develop new policy in consultation with native
bodies and the Mulroney government's futile attempts to negotiate
a definition of 'existing aboriginal and treaty rights,' enormous
changes have occurred in native-government relations in Canada.
The experience of being promised consultation and then denied it
in 1968–9 drove Indian and native organizations together in
powerful and effective national political bodies. Headed by a new
generation of leaders, most of them relatively well educated and all
of them articulate and committed, these organizations advanced
the native political cause dramatically. They defeated both the
white paper of 1969 and the Nielsen task force proposals of 1985–6,
and in between they managed to persuade the Penner committee
to endorse their concept of self-government. In the 1970s their
united political action won them funding and greater influence,
although they did not achieve the breadth of control and adequacy
of funding that they consider necessary.

The Indian political drive in the years since the white paper has
had its setbacks, too. Indian Affairs officials resisted most of their
initiatives in the 1970s, and in 1978 these bureaucrats embarked on
the promotion of a municipal style of Indian government that
probably constituted a danger to the native cause in the long run.
Furthermore, if natives managed to convince the Penner committee to endorse their notion of self-government, they were not able

to persuade the Trudeau cabinet to commit itself fully to it. The successor Mulroney government, to judge by the Nielsen task force and the agreement with the Sechelt band, is pursuing a policy that bears more resemblance to the less enlightened 1970s policies of the Trudeau government than to the Penner committee's report.

Perhaps the most serious setback of all to the Indian and native political campaign of the 1970s and early 1980s was not a political but an economic event. The dramatic downturn in the economy that began in 1982 and lasted in most parts of Canada at least until 1984 dealt a crippling blow to aboriginal peoples by hobbling a number of economic ventures that they had begun in the hopes of making themselves not just self-governing, but also economically self-sufficient. In the prairies, west coast, and far north, the recession lingered on well after 1984, holding back the economic development and muting the political militancy of those native organizations that had been the most assertive during the Trudeau years. And in the later 1980s it looks as though it will be issues of economic development policy and the closely related area of claims that will determine the success or failure of the native peoples.

14

Aboriginal rights, land claims, and the struggle to survive

The social and economic conditions in which natives in Canada live – or, more accurately, exist – are a national disgrace. Indian children are more likely than the general population to be born outside a stable nuclear family, are far less likely to complete enough schooling to obtain a job and become self-sustaining, are much more highly represented in the figures of unemployed and incarcerated people than the rest of the population, and have shorter life expectancy than most others in the country. What is worse is the fact that these conditions have existed for close to a century, and have been known by governments and churches to exist for most of that time. Ottawa and the missionaries have tried unsuccessfully to impose their programs of economic development on Indians, Métis, and Inuit.

In the last few decades natives have begun to assert themselves about how economic development should take place. They have forced governments to listen to them in large part because economic development since the end of World War II has focused on regions that are occupied by native groups, areas that often were not covered by the treaties of the nineteenth and early twentieth centuries. Because Euro-Canadian entrepreneurs and governments found that they wanted access to the resources in Indian and Inuit country, and because natives were insistent that they control change in their regions, development has emerged as

a major point of confrontation. Disputes over economic development, as much as the political battles since 1969, have contributed
to the natives' emergence from their age of 'irrelevance.'

It was the natives' good fortune to find themselves occupying
lands containing valuable resources as the North American economy came alive during World War II and expanded dramatically in
the resource boom of the 1950s and 1960s. Their location was also
their misfortune in that period. Being situated atop or adjacent to
increasingly valuable resources was beneficial because it provided
an opportunity to enrich themselves and create jobs. It was
unfortunate in the early period because their rights were often
ignored and their demands refused, and in later years because
economic development often meant the disruption and destruction of their traditional economy and way of life.

The expansion of the economy in the 1940s was focused on
energy and base minerals. To a considerable extent these resources
were found in areas controlled by Indians, whether it was the
Alberta Indians whose lands were in the area where Leduc #1
gushed to life in 1947, or more northerly Indians who found
themselves in the path of the Alaska Highway that the u.s. Army
Corps of Engineers constructed during World War II. The pattern
persisted after the coming of peace. The Woodland Cree discovered that their district near Lake Athabasca in Saskatchewan
contained valuable deposits of uranium that Eldorado Nuclear
began to develop in the early 1950s. Later Indians in neighbouring
Manitoba found that projects, such as the Churchill Forest
Industries complex or new hydroelectricity developments on
northern rivers, provided both opportunities for employment and
disruption of the habitat of the animals and fish on which they had
previously depended. Much the same pattern held true in the
resource-rich territories in Labrador, northern Quebec, and
Ontario, the northern interior of British Columbia, and the
Northwest Territories. The wartime and postwar boom that was
based on new sources of energy, minerals, and forest products
brought rapid development to the doorstep of many Indian, Métis,
and Inuit people who hitherto had resided in economically
marginal lands beyond the awareness of most of the southern
population.

In the early years of this boom – and in some cases for many years – the tendency of governments and developers was to ignore the interests of the native peoples. To some extent this high-handed approach to development of resources in Indian territory could be explained by the fact that the written portion of Canada's constitution, the British North America Act, gave jurisdiction over resources to the provinces. The provinces were little inclined to pay much heed to 'Indians and lands reserved for Indians,' which was an area of federal responsibility, as they set about authorizing the entrepreneurs to go after the new riches. In cases such as the Hobbema band in the Edmonton area, Indians were able to profit from the development by virtue of general rights under existing legislation, in this case provincial provisions for compensating those who held lands in which oil was found. But such materially successful bands were the minority, and even they often discovered that the problems of wealth, though different from those of poverty, were no less disturbing.

Most of Canada's native peoples who were in the path of development found that they were ignored in the process of going after the resources and left out of the division of the proceeds of their sale. Aside from some relatively low-paid jobs in unskilled categories, the Cree of north-central Saskatchewan benefited little from Eldorado's Beaver Lodge mine. Still, they were luckier than the Lubicon band of central Alberta, who were not only ignored but seriously threatened by energy developments on lands that traditionally had been theirs. Though the Lubicon had much earlier been promised a reserve, the commitment was not honoured. And when an oil company began to disrupt their territories in the 1980s, their protests were ignored by a provincial government obsessed with economic development. The plight of the Lubicon attracted the attention of Canadian and international church groups, which charged that corporate and government insensitivity during development had had 'genocidal consequences' in Alberta.[1] In British Columbia, down to and during the 1980s, similar provincial refusal to consult the Indian peoples about logging of lands that they consider theirs has led to confrontations.[2] In general, BC Indians did not prosper from the resource boom of the 1950s and 1960s as wage workers, either.[3]

Even worse were some of the government-supported programs

of economic development by Indians, or adjustment to economic development by others. A depressingly large number of Indian bands found themselves moved at the whim of bureaucrats who thought that their presence impeded exploitation of a resource, as in the case of those at South Indian Lake in Manitoba who stood in the way of a hydro project, or who were deemed to require a move to another location in order to become self-sufficient. The Ojibwa of Grassy Narrows in northwestern Ontario were removed in 1964 to a new reserve where they found it very hard to make a living, and then six years later learned that the English-Wabigoon River system from which they took water and fish was polluted with mercury from industrial establishments in nearby Dryden. The closure of the waterway for fishing destroyed the band's fragile economic base, and social problems soon followed economic troubles in a depressing cascade of misery.[4] Similar horror stories from the postwar period, though fortunately not all featuring medical problems such as mercury poisoning, could be multiplied almost endlessly.[5] Whatever the type of development, the impact of socio-economic change during the thirty-year boom that followed the Great Depression was the same: the native peoples did not benefit to any great extent from expansion.

Gradually, as natives organized themselves into more effective provincial and national political bodies, they began to assert themselves to resist development or to control the way in which it occurred and the pace at which it wrought its effects. The prime examples of this new assertiveness have been the James Bay and Mackenzie Valley projects of the 1970s.

The story of the James Bay hydro project began with the election in 1970 of a Quebec Liberal government headed Robert Bourassa. The new premier had campaigned on a platform that promised the creation of 100,000 jobs, and the key to the realization of his dream was a gargantuan project to harness the electricity potential of northern rivers. Unfortunately, Bourassa's cabinet gave no thought to the rights and interests of the approximately 10,000 Inuit and Cree who lived in the region, and who hunted and fished for their livelihood. The government established a James Bay Corporation to carry out the development and then sat back to await the political benefits.

What they got instead, at least in the short run, was one of the first effective legal actions by a native group against southern developers of their homeland. Late in 1972 a coalition of Indians and Inuit from northern Quebec sought an injunction against construction of dams and generating stations until the courts could establish what rights the indigenous inhabitants had in the lands. Their case pointed out that land surrender treaties had never been signed in northern Quebec, and that whatever their rights to the territories were before the white man came were undiminished. The case lasted more than six months and heard the testimony of more than 150 witnesses. About eleven months after the native groups initiated the case, the judge issued an order to the various companies involved 'to immediately cease, desist and refrain from carrying out works, operations, and projects in the territory' and 'to cease, desist and refrain from interfering in any way with petitioners' rights, from trespassing in the said territory and from causing damage to the environment and the natural resources of the said territory.'[6] Appeals got the order to stop work lifted, but they did not remove the notion of native rights to the land that had underlain the original court order.

Eventually, government, companies, and the native peoples decided that a negotiated settlement would be preferable to more litigation. The judgment confounded developers and government, and made the Bourassa cabinet anxious to negotiate a settlement that would permit work to continue legally. For their part the native groups, unsure of the final outcome of a case based on notions of aboriginal title, also concluded that negotiations would be preferable to further litigation. The result was a massive agreement signed late in 1975 by which the Inuit and Cree surrendered their rights and claims to 400,000 square miles of northern Quebec in return for a commitment from the two senior levels of government to pay them over ten years $150 million in grants and royalties from the electricity that was to be generated, one-quarter of the royalties the province would receive for the next fifty years, control of those sites they occupied that would not be flooded, and hunting and fishing rights. Chief Billy Diamond described it as a 'big victory' when the deal was announced.[7] The general public reacted as though the native peoples of northern Quebec had received an incredible windfall. But there was much less attention paid years later when a federal study showed that the natives of James Bay were living in poverty and with inadequate educational, medical, and social services.[8] The James Bay Agreement turned out not to be an antidote to the poisonous effects of development. However, it did constitute an important precedent – a negotiated settlement to litigation that aimed at stopping development by appeal to natives' claims to the land – that would affect later events.

Three other northern incidents helped to establish the notion that native peoples who had not entered treaty had an aboriginal title that could not lightly be ignored. In 1973 the Supreme Court of Canada ruled on an argument by the Nishga of the Nass Valley, represented by lawyer Thomas Berger, that they had aboriginal title to their lands and that they could not be dispossessed of it unilaterally by legislative action. The argument fell, but in the process an important concept was established. Although the court rejected the main argument, most of the judges acknowledged that aboriginal title existed in law. A minority of them even held that Nishga aboriginal title had not been extinguished. A few years later another piece of litigation known as the Baker Lake case advanced the process of establishing and defining aboriginal title. The Inuit of the Hamlet of Baker Lake in the Northwest Territories (NWT) sought a prohibition on economic development on their traditional lands in order to protect their hunting economy. In considering the case the court laid down four criteria for establishing the validity of aboriginal title: 'first, that they (the Indians or Inuit) and their ancestors were members of an organized society; second, that this organized society occupied the specific territory over which they claimed aboriginal title; third, that the occupation was to the exclusion of other organized societies; and finally, that the occupation was an established fact at the time sovereignty was asserted by England.' The judge concluded that these criteria had been satisfied, and he agreed that the native peoples had an aboriginal title that gave them an interest in the lands for hunting and fishing, though he would not block other forms of economic development as the petitioners had asked.[9]

A political dimension was added to these legal methods by which native peoples in Canada in the 1970s began to protect their interest in their lands by two northern pipeline inquiries. In 1977

Thomas Berger, then a judge of the BC Supreme Court sitting as a federal commissioner, reported on the impact of a proposed pipeline up the Mackenzie Valley, and in the same year Ken Lysyk (then a law professor and now a judge of the BC Supreme Court) conducted an inquiry into the likely effect of an Alaska pipeline on the southern Yukon. Both men warned against rapid development that would damage native economies and ways of life. Lysyk argued that four years would be necessary for the natives to prepare for the impact of the construction of an Alaskan pipeline, while Berger suggested that 'a period of ten years will be required in the Mackenzie Valley and Western Arctic to settle native claims, and to establish the new institutions and new programs that a settlement will entail. No pipeline should be built until these things have been achieved.'[10]

Perhaps more important than the conclusions of these investigations was the process of making the inquiries. Both commissioners spent a long time listening to the native peoples' expectations and fears about their lands and the proposed development. Berger's inquiry in particular attracted a great deal of attention, and the commissioner quite deliberately extended his hearings to the south to bring northerners' views to the attention of the southern Canadians who had the political influence to affect government decisions in the sparsely populated north. Southerners were exposed to poignant statements of the natives' fear of the changes that might overwhelm them. 'Steel kills,' testified Alfred Nahanni. 'With more steel products coming in we will eventually die because we will be overpowered by something that doesn't feel the cold.'[11] Ultimately, it was a downturn in the demand for energy that accounted for the failure to proceed with northern developments. But the work of judges Lysyk and Berger, and the dozens of northerners who testified before them, helped to make rapid development of the north over the protests of its inhabitants politically unacceptable in the 1970s and early 1980s.

These new political factors, coming on top of the creative legal aspects of the Nishga and Baker Lake cases, firmly established during the 1970s that something called aboriginal title existed and had to be considered. The clearest proof that these developments had their political impact was found in the response of the federal government to the Nishga case in 1973. This was a government headed by Pierre Trudeau, a man who had claimed that political communities could not make policy on the basis of historical might-have-beens, who had argued for ignoring past wrongs in the search for a just program in the present, and who could not understand how a liberal democratic society such as he championed could have a treaty with one of its constituent elements. The Nishga case, coming fairly soon after the political firestorm over the white paper, shook the Trudeau government's confident belief in the ultimate triumph of individualism. In mid-1973 Trudeau's minister of Indian affairs and northern development, Jean Chrétien, said that the government would now deal with Indian claims to land in areas that had not been surrendered by treaties. The government was prepared to consider two types of land claims: comprehensive claims that were based on aboriginal title, and specific claims that were allegations that the government had not lived up to promises it had made, usually in treaties. Ottawa would also fund research by native bodies to support their claim cases, and the next year it set up an Office of Native Claims (ONC) with responsibility to assess the validity of native claims and to advise the Department of Indian Affairs and Northern Development (DIAND) on how to settle them.

A new procedure for handling claims was developed in the 1970s. If the ONC thought that a claim was valid, and if DIAND decided that a negotiated settlement of the claim was in order, then officials from the ONC would participate in a government team that attempted to negotiate a settlement. Following a negotiated settlement of a native claim, the ONC would help with the implementation of, and monitor compliance with, the agreement.[12] In other words, the Trudeau government in 1973 and 1974 initiated an important new method of dealing with claims from status Indians, Inuit, Métis, and non-status Indians. This shift marked a definite retreat by Trudeau and a significant advance for aboriginal peoples.

Then ensued a protracted period of researching, presenting, and negotiating settlement of claims. The impetus that was given to this process by the events of the 1970s was strengthened by the native groups' frustrations over the constitution-making process from 1977 to 1981. Failure to reach agreement in the later constitutional talks that were supposed to determine what 'existing aboriginal and treaty rights' were simply reinforced the tendency among some native groups to emphasize the claims process along with, or instead of, the drive to establish native self-government through political means. The two categories – self-government and claims – intersect because natives have long recognized that without an economic base in the ownership of extensive territories political control of their own affairs is meaningless. In the 1980s the search for political sovereignty and drive for economic self-sufficiency marched together behind the banners of aboriginal title and land claims.

Perhaps the most difficult thing for non-natives to understand is the notion of aboriginal title that underlies both land claims and the contention that native peoples have the right to govern themselves. What is aboriginal title, and how does it relate to sovereignty? Aboriginal title is simply the right to lands that an indigenous people has by virtue of its occupation of an area 'from time immemorial.' It is a notion that Indians and other natives have always held to, though they did not always articulate it; but a notion that until recently Euro-Canadian society did not recognize or respect. European nations usually maintained that discovery or intensive use in agriculture gave them a superior right over indigenous peoples to occupancy and use of the land. (In 1988 an Australian aborigine mocked these notions by landing at Dover and claiming Britain for the first people of Australia.) This presumption was taken to its extreme in the Papacy's division of the Western Hemisphere between Spain and Portugal early in the era of Europe's expansion, without reference to the interests of either the native peoples or of other Catholic powers such as France.

But the French, while they challenged the pope's decision and the Iberian states' claim to the hemisphere, did not assert title to land and political sovereignty over the indigenous peoples of the regions with whom they came into contact. France set about the exploration and economic utilization of the eastern half of North America without much concern for pope or other European powers. But of necessity her explorers had to behave in a more circumspect manner in their relations with indigenous peoples, whatever Christian theorists may have held about the legitimacy of ignoring the rights of natives. For the most part, Frenchmen's intensive use of land was restricted to areas that the Iroquoians and Algonkians had vacated, with the result that their penetration of the continent did not threaten any aboriginal interest. French claims to title to New France were assertions made, not in the face of aboriginal title, but to forestall claims by other European powers. French pretensions to political sovereignty over the regions they explored and utilized were legal fictions based on decaying concepts of divine-right kingship; they were not assented to, much less accepted by, the Indian peoples with whom the French traded and warred. The French period did not weaken aboriginal title to the land or the indigenous peoples' powers of self-government. [13]

The coming of British rule in the eighteenth century both strengthened and threatened aboriginal title and Indian sovereignty. The Royal Proclamation of 1763 established the concepts of Indian territory, Indian title, and the necessity of newcomers to arrange the extinguishment of that title by direct negotiations with the crown. Although the Royal Proclamation did not apply everywhere in present-day Canada – its application was technically only to the narrow parallelogram along the St Lawrence that constituted the Province of Quebec from 1763 to 1791 – it has had an important historical influence throughout all of Canada. By and large, as already noted, colonial and then dominion governments operated on the assumption that there was an obligation to negotiate for title to land in their dealings with Indians in Ontario, the prairies, and parts of northern Canada. While governments might have acted as though they could limit Indian self-government in various Gradual Civilizing acts and Indian acts, they, with the exception of colonial British Columbia, did not pretend that they could simply take territory without prior negotiations with the first occupiers.

This tradition has had the effect of continuing the influence of the proclamation concept into post-Confederation Canada. An important step in this process was the legal decision in 1888 in the St Catharine's Milling Case. In that important ruling the Judicial Committee of the Privy Council held that there was such a thing as aboriginal title. Under the proclamation, the decision held, Indians enjoyed 'a personal and usufructuary right, dependent upon the good will of the Sovereign.'[14] This was a minimal version of what aboriginal title meant. In the first place, a usufructuary right is merely the right to *use* something that someone else *owns*. Furthermore, the Judicial Committee's decision that even this diminished title was 'dependent upon the good will of the Sovereign' meant that the crown – and, by extension, all legislative bodies of which the crown was a part – could extinguish this title unilaterally. The Supreme Court judges who held in the Nishga case in 1973 that there was such a thing as aboriginal title but still concluded that the Nishga had no case did so largely because the BC legislature was held to have nullifed the Indians' title by statute. But, as already noted, the political cost of holding to this legalistic view after granting the important point that aboriginal title existed in law was simply too great for federal governments to pay. After this decision, consonant with the proclamation and in expansion of the St Catharine's Milling Case definition of aboriginal title, the government of Canada conceded that it recognized aboriginal title. This concession was embodied, belatedly, in the 1982 Constitution Act's confirmation of 'existing aboriginal and treaty rights.'

From this important base of aboriginal title, important claims flow. In those regions of Canada where title was not extinguished, native groups argue that the land is theirs and cannot be used by anyone else without their agreement. This was the basis of the case put forward early in the 1970s by the Cree and Inuit of northern Quebec to halt the development of the James Bay project until their agreement was acquired by negotiation. It also underlay the cases of the Inuit and of the Dene Nation, as the Indian and Métis of the western Northwest Territories called themselves, in the far north who made similar arguments to the Lysyk and Berger pipeline inquiries. In the 1980s it continues to serve as the foundation of northern native claims to control their land.

Dene and Inuit maintain that southerners cannot intrude on their territories for economic development without securing the agreement of the indigenous peoples. And they also argue that they have the right to determine how their northern homeland will be governed. The Dene Declaration, a statement by the native peoples of the Territories issued in 1975, makes the point:

We the Dene of the N.W.T. insist on the right to be regarded by ourselves and the world as a nation.

What we seek then is independence and self-determination within the country of Canada. This is what we mean when we call for a just land settlement for the Dene Nation.[15]

The case for Dene control of their own political institutions is based on the argument that they were self-governing peoples before the white population arrived, that they did not sign any treaties that required recognition of Canadian sovereignty, that they were never conquered, and that, therefore, they are still sovereign and hold title to their lands.

Finally, the same arguments based on aboriginal title are at the heart of the comprehensive land claims of British Columbia's Indians. With a few exceptions, Indian groups in the Pacific province did not enter treaty with either colonial or dominion governments for title to land. Accordingly, BC Indians argue today as they have for a century that most of British Columbia is still Indian country. Here, as in most of the other cases mentioned above, solution of these claims will most likely come by negotiation rather than litigation. Neither side can afford to take the chance of losing in the courts; neither side wants to incur the costs of resolution by litigation. Thus far one comprehensive land claim has definitely been settled, while two others have reached the stage of agreement in principle. In 1984 a settlement with the Committee of Original People's Entitlement (COPE) provided 242,000 square kilometres and $45 million in 1977 dollars to the Inuvialuit, the approximately 2500 Inuit of the Mackenzie River Delta. In 1988 two other northern claims proceeded as far as agreement in principle. In September the 13,000 Dene and Métis of the Mackenzie River Valley agreed to a settlement of their claims that yielded 180,000 square kilometres of land, $500 million, and a share of royalties from energy extraction on some of their lands. In November, in the middle of the federal general election campaign, Ottawa concluded a pact with the Yukon Council of Indians that promised the transfer to the 6500 members of the body 41,000 square kilometres, or approximately 9 per cent of Yukon Territory, and $230 million. The Yukon Indians, however, agreed to give up their exemption from federal income tax.[16]

The Métis make an argument similar to the Indians' case for com-

prehensive land claims, though there are some significant differences in the foundation of their case. It is clearly a logical
impossibility that the Métis argument can be one based solely on
aboriginal rights if aboriginal is equated, as is usually the case, with
existence and occupancy 'since time immemorial.' Even a sympathetic study of the Métis argues, obviously with tongue partly in
cheek, that the mixed-blood people was not created until 'Nine
months after the first White man set foot in Canada.'[17] So far as
strict logic is concerned, the Métis cannot be an aboriginal people
holding aboriginal title for the simple reason that they have not
existed 'since time immemorial.' But history is not always logical.
Since at least 1870 the mixed-blood population of Manitoba and the
prairies have had a basis for claims to aboriginal status, and since
1982 the Métis and non-status Indians throughout Canada have
enjoyed an even stronger case. In 1870 the Manitoba Act conferred
on the mixed-blood populations of Red River a claim to land based
on their share of Indian blood.[18] And the agreement on aboriginal
rights in the 1982 constitution explicitly included the Métis and
non-status Indians. Since then these groups have participated in
first ministers' constitutional talks along with Indians and Inuit.
And in the 1980s the Métis of Manitoba have asserted an extensive
land claim based on the unfulfilled provisions for land grants to the
offspring of mixed-blood parents under the Manitoba Act of 1870.
The land claim of the Manitoba Métis is in part a comprehensive
claim in that it is based on their status as an aboriginal people, and
in part a specific claim based on allegations that the promises of
1870 were not carried out.

Specific claims are more limited than comprehensive land
claims, and not all specific claims deal directly with land matters.
Specific claims are demands for compensation or restitution based
upon an allegation that a promise, usually a treaty undertaking,
was not fulfilled. The cases in this category that are coming
forward usually concern bands that never received any, or all, of
the lands that they were promised during negotiations. In a sense,
the claim of the Lubicon Indians of Alberta that was referred to
earlier is such a specific claim. So far almost 300 specific claims have
been preferred, but only a few have been resolved by negotiation,
and they have affected small groups and limited tracts of land.
Both sides are being cautious in these negotiations. The Indians

recognize that any settlement must stand for a long time, and governments are aware that there are often political recriminations from white populations residing in areas where Indian reserves are expanded as a result of settling a specific land claim. Attempts in Saskatchewan to resolve some specific claims during the life of the Blakeney government (1971–82) were slowed or stopped by strong non-Indian opposition to seeing crown lands or community pastures handed over to bands. In some cases, the non-Indian neighbours were utilizing the lands that were proposed for settlement of the claims; in others they simply opposed the growth of Indian reserves. A particularly thorny instance occurred in the city of Prince Albert, where a federal-provincial proposal to grant a band a reserve within the city limits evoked ferocious opposition from the municipal council. The Prince Albert case was merely the worst example of a general disenchantment and opposition among the non-Indian population to the resolution of specific claims.

Other claims resemble specific land claims in that they are based on allegations that the government has not carried out its promises. Sometimes these are based on literal readings; othertimes on loose constructions of the language of the treaties. An instance of the latter was the argument of Indians in Treaty 6 that the promise of 'a medicine chest' in their treaty should be interpreted in the late twentieth century as embracing free medical care. The courts have not been persuaded to extend the meaning of Treaty 6 in this way. Claims demanding enforcement of literal promises include those that refer to the commitments in some of the numbered treaties to provide implements, ammunition, and twine. A number of Indian bands have extensive claims based on the federal government's failure to provide twine for nets and ammunition for hunting, the value of these supplies being greatly increased thanks to the magic of compound interest. Thus far claims of this nature have generally proved unsuccessful.

The final type of contemporary claim, one example of which was settled in 1985, flows not directly from aboriginal status or treaty promises, but from the special relationship in which Indians stand to the federal government by virtue of the Indian Act. The obverse of government's persistent treatment of Indians as wards, or legal minors, is the notion that Ottawa stands in a special trust relationship to Indians whose affairs it controls. From a legal standpoint, then, the role of the Department of Indian Affairs in relation to Indians is like that of a trustee administering the affairs of a minor. For more than a century Indians suffered the negative effects of this relationship: their lives were directed and their property controlled by others. But in 1985 the courts confirmed that there were certain protections inherent in this unequal relationship.

The 1985 Supreme Court of Canada decision in the Musqueam case confirmed that Ottawa had a legal obligation to discharge its trust responsibilities in a manner that advanced the interests and protected the rights of its 'wards.' The litigation stemmed from an 1958 lease that the department had negotiated on behalf of the Musqueam band with a Vancouver golf club for 160 acres of land. The lease, which was initially for fifteen years, allowed the golf club to extend it in instalments up to another seventy-five years, while limiting the increases in rent that the band could get on renewal. When band officers finally were able to see the lease some twelve years after it came into effect, they concluded that they had been misled and their interests had been abandoned by the government. The terms had not been reported accurately to them, and the rental had fallen far below the market value of the land. They took their case to court, where they were awarded $10 million. On appeal the Supreme Court upheld the financial award and stated anew the notion that DIAND had a trustee relationship. Where Indian Affairs failed to discharge the duties of that role properly, it was liable for the damages those in its trust incurred.[19]

The interpretation that the Musqueam case confirmed in 1985 is a fruitful source of support for Indian claims. The concept of trust obligation on the part of the government provides those Indian bands who were deprived of their reserve lands during the western boom of the early twentieth century with an avenue for redress. If, as is often the case, they can demonstrate that the Indian Affairs officials did not properly inform their ancestors who were induced to agree to sales or leases at derisory rates, or if they can demonstrate that their band was not consulted at all, they have a good base from which to argue that the federal government is liable for the damages the band has incurred as a consequence of the unprofitable lease or fraudulent sale.

There has already been one major settlement of such a case for the White Bear reserve of southeastern Saskatchewan. In 1901 over 200 Assiniboine were moved off their reserves by mendacious department officials and forced to move onto a Cree reserve, known as the White Bear. In 1984 Ottawa was persuaded that the dispossession of the Assiniboine had been fraudulent, and a commitment was made by the short-lived Turner government to compensate them for their losses. In 1986 land was transferred to them. Some idea of the potential for other large-scale settlements can be garnered from the fact that the Federation of Saskatchewan Indian Nations estimates that in that province alone Indians were defrauded of 416,000 acres of reserve land before World War I.[20] There is every reason to believe that other provinces, particularly on the prairies, have similar situations.

All these claims have added up to a vast and troubled area that has absorbed Indian and federal government efforts, not to mention tens of millions of dollars of Canadian taxpayers' money, for decades. Specific claims concerning unallotted reserves, missing twine, or annual payments continue to mount. Claims based on Ottawa's perversion of the trust relationship seem likely to increase dramatically in the wake of the Musqueam decision. But the potentially most intractable of the claims are those that fall under the heading of comprehensive claims, which are, in reality, latter-day attempts to negotiate treaties where they do not exist. The argument that various native groups have claims to extensive lands by virtue of unextinguished aboriginal title is potentially revolutionary. It is revolutionary in its scope alone, for such claims could embrace most of British Columbia, the Yukon, and the Northwest Territories. One, by the Golden Lake Algonkin band in Ontario, embraces Parliament Hill and the Petawawa armed forces base.[21] The argument on which comprehensive claims are based is also dramatic in another sense. Claims based on aboriginal rights are not only about land; they are also connected to native claims to unsurrendered political sovereignty. These contentions that Indians, Inuit, and Métis have a right to establish their own order of government within Canada, as noted in the previous chapter, are unsettling to many Canadians because they are based on assumptions about political organization that many Canadians find uncongenial and perhaps unacceptable. The prospect for Indian-white relations over claims seems troubled, and the confrontation over the intertwined issues of comprehensive land claims and native efforts to establish their own order of government seems likely to be protracted and painful.

For most native peoples, however, the question of what will become of comprehensive land claims and arguments over native political sovereignty must seem like idle preoccupations. For many bands the problems of maintaining or restoring an economy that will sustain them and provide a release from the stultifying welfare culture in which two-thirds of them find themselves are the most pressing concerns. Native leaders have argued that there is no such thing as a purely economic issue, that land claims and political sovereignty are essential to end natives' economic problems once and for all by giving them the resources and political control to make use of them as they see fit. For a time it seemed as though those arguments had persuaded the native communities. The fact that political leaders could carry their followers with them was the result in part of the successes they won through united action and in part the side-effect of an improving economy. But the 1980s have been much less buoyant.

Interesting case studies of the economic problems Indians are facing in the harder times of the 1980s can be found in Saskatchewan. The Federation of Saskatchewan Indians, now the Federation of Saskatchewan Indian Nations (FSIN), was one of the most aggressive Indian organizations in pressing the political case and trying to advance the economic lot of Indians by their own actions. In the 1970s the FSIN established its own holding company, Sinco, to control a series of service companies based principally in the resource sector. These companies were to provide employment for Indians and to begin the process of lifting Saskatchewan's Indians out of the economic morass. After the collapse of the western resource economy in the recession of 1982, the constituent companies in Sinco began falling one by one. By 1986 only Sinco's trucking company was still in operation. Another example of attempted economic development based on the resource economy and increasing Indian political power was a technical training institute on the Thunder Child reserve in west-central Saskatchewan in the early 1980s. It was designed to train skilled Indian workers for high-paying jobs in the oil and gas industry that was booming in neighbouring Alberta. By the time the school was ready to produce its first graduates in 1986, there were no jobs to be had in the prostrate energy industry.

As these two incidents from recent western history illustrate, the economic advancement of Indian and native groups depends not just on securing a land base and political control of their own affairs. As long as most natives are located in what is sometimes called the 'Mid-Canada Corridor,' a northern region in which resource extraction and processing constitute almost the entire economy, natives also need the return of prosperity to resource industries in order to begin the long march from poverty to comfort. Just as Canada's Indians began to move out of 'irrelevance' by a combination of political assertiveness and the increase in value of the resources on which they found themselves located, a sharp economic downturn threatened to knock them back.

It was bitterly ironic that aboriginal peoples around the world found themselves in almost exactly the same position in the 1980s. The leaders of Canada's native communities began to reach out to others in similar circumstances to form a Fourth World alliance in the 1970s. Canada's Indians, Métis, and Inuit wanted to join the Saami of Scandinavia, the Maori of New Zealand, and the Melanesians and Polynesians of south Pacific states in a vast anti-imperial coalition of colonized peoples. Thanks to the recession of 1982 they also joined them in renewed poverty. Fijians saw their income from sugar collapse and Maoris participated in New Zealand's agricultural recession at the same time as lucrative jobs in the Alberta oilfields disappeared.

15

Do we learn anything from history?

'While skyscrapers hide the heavens, / They can fall.' The history of Indian-white relations in Canada demonstrates that the links between human groups, like the ties between humans and nature, are part of a single ecology. A growing awareness of the soundness of aboriginal values about nature and its use in an age of increasing anxiety over waste disposal and the effects of acid rain is one sign that change might now be possible. Today there is a glimmering of understanding that the elements of a society are interdependent, bound together for good or ill. Slowly the awareness that one group's problem is everyone's is spreading. Economic disadvantages among natives are a drain on the whole community's wealth at a time of high deficits. Social ills in northern settlements, on reserves, and in the steadily expanding native ghettoes that western Canadian cities harbour affect the general citizenry. Urban populations are uneasily aware of rising crime statistics, and fearful that Canada in the 1990s is about to experience the racial problems that thirty years ago confronted their southern neighbour. A 1988 report of the Canadian Bar Association on the criminal justice system's impact on natives provides a little hope that something might be done. Canadians are becoming conscious that they should do something about the conditions in which too many natives find themselves.

Perhaps it is worth asking if the history of five centuries of relations between newcomers and indigenous peoples offers any clues for people in Canada, native or non-native, who are concerned about these ills. The philosopher Hegel once suggested that there is but one thing to be learned from history: 'What experience and history teach is this – that people and governments never have learned anything from history, or acted on principles deduced from it.' Later a highly unphilosophical American, Henry Ford, concluded that 'History is more or less bunk.' But, as one of Ford's contemporaries, George Santayana, argued, 'Those who cannot remember the past are condemned to fulfil it.'[1] Canadians who want to avoid a repetition of past mistakes in relations between Indians and others might want to consider some of the lessons that can be gleaned from the past.

The most obvious conclusion about the history of Indian-white relations in Canada is that the motives the two parties have had for making contact have usually shaped their interaction. Europeans came to North America for three reasons in the fifteenth and sixteenth centuries: exploration, fish, and fur. The first contacts after the abortive Norse attempt at colonization occurred when fishermen arrived on the Grand Banks off Newfoundland. The fishery led to the development, first as an ancillary enterprise and later as the main economic activity, of a trade in furs with the indigenous population of the region. During the early sixteenth century Europeans also came in search of Asian gold and spices. By the seventeenth century explorers realized that North America was not, as they had first thought, the 'Indies,' but a land mass between Europe and Asia. Now they bent their efforts to finding a passage through the new continent to the Orient. Finally, a massive European effort to spread Christianity in the seventeenth century brought missionaries to proselytize the aborigines of North America. In sum, Europeans came to Canada for fish, fur, exploration, and evangelization.

For each of these purposes the Indian was indispensable; and the native peoples were prepared to cooperate in each of these activities. Fishing and fish-curing would have been impossible if the aboriginal population were hostile and drove the fishermen off. In the fur trade the Indians' foodstuffs, transportation methods, and labour were vital for the success of the trade. The Indians' sweet corn was a portable, protein-rich food that enabled trading parties to undertake long trips to fur-bearing regions; the canoe in summer and snowshoes in winter were essential for travelling in the interior; and the Indians caught, skinned, and processed the beaver pelts by wearing them next to their bodies as robes. In similar ways the Europeans found themselves dependent on the Indians' knowledge and transportation technology when probing the continent in search of a passage to Asia. For the missionary, too, Indian cooperation, food and transportation, and toleration of his presence were essential if the black robe was to win souls for Christ. Indians had their own reasons for cooperating with the European newcomers along a frontier of commerce, exploration, and faith in the fifteenth and sixteenth centuries. The strangers had wonderful products of a more advanced technology than existed in North America. Iron revolutionized and simplied the natives' hunting, warfare, and household chores. If toleration of black-robed shamans was a means to strengthen the commercial bonds with the men who made these products available, then the missionary presence would be endured. If cooperation in exploration also seemed expedient, then Indians would cooperate with the forays of a La Salle. They would always try, however, to prevent direct European contact with those peoples in the interior who supplied the best furs.

In this generally harmonious relationship there was no doubt about who was the dominant partner. The fact that French traders had to learn and use Indian languages, especially Huron in the early years, was one clear indicator of where the power lay. That trade had to conform to Indian rituals was another sign that the newcomers were compelled to adapt to the patterns and values that they encountered. This was all the easier to do because the Europeans regarded the Indians whom they encountered along a frontier of commerce and faith as a means rather than an impediment to the realization of European objectives. The fact that newcomers lacked the numbers, as well as the motivation, to interfere with Indian society or attack Indians directly also explains the relative harmony of early Indian-European relations. Not even French missionaries of the seventeenth century posed a direct threat to indigenous culture, for Jesuits sought only religious conversion, not total assimilation. Still, it is true that there were negative consequences of contact for Indians. Most serious was disease, followed by more destructive warfare and the debilitating effects of alcohol. The serious weakening, and eventually destruction, of the Huron confederacy as a consequence of disease, internal divisions, and attacks by the Iroquois is the clearest example of the dark side of relations in New France.

The first phase of mutually beneficial contact, in which non-directed cultural change occurred on both sides of the relationship, was modified significantly at the beginning of the eighteenth century. Europeans continued to pursue fish and converts, but they now knew that there was no accessible passage through the temperate part of America to Asia. Moreover, the commerce in furs changed greatly after 1700. The eighteenth century was an era of rivalry between Britain and France, and in the Western Hemisphere that contest was reflected in a struggle for control of North America. Neither Euopean power wanted to field large numbers of its own troops, but the Indians were on site, had vital navigational and martial talents, and were favourably disposed thanks to the ties that had already been established by the fur trader and the missionary. From the Europeans' perspective, the edge of contact in the eighteenth century changed from a commercial to an imperial frontier, the Indians from trading partners to allies. The southwestern fur trade became a means of maintaining alliances with Indians, and not, for the most part, an economic pursuit in its own right.

The shift from a commercial to a strategic motive for contact did not seriously disrupt the harmonious coexistence of Indians and the French or *Canadiens*. The topography of the continent had created the partnership of the French and those Algonkians who controlled the fur regions oriented to the St Lawrence watershed; the English had established business contacts with the Iroquoians and other Indian nations of the regions that found their trade egress in the Hudson River. When commerce gave way to imperial warfare, the same patterns persisted, as both European powers lavished gifts on their Indian friends to retain their support. But the French found it easier to hold the allegiance of their allies, because the strangers in the valley of the St Lawrence were still primarily merchants and missionaries rather than farmers and burghers.

Consequently, the Indians regarded the French and Canadians

as less of a threat to their traditional economy than the Anglo-Americans. On the Indian side the contrast between American and Canadian experience was manifested in the stereotype view that the Indians held of the newcomers in the seventeenth century: they thought of 'the Englishman as a farmer or towndweller whose activities gradually drove the original agriculturalists deeper into the hinterland, whereas the stereotype of the French was a trader or soldier.'[2] The fact that the French in Canada had dealt with the Indians along a frontier of commerce and faith made it easier for them than it was for the British to win the support of Indian allies in the eighteenth century.

A consistent pattern developed during the century of struggle. From the initiation of the French strategy of encirclement by means of interior posts and Indian alliances in 1700 to the death of Tecumseh in 1813, most Indians found alliance with the Europeans north of the St Lawrence system more attractive than military association with those in the Thirteen Colonies. This was true during the Seven Years' War, when the French benefited from Indian alliances while colonies such as Virginia regarded the indigenous peoples as another enemy. It was still true at the end of that contest when Pontiac tried unsuccessfully to organize an Indian resistance to the assertion of British and American rule. The same pattern held in the American Revolutionary War, although the influences of geography and religion this time modified the patterns by inducing some Iroquois to seek neutrality. Finally, the War of 1812 – the last phase of the century-long struggle – illustrated the same alignment of forces. The overwhelming proportion of Indians who participated did so on the side of the British and Canadians. Alliance with the British in the War of 1812 offered Tecumseh and the Prophet the same chance that cooperation with France had given Pontiac earlier.

This second major phase of Indian-European relations, the era of alliance, produced important developments of great relevance for both Indians and Euro-Canadians in later ages. The first was the Royal Proclamation of 1763. The proclamation in the short term meant maintaining Indian support for Britain by not threatening their lands, and in the longer term formed part of the foundation of claims for land and self-government. After the conclusion of the revolutionary war, the need to provide for angry warriors who insisted that they were allies, not subjects, of the British king led to the initiation of negotiations with Indians in the lower Lakes region for the surrender of tracts for both red and white Loyalists. The process of settling Upper Canada at first was carried on in a manner consistent with the proclamation policy, as was only to be expected in an era when the British and Canadians continued to regard the Indians as military allies and commercial partners.

On the whole, the same pattern that had been observable in eastern Canada from the fifteenth century to Victoria's age was found in due course in the more westerly and northerly regions of what became the Dominion of Canada. In the Hudson's Bay Company lands the imperatives of commerce led the English to cooperate with their Indian trading partners. In a second phase of the fur-trade frontier in the west, the intense competition between the Bay and the Nor'westers provided a brief economic golden age for both Indians and Métis who traded with and provisioned the commercial interests. The struggle for control of the region between these two companies also produced the only instances in western Canadian history of Indians acting as allies to European powers. The same pattern, minus the military dimension, was found on the Pacific coast and in the British Columbia interior between the 1770s and 1850s. The relationship that developed was a commercial one, whether the trade occurred aboard ships or at posts on land. The relationship remained cooperative and mutually beneficial, and the changes induced in both parties were non-directed and did not seriously disrupt the respective societies.

In the nineteenth century a third phase of the relationship that was to be anything but beneficial to the native peoples began. Hitherto, Indians and Europeans had cooperated with each other along frontiers of commerce, faith, exploration, and alliance. In all these associations the two parties had found that they needed each other; in none had they had any reason to seek fundamental changes in each other. However, in the third era of the relationship the association was not mutually beneficial, and one party did definitely try to coerce the other to change.

The onset of this troubled era was uneven across the country. In Maritime Canada it had already begun while interior Indians were still fighting as allies against the Americans. Certainly for the indigenous population of Newfoundland, the Beothuk, it was a reality by the early nineteenth century. In the interior regions of present-day Quebec and Ontario, this third epoch began with the making of peace subsequent to the War of 1812 and with the Rush-Bagot Convention of 1817 that ushered in enduring peace between the United States and British North America in the interior. In the Pacific region, this third phase commenced with the arrival of prospectors, agricultural settlers, and missionaries in the late 1850s. And on the plains and in the parklands immediately to the north of them the Indian became increasingly irrelevant to the European population as the fur trade shifted northward. The arrival of missionaries in Red River in the 1820s and 1830s is one measure of the evolution; the decline of the bison in the 1860s and 1870s a second; and the completion of the transcontinental railway in the 1880s the final indicator of the change in the western interior. Across the continent in the nineteenth century, the commercial frontier shifted far to the north, the military preoccupations of the European powers declined, and the natives increasingly were perceived as a 'problem' by the now-dominant European population.

So far as nineteenth-century Canadians were concerned, the Indians were an impediment that had to be cleared away much as the pine forests in the east had to be reduced before production of surplus wheat crops for export was possible. But because of history, geography, and demography, the native peoples could not be cleared as bloodily in Canada as they were being removed at the same time in the United States. Canadians, unlike their southern neighbours, had not learned to regard Indians as hostile forces to be crushed. Moreover, by the time the Dominion of Canada had to deal with Indians in western Canada, a strong tradition of erecting political and legal institutions prior to intrusion by the general agricultural population had been established. In any event, the vast extent of the dominion made destructive policies horrendously expensive and probably impossible of completion. Finally, the sparseness of Euro-Canadian population in the west and north made such a bloody policy as problematical as history made it unacceptable. Even if the Indians were now perceived as an obstacle, they could not be shifted by force.

The means to remove them was a coercive policy of land

acquisition and directed cultural change. First in Upper Canada and then in the west, the proclamation policy of negotiating with Indians for access to their traditional lands in advance of Euro-Canadian penetration was followed. Land surrender treaties – or what government interpreted as land surrender treaties – were intended to remove Indians from resources that newcomers wanted to use in their own, exclusive, and frequently destructive ways. The second policy was a concerted effort to remove the Indian from Canadian society as a distinctive racial and social type. As an American Indian Affairs official put it, the objective of treaties, reserves, and educational programs was 'the extinction of the Indians *as Indians*.'[3] Schooling would assimilate them to Euro-Canadian values as it prepared them for husbandry, trades, or wage employment. Missionaries, Indian agents, and farming instructors would remove the Indians by changing them. Gradually Indians would become enfranchised, taking their allotment of reserve land with them in freehold tenure. The reserves would dissolve as the distinctive Indians disappeared into Euro-Canadian society. This policy of directed change reached its nadir in the federal government's white paper of 1969, which claimed that the Indians' problems were a consequence of their distinctiveness, and recommended the dismantling of their special status.

These changes in Canada's attitudes and policies towards Indians were the product of the changed relationship between a Euro-Canadian majority and the native population. No longer was the Indians' relationship with the newcomers that of dominant commercial partners who could compel the newcomer to learn their languages. Nor was it that of a military equal who could angrily inform a government emissary that the Indians were allies, not subjects, of the British crown. The new situation reflected the Indians' dependence in an age when they were viewed as an obstacle to be removed from the newcomers' path. This destructive treatment was the consequence of the fact that the relationship was now between a dominant group and another people regarded as superfluous to the needs of the majority population.

Indians began to emerge from irrelevance after World War II, and their emergence accelerated in the 1960s. The explanation was in part intellectual or ideological: wartime experiences and postwar intellectual fashions made the racist bases of government Indian policy increasingly untenable. Indians emerged for economic reasons as well: they occupied territories that the dominant society now realized contained valuable and needed resources. The explanation was also certainly political: Indians now had effective political bodies that confronted and put pressure on the political parties to modify policies.

In this fourth phase of relations – the era of the Indians' emergence from irrelevance to the larger population – no single type of relationship has developed. There is no consensus on either side of the relationship as to what should be done. On the native side there are numerous reasons for division. Regional differences set the various native groups apart. Historical distinctions are important, too. Those Indians who have signed treaties have a contractual basis from which to litigate and agitate for compliance with promises made. Others who for any number of reasons never entered treaty with the crown find that their most effective basis for action is the concept of aboriginal status. These differences have resulted in the fragmentation of native political action into a multiplicity of organizations, with a resulting weakening of their political voice. On the non-Indian side of the relationship, there also continues to be no unity. In a secular and urban age, the policy of the Bible and the plough is not acceptable to most Canadians. While the assimilative policy of the white paper still attracts liberal ideologues and secular missionaries, it offends champions of cultural and racial pluralism. Since the federal government adopted multiculturalism in 1971 and had the policy enshrined in the 1982 constitution, assimilators have had to face another barrier. On the non-native side of the relationship no consensus has developed to replace the nineteenth-century program of economic adaptation and assimilation.

What, if anything, can be learned from this historical record? First, that the relationship between the indigenous peoples and non-natives has been shaped by practical, often economic, factors. The record of Indian-white relations in Canada is one moulded by the reasons that the various parties have had for making contact and maintaining relations. When their motives were complementary, the relationship was harmonious and the consequences mutually advantageous. The best example of that was the fur-trade era, in which the two groups cooperated for their mutual material advantage without inflicting hardship on each other. Conversely, when their motives were antagonistic or competitive, the relationship became unhappy and the consequences unfortunate. This tendency is found most starkly in the long third phase of the relationship, when the newcomers regarded the natives not as commercial partners or military allies, but as obstacles to new forms of economic development. The result was the dispossession from the land of the native peoples, as well as coercive efforts to change them. The efforts have proven unavailing; all they have accomplished is the demoralization as well as impoverishment of the native peoples and the creation of a climate of confrontation. If the native and non-native populations of Canada are to restore harmonious and mutually beneficial relations, they must find a new and complementary reason for interacting.

The historical record also indicates something about what ought not to be included in that new relationship. A century and a half of attempts by Euro-Canadian society to define the role of natives and to impose that destiny on them have added up to miserable failure. Aside from the effective removal of Indians from the land, none of the policies of the Bible and the plough has been successful. And now, with the recognition by the courts and governments of the validity of aboriginal title in the hands of non-treaty natives and the obligations of government's trustee relationship with those who made treaty, even that record of dispossession may be in the preliminary stages of reversal. Attempts by governments, churches, and the general population to change Indians, Métis, and Inuit into just another ethnic group in the multicultural mosaic have failed. It is past time that these policies were abandoned.

The reason that assimilationist policies have failed holds another clue to the direction in which a new relationship should be sought. To some degree these policies failed because they were perverted to other ends. The efforts in colonial New Brunswick to assimilate the Micmac failed because New Brunswickers diverted British donations to colonial development and exploited the apprenticeship programs to secure cheap labour. Perhaps more significantly, these policies failed in part because they were never adequately funded and supported. The attempt to encourage and facilitate western Indians' shift to agriculture was sometimes met with enthusiastic cooperation by the Indians themselves. But in at least some instances, as in Manitoba's Oak River reserve, enthusiasm for agriculture was killed by bureaucratic obtuseness and racist assumptions. Elsewhere throughout the west in the 1880s and 1890s the agricultural programs failed because they were not adequately funded and because governmental support and instruction were not maintained long enough to enable the native population to make a satisfactory transition. Governments, especially when pressed for funds for development projects that the non-native majority considered important, found it all too convenient to forget that they were asking Indians to complete in a few years a transformation that had taken Europeans centuries. Racism, parsimony, and obtuseness go far to explain the failure of coercive assimilation in the third phase of the relationship. But none of these is the most important reason.

The policies that aimed at the conversion of natives into Euro-Canadians have failed principally because native peoples have resisted them tenaciously and persistently. Whether one looks at Upper Canada in the 1830s and 1840s, the prairies in the 1880s and 1890s, or the north in the twentieth century, the record is the same. Native groups recognized the inevitability of change and sought only to control it so that it would not prove destructive to their identity and social cohesion. Upper Canadian Indians agreed to support education with a portion of their annuities; they fought schooling when it turned out to be more concerned with turning their children into British Americans than into literate farmers. Western natives sought treaties to establish a relationship with government that would provide them assistance in a difficult transition; they resisted or lapsed into apathy when they realized that the government was more interested in asssimilating them than in helping them.

To a considerable extent the process of native disillusionment is seen most clearly in their reaction to the attempts by government and churches to interfere with their traditional political institutions. The Indians of Upper Canada complained about provisions in legislation of the 1850s that presumed to give administrators suzerainty over their councils. Big Bear attempted to put together a political front to stand firm against the likes of Edgar Dewdney and Hayter Reed. For well over a century the Six Nations have resisted first colonial and then national governmental pretensions to be able to determine their political institutions. In the later twentieth century they are being joined in this rejection of political interference by treaty Indians, Métis, and non-status Indians and Inuit in the north. The record is absolutely clear and consistent: the native peoples reject efforts to change them – whether economically, culturally, or politically – into imitation Euro-Canadians. Programs such as the white paper of 1969 or the 1985 Nielsen task force that aim at such change will fail as have all such earlier initiatives.

If there is a conclusion that can be drawn from these patterns in the historical record, surely it is that new policies that benefit natives and non-natives alike can be developed only within a real partnership. Only cooperative policies that have the support of government, native organizations, and the general population have any chance of helping native groups to free themselves from their social and economic morass. And real partnership has two aspects. First, there must be meaningful consultation. Second, non-natives must not only listen to natives; they must also agree to try solutions that the aboriginal peoples consider desirable.

Meaningful consultation is not a process of discussion but the act of listening and considering seriously what is being said. The travesty of the 'dialogue' of 1968–9 that preceded the white paper had a devastating effect on Indian-white relations. Not only was it dishonest to pretend to listen to native leaders and then produce a document that reflected purely bureaucratic and political considerations, it was also counter-productive. All that the duplicity accomplished was the disillusionment and political unification of the native peoples in opposition to the white paper. The decade of the 1970s was disfigured by the distrust that the process leading up to the white paper, as well as the policy document itself, engendered. And the making of the new constitution in 1980–2 was similarly disillusioning for native peoples. In spite of the professions that governments had offered, in spite of the progress that supposedly had been made, when the first ministers got together in the autumn of 1981 they betrayed the natives. And, finally, the Mulroney government's task force on public expenditure similarly shut the native people out of the evaluation of the policies that supposedly were for their benefit. Outside 'experts' from the private sector were considered more essential to the evaluation process than the recipients of the programs under review. Unless a change occurs in governments' attitudes about talking to Indians and other natives, the country will never find viable policies.

Meaningful consultation means more than just listening, however. It means listening with the intention of considering seriously what is being said, and with an open mind as to its merits. George Manuel, chief of the Assembly of First Nations, wrote scathingly of the usual way in which government 'considered' spending economic development funds in 1973: 'Band councils have submitted lists of thoroughly researched proposals, in consultation with professional economic advisers, for using the money for our own economic development. No dice. The industries that have gotten federal support, set up on reserve land, have employed no more than a token number of Indians in skilled or managerial positions. The department just cannot conceive of an Indian being able to run his own show.'[4] A case study of the failures of the 1970s economic development program by two white experts confirms what Manuel says: 'Instead of beginning with a clear set of workable objectives that were consistent with what the people wanted, government agencies such as DIAND and Manpower almost always worked at cross-purposes, failed to monitor and assess their programs, and, worst of all, never really consulted with the people they were supposed to be serving. The outcome was that band members were rewarded for becoming dependent, stymied in their attempts to become independent, and left in a position where vulnerability to government cut-backs is now the one overriding feature of their lives.'[5] Not consulting properly has resulted in the failure of programs, the frustration of bureaucrats, and the cynicism of natives.

Surely there cannot be any defensible argument for refusing to consult native peoples about policy and allowing them to control the administration of the programs that are supposedly for their benefit? Can anyone point to the consequences of a century and more of paternalistic administration in which programs were decided by people remote from the Indians and administered by officials who were not answerable to them and argue that they were at all successful? In the face of the chilling statistics on school drop-outs, unemployment, poverty, ill health, family breakdown, incarceration, and early deaths, such an argument seems impossible. The record shows no reason to refuse natives control over the development and administration of policies that affect them. They can hardly fail more abysmally than the thousands of Euro-Canadian politicians, bureaucratic planners, missionaries, and officials have during the past 150 years. There might even be modest reason to hope that the experiments of the last decade in native control of education and the administration of social policy provide proof that native direction produces better results. By 1988, over two-thirds of the schools on reserve were band-operated.[6] Drop-out rates, while still too high, were coming down among the prairie Indian communities with band-controlled schools or urban Native Survival Schools. Indian and Métis children no longer leave Manitoba for adoption by white Americans. Perhaps such initiatives provide a case for expanding the scope of native peoples' control of the policies that affect them? If so, that in itself is an argument for greater native self-government, an argument to which the two senior levels of government and the bulk of the Canadian population should listen.

It hardly follows from the historical record that all the changes should be made by the non-natives. There are aspects of the way in which Indians and natives have conducted their relations in recent decades, as they emerged from the irrelevance into which economics had cast them in the nineteenth century, that could stand improvement. These include the need to avoid the siege mentality, the desirability of re-establishing political unity, and the necessity to develop a clear strategy for advancing their various causes in negotiations with the larger Canadian community.

Increasingly of late various native groups have, understandably perhaps, edged towards a mind-set in which anyone who is not completely with them in their cause of the moment is deemed to be against them. A political science professor at the University of Calgary who wrote a book that Alberta natives considered critical of Louis Riel was denounced; his dismissal by the Board of Governors of the university was demanded, fortunately in vain. Such behaviour is both contrary to native social and political traditions, and harmful to their image in the broader community. There is criticism that is intended to be constructive; natives, before attacking, should attempt to distinguish it from negativism. Natives and their political organizations should also remember that they, too, can change policy and tactics, and, when they do, they may find themselves in the company of people whom they earlier denounced for differing with them. For example, in the late 1970s the Association of Metis and Non-Status Indians of Saskatchewan petitioned the federal government for a pardon for Louis Riel; by the mid-1980s the same people were saying that such a pardon was unnecessary. Previously citizens who called for a pardon were allies; now they are fools or knaves who wrongly imply that Riel did wrong. Incidents of that sort do not add to the credibility of native political organizations.

If natives should be more selective in their criticism of non-natives, they should also attempt to be more united among themselves. Such behaviour is, obviously, easier to counsel than to effect. But surely Canada's native leaders know better than anyone that it was during the decade following the white paper of 1969, when they were united, that they made their greatest gains in persuading the general public and, through it, governments to see some matters as the native peoples did? The divisions that have recurred within the native community since the failure of the first ministers' conferences on the definition of aboriginal and treaty rights and on native self-government have, unfortunately, encouraged a split into Assembly of First Nations and Prairie Treaty Nations Alliance, a division that is accompanied by further splinterings of Métis, non-status Indians, and Inuit.

There are hopeful exceptions to the general picture of disintegration of natives' political movements. The Dene Nation in the north is an apparently effective unification for political purposes of Indian, Métis, and non-status peoples. The fact that all the aboriginal groups represented at the 1987 first ministers' conference agreed to table a 'Joint Aboriginal Proposal for Self-Government' suggests that unity on some items of the constitutional agenda has been restored. Another inclusive model might be the Fourth World concept championed by George Manuel. If all aboriginal groups in Canada see themselves as parts of a Fourth World of indigenous peoples in collision with the other three worlds (capitalist, communist, and emerging), there is a basis for restoring political unity.

Once the native groups have re-established the political unity that served them so well in the 1970s, they should work to develop a clear strategy and a set of tactics. Is aboriginal status the basis of native claims, or is it contract with the majority community? Is their most effective argument that they have not made treaties or that promises made to them have not been kept? At the moment, with two major political bodies pursuing their separate strategies, both arguments are being advanced. The result is confusion in the general population, and, in some quarters, also a suspicion that natives are not playing a fair game. With organizations arguing both aboriginal and treaty rights, there is sometimes an exasperated reaction that the groups are trying to eat their cake and have it too. Perhaps it will remain necessary to pursue both the aboriginal rights and treaty rights paths. But, if so, it would behoove the native community to develop a coherent rationale for such an approach and to work at communicating it to the general population.

Tactics as well as strategy deserve consideration. Do the native leaders intend to proceed by the political or judicial route? Whether they make their case by negotiation with the heads of senior governments or by seeking court decisions on their claims depends in part on whether they are going to rely on aboriginal status or treaty obligations as their strategy. It also depends in large part on the extent to which native leaders think they can get the politicians to consult meaningfully with them. And that, in turn, depends on the extent to which the native communities can make their case to the general public. At present Canadian political leaders are dealing with the various native communities within a model of interest-group politics. They regard the Inuit, Métis, and Indians as specific interest groups and themselves as a broker adjudicating among the demands of many such groups. They are inclined to treat native political organizations as they would the agrarian community, labour, or manufacturers.

Native leaders reject the interest-group or brokerage politics approach and insist that they be treated as the representatives of First Nations. So far, in spite of some rhetoric to the contrary, they have not succeeded, and it seems unlikely that they soon will. That being the case, certain considerations follow. First, if native causes are going to be treated as the demands of interest groups, then the more unified they are the better. One native interest group will have more effect in negotiations than a series of Inuit, non-status Indian, Métis, and Indian pressure groups. Second, the attitude of the general electorate will determine the extent to which the leaders of the senior levels of government respond positively to the pressure of native groups.

Native leaders have drawn some, but not all, of the necessary conclusions from the fact that they are participating, like it or not, in a forum in which interest groups are competing for attention and funds. They have recognized that they often must make their case over the heads of premiers and federal ministers to the national electorate, or even, in some instances, an international community of consumers. The have learned the techniques of street theatre, staging media events and organizing political confrontations so as to maximize the photo and television opportunities on which modern news coverage – and, hence, political influence – turns. Demonstrations on Parliament Hill and native caravans have attracted publicity to their causes within Canada. The Inuit campaign in Europe against the Greenpeace Foundation's attack on the hunting of fur-bearing animals is an instance of the same approach used internationally. But native leaders have not always recognized that these techniques, which are designed to move politicians by first influencing the general public, have their drawbacks.

Many members of the general population resent some of the tactics that native groups use. Appeals beyond Canada's borders offend many voters without advancing the natives' cause much. The appeals to the British parliament against the Trudeau initiative on constitutional renewal around 1980 made good television but bad politics. The United Kingdom, as its prime minister made clear, had neither the legal right nor the will to interfere in what she regarded as a Canadian affair. The post-Confederation treaties were made with the Queen 'in right of Canada,' and legal and political responsibility for those that had been made in the colonial period with the 'Queen in right of the United Kingdom' were transferred at Canada's achievement of autonomy within the Commonwealth to Canada. Appeals to Britain are unhistorical and legally counterproductive. Similarly, appeals to the Bertrand Russell Human Rights Tribunal in Brussels offend Canadian voters without accomplishing anything. Canadians do not particularly

enjoy turning on the television news to see their country denounced for its treatment of aboriginal peoples in company with
Central American countries that have undertaken campaigns of
genocide. The international tribunal cannot provide relief; it can
arouse political resentment in Canada.

Such considerations lead to the matter of rhetoric. One of the
most striking features of Indian-white political relations in Canada
since the late 1960s has been the escalation of rhetoric on the native
side. Out of frustration at a lack of progress and out of calculation
that charges of 'racism' and 'cultural genocide' attract public
attention and embarrass politicians, native leaders have tended
increasingly to respond to every abortive political meeting with
denunciations and threats. But, again, if such anger is understandable, it is also pointless. Canadians do not like to see their prime
minister and premier, whatever they themselves might think of
the politicians, denounced on television when a first ministers'
meeting on native self-government has broken down. If native
political leaders are to move the people with whom they deal
politically, they must first inform and then convince the general
electorate to which those politicians answer. Ritualistic denuncia-
tion, oratorical hyperbole, and made-for-television histrionics
have only a negative effect.

George Manuel has argued that Indians will achieve political
victories that do not entail political losses for the rest of the
Canadian community. If, he has written, 'we can resolve the
contradictions between your values, white values, and our own,
then our victory will be complete. And it will be *our victory* not your
loss. Indian victories only rarely demand that there be a loser.'[7]
Manuel was referring to the cooperative, consensual, non-competi-
tive tradition of Indian decision-making. He recognized that it was
different from the adversarial, competitive, and, not infrequently,
confrontational political style of the Euro-Canadian majority in
Canada. The problem for the electorate at large is that it cannot
perceive an Indian victory that does not entail a corresponding loss
for non-natives in the overheated rhetoric and guerilla theatre that
has accompanied recent political confrontation.

George Manuel's point also reminds us that Indian-white
relations involve societies that differ in their values and aspira-

tions. There is a society of skyscrapers and one that focuses on the heavens. Manuel says what Indians from Pontiac to Big Bear and the opponents of the white paper have said: while they want to cooperate with and benefit from Canadian society, they do not want to be submerged in it. They want to participate, not assimilate. They want to remain one of the many distinct entities – what one historian has called 'limited identities'[8] – that make Canada the unique human community that it has become over the past 500 years.

'I wonder,' Indian actor Dan George once said, if 'My white brother … has ever really learned to love at all.' It is important that his white brothers learn to love before his red brothers learn to hate. 'Love is something you and I must have. We must have it because our spirit feeds upon it. We must have it because without it we become weak and faint. Without love our self esteem weakens. Without love we can no longer look out confidently at the world. Instead we turn inwardly and begin to feed upon our own personalities and little by little we destroy ourselves.'[9] Both Dan George and George Manuel are saying implicitly what the poet observed more than eighty years ago: 'love … consists in this, that two solitudes protect and touch and greet each other.'[10] The best hope of Canadians and the native peoples who dwell with them in what has become Canada lies in the possibility that a mutually beneficial, interdependent relationship between Indians and Euro-Canadians can be re-established. 'While skyscrapers hide the heavens, / They can fall.'

Notes

CHAPTER 1 Indians and Europeans at the time of contact

1 Cartier's narrative of 1534, in H.P. Biggar, *The Voyages of Jacques Cartier* (Ottawa: King's Printer 1924), 64–5
2 B.G. Trigger, *The Indians and the Heroic Age of New France* (Ottawa: Canadian Historical Association 1977), 3
3 B.G. Trigger, *The Huron: Farmers of the North* (New York: Holt, Rinehart and Winston 1969), 6
4 J. Rousseau and G.W. Brown, 'The Indians of Northeastern North America,' *Dictionary of Canadian Biography*, volume I: *1000 to 1700* (Toronto: University of Toronto Press 1966), 7
5 See, for example, Trigger, *Farmers of the North*, 50–1
6 Ibid., 51
7 Ibid., 106–12
8 Trigger, *Indians and the Heroic Age*, 8
9 C.J. Jaenen, 'French Sovereignty and Native Nationhood during the French Regime,' *Native Studies Review* 2, no. 1 (1986), 92

CHAPTER 2 Early contacts in the eastern woodlands

1 M. Trudel, *Introduction to New France* (Toronto/Montreal: Holt, Rinehart and Winston 1968), 253
2 Cartier's narrative of 1534, in H.P. Biggar, *The Voyages of Jacques Cartier* (Ottawa: King's Printer 1924), 49
3 Ibid., 53. For Henry Hudson's similar experience in James Bay in 1611 see

G.M. Asher, ed., *Henry Hudson the Navigator* reprint ed. (New York: Burt Franklin 1953; first published 1860), 114–15

4 Cartier's narrative of 1534, 56

5 See above, page 3.

6 W.J. Eccles, *The Canadian Frontier 1534–1760* (New York: Holt, Rinehart and Winston 1969), 15. See also C.J. Jaenen, *Friend and Foe: Aspects of French-Amerindian Cultural Contact in the Sixteenth and Seventeenth Centuries* (New York: Columbia University Press 1976), 12–13.

7 Cartier's narrative of 1534, 60

8 P.F.X. de Charlevoix, *History and General Description of New France*, trans. J.G. Shea, 6 vols (Chicago: Loyola University Press 1870; first published Paris 1743), IV, 198

9 Gabriel Sagard-Théodat, *Le grand voyage au pays des Hurons*, 2 vols (Paris: Librairie Tross 1865), I, 67; G.M. Wrong, ed., *The Long Journey to the Country of the Huron* by Father Gabriel Sagard (Toronto: Champlain Society 1939), 74, 183

10 W.F. Ganong, ed., *Description and Natural History of the Coasts of North America (Acadia)* (Toronto: Champlain Society 1908), 440–1

11 E.H. Blair, ed., *The Indian Tribes of the Upper Mississippi Valley and Region of the Great Lakes as described by Nicolas Perrot*, 2 vols (Cleveland: Arthur H. Clark 1911), I, 177

CHAPTER 3 Commercial partnership and mutual benefit

1 C.J. Jaenen, 'French Sovereignty and Native Nationhood during the French Regime,' *Native Studies Review* 2, no. 1 (1986), 84

2 R.G. Thwaites, ed., *The Jesuit Relations and Allied Documents*, 73 vols (New York: Pageant Books 1959), V, 119–21

3 B.G. Trigger, *Natives and Newcomers: Canada's 'Heroic Age' Reconsidered* (Kingston: McGill-Queen's University Press 1985), 225. See also C.J. Jaenen, *Friend and Foe: Aspects of French-Amerindian Cultural Contact in the Sixteenth and Seventeenth Centuries* (New York: Columbia University Press 1976), 23–4.

4 Trigger, *Natives and Newcomers*, 192–3, 219

5 T.R.L. MacInnes, 'History of Indian Administration in Canada,' *Canadian Journal of Economics and Political Science* 12, no. 3 (Aug. 1945), 387. Ramsay Cook, 'The Social and Economic Frontier in North America,' in H. Lamar and L. Thompson, eds., *The Frontier in History: North America and South Africa Compared* (New Haven: Yale University Press 1981), 188–9, argues that much higher initial population figures should be used. Estimates of contact population range up to three-quarters of a million. For a thoughtful discussion of the difficulties of establishing pre-contact population figures see Trigger, *Natives and Newcomers*, 231–42.

6 A. Vachon, 'L'eau-de-vie dans la société indienne,' Canadian Historical Association, *Annual Report 1960*, 22–32

7 N.O. Lurie, 'The World's Oldest On-Going Protest Demonstration: North American Indian Drinking Patterns,' *Pacific Historical Review* 40, no. 3 (Aug. 1971), 311–32. It is important to note that Lurie's analysis is based on evidence from a much later period when conditions in which Indians and Europeans interacted had changed dramatically.

8 Thwaites, ed., *Jesuit Relations and Allied Documents*, v, 49

9 Jaenen, *Friend and Foe*, 17

10 Ibid., 33

11 An excellent summary of these early reserves is G.F.G. Stanley, 'The First Indian "Reserves" in Canada,' *Revue d'histoire de l'Amérique française* 4, no. 2 (Sept. 1950), 178–210.

12 Trigger, *Natives and Newcomers*, 108, 110, 117, 162

13 W.J. Eccles, *The Canadian Frontier 1534–1760* (New York: Holt, Rinehart and Winston 1969), 9

14 Trigger, *Natives and Newcomers*, 224

15 Ibid.

16 For a useful summary of Indian responses to Christian missions see C.J. Jaenen, 'Amerindian Responses to French Missionary Intrusion, 1611–1760,' in W. Westfall and L. Rousseau, eds., *Religion/Culture: Comparative Canadian Studies/Etudes canadiennes comparées* (Ottawa: Association for Canadian Studies 1985), 182–97

CHAPTER 4 Military allies through a century of warfare

1 R.G. Thwaites, ed., *The Jesuit Relations and Allied Documents*, 73 vols (New York: Pageant Books 1959), v, 53. Allowance should be made for the fact that the author was not reporting events he had witnessed, but rather quoting others.

2 Ibid., ix, 269

3 C.J. Jaenen, *Friend and Foe: Aspects of French-Amerindian Cultural Contact in the Sixteenth and Seventeenth Centuries* (New York: Columbia University Press 1976), 143

4 Ibid., 122–3

5 Unidentified chief quoted in W.J. Eccles, *Canada under Louis XIV, 1663–1701* (Toronto: McClelland and Stewart 1964), 4

6 Jaenen, *Friend and Foe*, 192

7 Quoted in W.J. Eccles, *The Canadian Frontier 1534–1760* (New York: Holt, Rinehart and Winston 1969), 158

8 L.F.S. Upton, *Micmacs and Colonists: Indian-White Relations in the Maritimes, 1713–1867* (Vancouver: University of British Columbia Press 1979), 26

9 Ibid., 36 ('betrayed by our most trustworthy Indians'). Note that this is

another instance of the inappropriateness of translating 'sauvages' as 'savages.'

10 Eccles, *Canadian Frontier*, 156

11 The text of the proclamation is reprinted in I.A.L. Getty and A.S. Lussier, eds., *As Long as the Sun Shines and Water Flows: A Reader in Canadian Native Studies* (Vancouver: Nakoda Institute and University of British Columbia Press 1983), 29–37.

12 Ibid., 33–6

13 The legal issues are analysed in D.W. Elliott, 'Aboriginal Title,' in B.W. Morse, ed., *Aboriginal Peoples and the Law: Indian, Metis and Inuit Rights in Canada* (Ottawa: Carleton University Press 1985), 56.

14 Quoted in Jaenen, *Friend and Foe*, 7

15 L. Chevrette, 'Pontiac,' *Dictionary of Canadian Biography*, volume III: *1741–1770* (Toronto: University of Toronto Press 1974), 530

16 Quoted in S.F. Wise, 'The American Revolution and Indian History,' in J.S. Moir, ed., *Character and Circumstance: Essays in Honour of Donald Grant Creighton* (Toronto: Macmillan 1970), 182

17 Quoted ibid., 185–6. Wise describes this as 'a relatively light-hearted sample' of the propagandists' work (185).

18 Quoted in J.M. Sosin, 'The Use of Indians in the War of the American Revolution: A Re-Assessment of Responsibility,' *Canadian Historical Review* 46, no. 2 (June 1965), 106. On the Oneida's sympathy for the Americans see also B. Graymont, *The Iroquois in the American Revolution* (Syracuse: Syracuse University Press 1972), 128.

19 R.S. Allen, 'The British Indian Department and the Frontier in North America, 1755–1830,' Canadian Historic Sites, *Occasional Papers in Archaeology and History* 14: 11. Johnson's appointment as superintendent constituted the beginnings of a 'Department of Indian Affairs.'

20 Graymont, *Iroquois in the American Revolution*, chap. 2

21 Ibid., 221 note

22 Quoted in Wise, 'American Revolution and Indian History,' 199

23 Ibid., 200

24 Quoted in D.C. Scott, 'Indian Affairs, 1763–1841,' in A. Shortt and A.G. Doughty, eds., *Canada and Its Provinces*, IV (Toronto: Glasgow, Brook and Co 1914), 708

CHAPTER 5 From alliance to irrelevance

1 E.P. Patterson, *The Canadian Indian: A History since 1500* (Don Mills: Collier-Macmillan 1972), 72

2 G. Brown and R. Maguire, *Indian Treaties in Historical Perspective* (Ottawa: Indian and Northern Affairs 1979), 22

3 R.S. Allen, 'The British Indian Department and the Frontier in North America, 1755–1830,' Canadian Historic Sites, *Occasional Papers in Archaeology and History* 14: 58–73

4 Quoted in G.M. Craig, *Upper Canada: The Formative Years 1784–1841* (Toronto: McClelland and Stewart 1963), 67

5 Patterson, *Canadian Indian*, 84

6 General Hull, quoted in G.F.G. Stanley, 'The Indians in the War of 1812,' *Canadian Historical Review* (CHR) 31, no. 2 (June 1950), 151–2

7 L.F.S. Upton, *Micmacs and Colonists: Indian-White Relations in the Maritimes 1713–1867* (Vancouver: University of British Columbia Press 1979), 145

8 The following synopsis is based on the excellent study by J. Fingard, 'The New England Company and the New Brunswick Indians, 1786–1826: A Comment on the Colonial Perversion of British Benevolence,' *Acadiensis* 1, no. 2 (spring 1972), 29–42.

9 This account is based on L.F.S. Upton, 'The Extermination of the Beothucks of Newfoundland,' CHR 58, no. 2 (June 1977), 133–53

10 R.J. Surtees, 'Indian Land Cessions in Upper Canada, 1815–30,' in I.A.L. Getty and A.S. Lussier, eds., *As Long as the Sun Shines and the Water Flows: A Reader in Canadian Native Studies* (Vancouver: Nakoda Institute and University of British Columbia Press 1983), 67; A.R.M. Lower, *Canadians in the Making: A Social History of Canada* (Don Mills: Longmans 1958), 189–90

11 Surtees, 'Indian Land Cessions,' 69–70

12 D.B. Smith, *Sacred Feathers: The Reverend Peter Jones (Kahkewaquonaby) and the Mississauga Indians* (Toronto: University of Toronto Press 1987), 124

13 Sir G. Murray to Sir J. Kempt, Jan. 25, 1830, *British Parliamentary Papers* [Irish University Press Series], 'Correspondence and other Papers Relating to Aboriginal Tribes in British Possessions,' 1834, no. 617, 88

14 Allen, 'British Indian Department,' 91

15 C. White, *Account of the Regular Gradation in Man* (London 1799), 135, quoted in L.F.S. Upton, 'The Origins of Canadian Indian Policy,' *Journal of Canadan Studies* 8, no. 4 (Nov. 1973), 52

16 For an example of the use of phrenology to 'explain' the alleged fact 'that all attempts to make gentlemen of them [Métis], have hitherto proved a failure,' see J. Tod to F. Ermatinger, 20 March 1843, quoted in J.S.H. Brown, *Strangers in Blood: Fur Trade Company Families in Indian Country* (Vancouver: University of British Columbia Press 1980), 188–9.

17 Quoted in Smith, *Sacred Feathers*, 27

18 Unidentified Mississauga, 1820, in D.F. McOuat, ed., 'The Diary of William Graves,' *Ontario History* 43, no. 1 (Jan. 1951), 10. I am indebted to a colleague, J.R. Handy, who made me aware of this item.

CHAPTER 6 Reserves, residential schools, and the threat of assimilation

1 Sir James Kempt to Lt-Gov. J. Colborne, 16 May 1829, *British Parliamentary Papers* [Irish University Press Series], 'Correspondence and other Papers Relating to the Aboriginal Tribes in British Possessions,' 1834, no. 617, 40–1
2 H. Merivale, *Lectures on Colonization and Colonies* (London 1928), 511, quoted in L.F.S. Upton, 'The Origins of Canadian Indian Policy,' *Journal of Canadian Studies* 8, no. 4 (Nov. 1973), 54
3 A useful, brief survey of missionary efforts in Upper Canada is E. Graham, *Medicine Man to Missionary: Missionaries as Agents of Change among the Indians of Southern Ontario, 1784–1867* (Toronto: Peter Martin Associates 1975). The Methodists are best examined in D.B. Smith, *Sacred Feathers: The Reverend Peter Jones (Kahkewaquonaby) and the Mississauga Indians* (Toronto: University of Toronto Press 1987). For the Jesuits see Regis College Achives, J. Paquin, 'Modern Jesuit Indian Missions in Ontario' (typescript), and [Anonymous] 'Synopsis of the History of Wikwemikong' (typescript).
4 J.R. Handy, 'The Ojibwa: 1640–1840. Two Centuries of Change from Sault Ste. Marie to Coldwater/Narrows' (MA thesis, University of Waterloo, 1978), 91–7
5 Minutes of a Speech, 19 July 1827, 'Aboriginal Tribes in British Possessions,' 16–17
6 Proceedings of a Council of the Chippewa Indians, 20 July 1827, ibid., 17
7 Handy, 'The Ojibwa,' chaps 9–12
8 H. Maclean, 'The Hidden Agenda: Methodist Attitudes to the Ojibwa and the Development of Indian Schooling in Upper Canada, 1821–1860,' (MA thesis, University of Toronto, 1978), 89
9 The best account is J. Leslie, 'The Bagot Commission: Developing a Corporate Memory for the Indian Department,' Canadian Historical Association, *Historical Papers 1982*, 38–52, on which this summary is based.
10 H.J. Vallery, 'A History of Indian Education in Canada,' (MA thesis, Queen's University, 1942), 37
11 Maclean, 'Methodist Attitudes,' 144
12 Smith, *Sacred Feathers*, espec. chaps 10–12
13 Maclean, 'Methodist Attitudes,' 144–8
14 *Statistics respecting Indian Schools with Dr. Ryerson's Report of 1847 attached* (Ottawa: Government Printing Bureau 1898), 73. I am indebted to Professor D.B. Smith of the University of Calgary and to John Leslie of the Treaties and Historical Research Centre of Indian and Northern Affairs for supplying me with a copy of Ryerson's report.
15 Lord Elgin to Lord Grey, 23 November 1849, in A.G. Doughty, *The Elgin-Grey Papers 1845–1852*, four vols (Ottawa: King's Printer 1937), IV, appendix VII, 1485, 1486. This account is based on Elgin's reports, ibid., II, 549, 553–4,

563–4; IV, 1485–6. Elgin blamed 'blackguard whites' for inciting the Indians, but the behaviour of the Indians was consistent with the resistance other Indians would show to white incursions in the north and west during the rest of the century.

16 W.B. Robinson to superintendent general, Indian Affairs, 24 Sept. 1850, in A. Morris, *The Treaties of Canada with the Indians* (Toronto: Belfords, Clarke 1880; Coles facsimile edition 1979), 17, 19

17 J. Leslie and R. Maquire, eds., *The Historical Development of the Indian Act*, 2nd ed. (Ottawa: Indian Affairs and Northern Development 1983; first edition 1975), 23–4

18 Ibid., 27. There are useful discussions of this important measure in J.S. Milloy, 'The Early Indian Acts: Developmental Strategy and Constitutional Change,' in I.A.L. Getty and A.S. Lussier, eds., *As Long as the Sun Shines and the Water Flows: A Reader in Canadian Native Studies* (Vancouver: Nakoda Institute and University of British Columbia Press 1983), 56–64; and J.L. Tobias, 'Protection, Civilization, Assimilation: An Outline History of Canada's Indian Policy,' ibid., 39–55.

19 Tobias, 'Protection,' 42

20 Milloy, 'Early Indian Acts,' 59

21 Smith, *Sacred Feathers*, 213–14

22 Milloy, 'Early Indian Acts,' 61

CHAPTER 7 The commercial frontier on the western plains

1 This description of the western and northern nations is based on the excellent brief account in G. Friesen, *The Canadian Prairies: A History* (Toronto: University of Toronto Press 1984), 23–7. A longer description can be found in D. Jenness, *The Indians of Canada*, 7th ed. (Ottawa: Supply and Services Canada 1977), espec. chaps 20 and 23.

2 Friesen, *Canadian Prairies*, 21

3 W.J. Eccles, 'A Belated Review of Harold Adams Innis's *The Fur Trade in Canada*,' *Canadian Historical Review* (CHR) 60, no. 4 (Dec. 1979), 429–34

4 A.J. Ray, *Indians in the Fur Trade: Their Role as Hunters, Trappers and Middlemen in the Lands Southwest of Hudson Bay, 1660–1870* (Toronto: University of Toronto Press 1974), 69

5 Ibid., 68

6 Ibid., 14, 16

7 Ibid., 188–92

8 S. Van Kirk, *'Many Tender Ties': Women in Fur-Trade Society, 1670–1870* (Winnipeg: Watson & Dwyer, nd), 4. The following account is based mainly on Van Kirk's study.

9 Quoted in R.A. Fisher, *Contact and Conflict: Indian-European Relations in British*

Columbia, 1774–1890 (Vancouver: University of British Columbia Press 1977), 42

10 A good starting point for understanding this phase of relations in the west is J.E. Foster, 'Program for the Red River Mission: The Anglican Clergy 1820–1826,' *Histoire sociale/Social History* 4 (Nov. 1969), 49–75

11 E.P. Patterson, *The Canadian Indian: A History since 1500* (Don Mills: Collier-Macmillan 1972), 122

12 James Douglas, quoted in Van Kirk, *'Many Tender Ties,'* 1

13 The case for division within the mixed-blood community at Red River has been argued most effectively by F. Pannakoek, 'The Anglican Church and the Disintegration of Red River Society, 1818–1870,' in C. Berger and R. Cook, eds., *The West and the Nation: Essays in Honour of W.L. Morton* (Toronto: McClelland and Stewart 1976), 72–90, and 'The Rev. Griffiths Owen Corbett and the Red River Civil War of 1869–70,' CHR 57, no. 2 (June 1976), 133–45. A recent, forceful restatement of the traditional view is I. Spry, 'The Métis and Mixed-Bloods of Rupert's Land before 1870,' in J. Peterson and J.S.H. Brown, eds., *The New Peoples: Being and Becoming Metis in North America* (np: University of Manitoba Press 1985), 95–118.

14 Friesen, *Canadian Prairies*, 101 ('Hurrah for freedom! Free trade is here!'). The Louis Riel involved in the Sayer case was the father of the man who led the resistance to the assertion of Canadian control in 1869–70.

15 A. Morris, *The Treaties of Canada with the Indians* (Toronto: Belfords, Clarke 1880; Coles facsimile edition 1979), 15

16 Friesen, *Canadian Prairies*, 130–2

CHAPTER 8 Contact, commerce, and Christianity on the Pacific

1 D. Jenness, *The Indians of Canada*, 7th ed. (Ottawa: Supply and Services Canada 1977), chap. 23

2 An excellent, easily accessible introduction to their art is J. Thompson, 'No Little Variety of Ornament: Northern Athapaskan Artistic Traditions,' *The Spirit Sings: Artistic Traditions of Canada's First Peoples* (Toronto: Glenbow Museum and McClelland and Stewart 1987), 133–68

3 See W. Duff, *The Indian History of British Columbia*, vol. 1: *The Impact of the White Man*, 2nd ed. (np: Royal British Columbia Museum 1969; first published 1966), chap. 1; Jenness, *Indians of Canada*, chap. 22.

4 H. Codere, *Fighting with Property: A Study of Kwakiutl Potlatching and Warfare, 1792–1930* (Seattle: University of Washington Press 1966)

5 This account is based mainly on the excellent study by Robin A. Fisher, *Contact and Conflict: Indian-European Relations in British Columbia, 1774–1890* (Vancouver: University of British Columbia Press 1977), espec. chap. 1.

6 Ibid., 23

7 Duff, *Indian History*, 56
8 Fisher, *Contact*, 40, 45–6. See also Duff, *Indian History*, 57.
9 Quoted in Duff, *Indian History*, 59
10 Fisher, *Contact*, 47–8
11 Quoted ibid., 24
12 The best account of this period is ibid., chap. 2.
13 The best brief treatment is found ibid., chap. 3, on which this account is based.
14 Quoted ibid., 117
15 Ibid., 107–8
16 J.W. Grant, *Moon of Wintertime: Missionaries and the Indians of Canada in Encounter since 1534* (Toronto: University of Toronto Press 1984), 125–6; D. Mulhall, *Will to Power: The Missionary Career of Father Morice* (Vancouver: University of British Columbia Press 1986), 8–9
17 The best account is J. Usher, *Duncan of Metlakatla* (Ottawa: National Museum of Man 1974).
18 A. Rettig, 'A Nativist Movement at Metlakatla Mission,' *BC Studies*, no. 46 (summer 1980), 28–39

CHAPTER 9 Resistance in Red River and the numbered treaties

1 J.S. Milloy, 'The Early Indian Acts: Developmental Strategy and Constitutional Change,' in I.A.L. Getty and A.S. Lussier, eds., *As Long as the Sun Shines and the Water Flows: A Reader in Canadian Native Studies* (Vancouver: Nakoda Institute and University of British Columbia Press 1983), 62. See also J.L. Tobias, 'Protection, Civilization, Assimilation: An Outline History of Canada's Indian Policy,' ibid., 43.
2 'Report of the Indian Branch of the Department of the Secretary of State for the Provinces, 1871,' Canada, *Sessional Papers (No. 23), 1871*, 4
3 Quoted in G.F.G. Stanley, *Louis Riel* (Toronto: Ryerson 1963), 114
4 Section 31 of Manitoba Act and Macdonald quoted in T. Flanagan, *Riel and the Rebellion: 1885 Reconsidered* (Saskatoon: Western Producer Prairie Books 1983), 60, 61 and 62
5 D.N. Sprague, 'The Manitoba Land Question, 1870–1882,' *Journal of Canadian Studies* 15, no. 3 (autumn 1980), 74–84; 'Government Lawlessness in the Administration of Manitoba Land Claims, 1870–1887,' *Manitoba Law Journal* 10, no. 4 (1980), 415–41
6 Quoted in D.G. Creighton, *Dominion of the North: A History of Canada*, new ed. (Toronto: Macmillan 1962; first published 1944), 360
7 J.L. Tobias, 'Canada's Subjugation of the Plains Cree, 1879–1885,' *Canadian Historical Review* 64, no. 4 (Dec. 1983), 520; G. Friesen, *The Canadian Prairies: A History* (Toronto: University of Toronto Press 1984), 137–8;

A. Morris, *The Treaties of Canada with the Indians of Manitoba and the North-West Territories*, reprint ed. (Toronto: Belfords, Clarke, 1880; Coles facsimile edition 1979), 37. Concerning Commissioner Alexander Morris's concern about Indian unrest, especially near Portage, see National Archives of Canada, Sir John Macdonald Papers, MG 26 A, vol. 252, 114028–32, 114133–7, Morris to Macdonald, 7 Feb. and 2 June 1873.

8 R.C. Macleod, *The North-West Mounted Police and Law Enforcement* (Toronto: University of Toronto Press 1976), 3

9 Canada, *Debates of the House of Commons*, 8 Feb. 1877, 3

10 *Oxford Dictionary of Quotations*, 3rd ed. (New York: Oxford University Press 1979; first published 1941), 505

11 Morris, *Treaties of Canada*, 174

12 Ibid., 170–1

13 G. McDougall to J. Ferrier, 17 Dec. 1875, in H.A. Dempsey, ed., 'The Last Letters of Rev. George McDougall,' *Alberta Historical Review* 6, no. 2 (spring 1967), 26

14 Friesen, *Canadian Prairies*, 138–9

15 Quoted ibid., 144

16 Morris, *Treaties of Canada*, 58

17 The different approaches and objectives are summarized by J.L. Tobias, 'Indian Reserves in Western Canada: Indian Homelands or Devices for Assimilation,' in D.A. Muise, ed., *Approaches to Native History in Canada* (Ottawa: National Museum of Man 1977), espec. 90–1.

18 J.L. Taylor, 'Canada's North-West Indian Policy in the 1870's: Traditional Premises and Necessary Innovations,' ibid., 107–8

19 Treaty 6, Morris, *Treaties of Canada*, 352, 355

20 Ibid., 351

21 The different understandings have been documented for Treaties 6 and 7 in J.L. Taylor, 'Two Views on the Meaning of Treaties Six and Seven,' in R. Price, ed., *The Spirit of the Alberta Indian Treaties*, 2nd ed. (Edmonton: Pica Pica Press 1987; first published 1979), 9–45.

CHAPTER 10 The Northwest Rebellion of 1885

1 The earliest, and still the best, treatment of the Rebellion as the clash of two ways of life is G.F.G. Stanley, *The Birth of Western Canada: A History of the Riel Rebellions*, 2nd ed. (Toronto: University of Toronto 1960; first published 1936).

2 G. Pennanen, 'Sitting Bull: Indian without a Country,' *Canadian Historical Review* (CHR) 51, no. 2 (June 1970), 123–41

3 Stanley, *Birth of Western Canada*, 220, 221; G. Friesen, *The Canadian Prairies: A History* (Toronto: University of Toronto Press 1984), 250

4 J.L. Tobias, 'Canada's Subjugation of the Plains Cree, 1879–1885,' CHR 64, no. 4 (Dec. 1983), 524, 527–8
5 This account is based on ibid., 526ff.
6 Quoted ibid., 534
7 Quoted in Friesen, *Canadian Prairies*, 227
8 The best account of Riel's millenarian thought is T. Flanagan, *Louis 'David' Riel: Prophet of the New World* (Toronto: University of Toronto Press 1979).
9 T. Flanagan, *Riel and the Rebellion: 1885 Reconsidered* (Saskatoon: Western Producer Prairie Books 1983), chap. 5. How accurate the priest's report was is impossible to determine.
10 United Church of Canada Archives, Presbyterian Church Papers, Home Missions Committee, box 1A, file 18, H. McKay to 'Dear Sir,' 13 April 1885
11 H.A. Dempsey, 'The Fearsome Fire Wagons,' in H.A. Dempsey, ed., *The CPR West: The Iron Road and the Making of a Nation* (Vancouver/Toronto: Douglas & McIntyre 1984), 65
12 Tobias, 'Subjugation,' 545–7
13 S. Bingaman, 'The Trials of Poundmaker and Big Bear, 1885,' *Saskatchewan History* 28, no. 3 (autumn 1975), 81–94; and 'The Trials of the "White Rebels," 1885,' ibid., 25, no. 2 (spring 1972), 41–54; Flanagan, *1885 Reconsidered*, 118
14 D.H. Brown, 'The Meaning of Treason in 1885,' *Saskatchewan History* 28, no. 2 (spring 1975), 65–73
15 Flanagan, *1885 Reconsidered*, 122–4, 126–9
16 A.I. Silver, *The French-Canadian Idea of Confederation 1864–1900* (Toronto: University of Toronto Press 1982), 153–79
17 See especially Flanagan, *1885 Reconsidered*, chap. 7.
18 Quoted in Association of Metis and Non-Status Indians of Saskatchewan, 'Louis Riel: Justice Must Be Done,' mimeograph, 1978, vi
19 *Colombo's Canadian Quotations* (Edmonton: Hurtig 1974), 597
20 R. Wiebe, *The Temptations of Big Bear* (Toronto: McClelland and Stewart 1973); National Film Board, *The Ballad of Crowfoot* (1968)

CHAPTER 11 The policy of the Bible and the plough

1 Return to an Order of the House of Commons, dated 2 May 1887, Canada, *Sessional Papers (No. 20b) 1887*, 37
2 H. Samek, *The Blackfoot Confederacy, 1880–1920: A Comparative Study of Canadian and U.S. Indian Policy* (Albuquerque: University of New Mexico Press 1987), 26
3 E.B. Titley, *A Narrow Vision: Duncan Campbell Scott and the Administration of Indian Affairs in Canada* (Vancouver: University of British Columbia Press 1986), chap. 7

4 Canada, *Sessional Papers (No. 12) 1890*, 165, Reed to Superintendent General, 31 Oct. 1889

5 Ibid., x

6 Canada, House of Commons, *Debates*, 1876, 752

7 S.A. Carter, 'Controlling Indian Movement: The Pass System,' *NeWest Review*, May 1985, 8–9; F.L. Barron, 'The Indian Pass System in the Canadian West, 1882–1935,' *Prairie Forum* 21, no. 1 (spring 1988), 25–42

8 National Archives of Canada (NA), Hayter Reed Papers, MG 29 E 106, vol. 14, file 'Reed, Hayter 1893,' H. Reed to T.M. Daly, 25 March 1893

9 Significantly, the printed 'General Instructions to Indian Agents in Canada' that the department issued in 1913 and reissued in 1933 nowhere mentioned passes. Glenbow Archives, Blackfoot Indian Agency Papers, box 3, file 15

10 SC 1884 (47 Victoria), c. 27, sec. 3

11 NA, Correspondence of the Secretary of State, vol. 54, no. 4355, Order in Council, 7 July 1883 (Gazetted 4 Aug. 1883). D. Cole and I. Chaikin, unpublished manuscript on the potlatch. I am deeply grateful to Professor Cole for providing me with this study, to which my account is greatly indebted.

12 Quoted R.A. Fisher, *Contact and Conflict: Indian-European Relations in British Columbia, 1774–1890* (Vancouver: University of British Columbia Press 1977), 206–7

13 H.A. Dempsey, *Red Crow, Warrior Chief* (Saskatoon: Western Producer Prairie Books 1980), chap. 19, espec. 213

14 Interview with Gordon Tootoosis, Poundmaker Reserve, 7 May 1987

15 E. Brass, 'The File Hills Colony,' *Saskatchewan History* 6, no. 2 (spring 1953), 57; *I Walk in Two Worlds* (Calgary: Glenbow Museum 1987), 13, 25

16 S. Cuthand, 'The Native Peoples of the Prairie Provinces in the 1920s and 1930s,' in I.A.L. Getty and D.B. Smith, eds., *One Century Later: Western Canadian Reserve Indians since Treaty 7* (Vancouver: University of British Columbia Press 1978), 39–40

17 Cole and Chaikin manuscript, 122 and 168

18 Ibid., chaps 6–9

19 Ibid., 233–4

20 Canada, House of Commons, *Debates*, 1885, 1575

21 Canada, *Sessional Papers (No. 14) 1892*, x

22 Canada, *Sessional Papers (No. 12) 1890*, xi

23 NA, Sir John Macdonald Papers, vol. 91, 35428, N.F. Davin, 'Report on Industrial Schools for Indians and Half-Breeds,' confidential, 14 March 1879, 1

24 Dan Kennedy [Ochankugahe], *Recollections of an Assiniboine Chief*, ed. James R. Stevens (Toronto/Montreal: McClelland and Stewart 1972), 54–5

25 Canada, House of Commons, *Debates*, 1883, 1377

26 Canada, *Sessional Papers (No. 14) 1892*, 291; Brass, 'The File Hills Colony'

27 Canada, House of Commons, *Debates*, 1904, 6948. Later Sifton elaborated: 'He has not the physical, mental or moral get-up to enable him to compete. He cannot do it'; ibid., 6956.

28 Toronto *Globe*, 4 July 1895. I.A. L. Getty, 'The Failure of the Native Church Policy of the cms in the North-West,' in R. Allen, ed., *Religion and Society in the Prairie West* (Regina: Canadian Plains Research Center 1974), 30, points out that the Blackfoot had three years earlier petitioned Ottawa to remove the missionary, whom they considered 'too bossy.'

29 'Sophie,' quoted in C. Haig-Brown, *Resistance and Renewal: Surviving the Indian Residential School* (Vancouver: Tillacum Library 1988), 102

30 'Josephine,' quoted ibid., 99

31 This account relies heavily on S.A. Carter, 'The Genesis and Anatomy of Government Policy and Indian Reserve Agriculture on Four Agencies in Treaty Four, 1874–1897' (phd thesis, University of Manitoba, 1987). I am greatly indebted to Dr Carter for providing me with a copy of her valuable dissertation.

32 M.J. Boswell, ' "Civilizing" the Indian: Government Administration of Indians, 1876–1896' (phd thesis, University of Ottawa, 1977), 218, 221

33 Reed Papers, vol. 14, 1349, H. Reed to T.M. Daly, 10 March 1893

34 Canada, *Sessional Papers (No. 12) 1890*, 162. See also Canada, *Sessional Papers (No. 14) 1892*, 193. Carter, 'Genesis and Anatomy,' chaps 5 and 7

35 Canada, House of Commons, *Debates*, 1888, 1610 (Macdowall referring to a petition from Battleford); *Regina Leader*, 20 Nov. 1884; *MacLeod Gazette*, 2 Aug. 1895, editorial, 'Indian Competition,' in Glenbow Archives, J.W. Tims Papers, box 4, file 51

36 Boswell, ' "Civilizing" the Indian,' 340–2

37 S.A. Carter, 'Agriculture and Agitation on the Oak River Dakota Reserve, 1875–1895,' *Manitoba History*, no. 6 (fall 1983), 4–8

38 Canada, *Sessional Papers (No. 18) 1891*, 250–7

39 Canada, *Sessional Papers (No. 14) 1896*, xxx. See also Samek, *Blackfoot Confederacy*, chap. 4.

40 D.J. Hall, 'Clifford Sifton and Canadian Indian Administration 1896–1905,' in I.A.L. Getty and A.S. Lussier, eds., *As Long as the Sun Shines and the Water Flows: A Reader in Canadian Native Studies* (Vancouver: Nakoda Institute and University of British Columbia Press 1983), 132–6. See also Boswell, ' "Civilizing" the Indian,' 350–6.

41 Kakeewistahaw, quoted in S. Raby, 'Indian Land Surrenders in Southern Saskatchewan,' *Canadian Geographer* 17, no. 1 (spring 1973), 46

42 J. Usher, *Duncan of Metlakatla* (Ottawa: National Museum of Man 1974), 125–6, 132–3; Regis College Archives, J. Paquin, 'Modern Jesuit Indian Missions in Ontario' (unpublished manuscript), 248

43 Samek, *Blackfoot Confederacy*, chap. 5

44 J. Leslie and R. Maquire, eds., *The Historical Development of the Indian Act*, 2nd ed. (Ottawa: Indian Affairs 1978; first published 1975), 97, 108–9; Titley, *Narrow Vision*, 40–3
45 Raby, 'Indian Land Surrenders,' 39
46 Ibid., 41–3; Hall, 'Clifford Sifton,' 134–5
47 G. Friesen, *The Canadian Prairies: A History* (Toronto: University of Toronto Press 1985), 159
48 Quoted in 'Mission de Qu'Appelle,' *La Bannière de Marie Immaculée*, 1895, 71. ('I never agreed to sell our lands to the whites.')
49 Commissioner of North-West Mounted Police, 1898, quoted in *Treaty Number Eight* (Ottawa: Indian Affairs 1900), 5
50 R. Fumoleau, *As Long as This Land Shall Last: A History of Treaty 8 and Treaty 11, 1870–1939* (Toronto: McClelland and Stewart, nd), 19, on which this account of Treaties 8 and 11, unless otherwise noted, is based.
51 The text of Treaty 8 is ibid., 70–3. See also Friesen, *Canadian Prairies*, 477–8n.
52 R. Daniel, 'The Spirit and Terms of Treaty Eight,' in R. Price, ed., *The Spirit of the Alberta Indian Treaties*, 2nd ed. (Edmonton: Pica Pica Press 1987; first published 1979), 79–82
53 Unidentified chief, quoted in Fumoleau, *As Long*, 356, 257
54 Ibid., 337–8
55 Quoted in Leslie and Maguire, *Historical Development*, 114

CHAPTER 12 The beginnings of political organization

1 A.B. Baird, quoted in J.W. Grant, *Moon of Wintertime: Missionaries and the Indians of Canada in Encounter since 1534* (Toronto: University of Toronto Press 1984), 191; General Synod Archives (GSA), Papers of the Missionary Society of the Church in Canada, GS 75–103, Special Indian Committee, Series 2–14, box 18, S.H. Blake to F. Oliver, 29 Dec. 1908 (copy)
2 J.J. McKenna, quoted in D.J. Hall, 'Clifford Sifton and Canadian Indian Administration 1896–1905,' in I.A.L. Getty and A.S. Lussier, eds., *As Long as the Sun Shines and the Water Flows: A Reader in Canadian Native Studies* (Vancouver: Nakoda Institute and University of British Columbia Press 1983), 137; GSA, GS 75–103, series 2–14, box 18, F. Pedley to Rev. L.N. Tucker, 21 March 1908
3 GSA, GS 75–103, series 2–14, box 19, A.Y. Blair to S.H. Blake, 27 March 1908
4 G.J. Wherrett, *The Miracle of the Empty Beds: A History of Tuberculosis in Canada* (Toronto: University of Toronto Press 1977), 103–5
5 D.C. Scott, 'Indian Affairs, 1867–1912,' in A. Shortt and A.G. Doughty, eds., *Canada and Its Provinces*, vol. VII (Toronto: Glasgow, Brook 1914), 16

6 *Annual Report of the Department of Indian Affairs for the Year Ended March 31, 1933* (Ottawa: King's Printer 1934), 54

7 United Church of Canada Archives, E.E. Joblin Papers, box 1, file 1, Memorandum re Deputation's Interview with the Honorable T.A. Crerar, Ottawa, 25 Nov. 1941

8 Quoted in W. Duff, *The Indian History of British Columbia*, vol. 1: *The Impact of the White Man*, 2nd ed. (np: Royal British Columbia Museum 1969; first published 1965), 67

9 Ibid., 67–8; R.A. Fisher, *Contact and Conflict: Indian-European Relations in British Columbia, 1774–1890* (Vancouver: University of British Columbia Press 1977), chap. 8; R.E. Cail, *Land, Man and Law: The Disposal of Crown Lands in British Columbia, 1871–1913* (Vancouver: University of British Columbia Press 1974)

10 United Church of Canada Archives, A. Sutherland Papers, box 5, file 87, Port Simpson Tsimshian to Dear Sir, 30 Jan. 1909

11 Quoted in E.P. Patterson, 'Nishga and Tsimshian Land Protests in the 1880s,' *Journal of Canadian Studies* 18, no. 3 (autumn 1983), 45

12 Quoted in Duff, *Indian History*, 67

13 Ibid., 69; E.P. Patterson, 'Andrew Paull and the Early History of British Columbia Indian Organizations,' *As Long*, 49

14 Duff, *Indian History*, 69 and note

15 *SC 1926–27 (17 Geo. V) c. 32*, sec 149A. See R. Daniel, *A History of Native Claims Processes in Canada, 1867–1979* (Ottawa: Indian Affairs 1980), 53–4.

16 Quoted in S. Cuthand, 'The Native Peoples of the Prairie Provinces in the 1920's and 1930's,' in I.A.L. Getty and D.B. Smith, eds., *One Century Later: Western Canadian Reserve Indians Since Treaty 7* (Vancouver: University of British Columbia Press 1978), 31–2

17 There is a good account of these developments in J. Goodwill and N. Sluman, *John Tootoosis*, 2nd ed. (Winnipeg: Pemmican Publications 1984; first published 1982 by Golden Dog Press), chaps 9 and 12.

18 Quoted in Cuthand, 'Native Peoples,' 34. See also Goodwill and Sluman, *John Tootoosis*, 156.

19 Quoted in H. Samek, *The Blackfoot Confederacy, 1880–1920: A Comparative Study of Canadian and U.S. Indian Policy* (Albuquerque: University of New Mexico Press 1987), 132

20 Cuthand, 'Native Peoples,' 40

21 Royal British Columbia Museum, Anthropological Picture Collections Section, nos. 250, 834, 2777 (examples only). Provincial Archives of British Columbia, Sound and Moving Images Division, tape 965-1, Mrs Edward Joyce interview

22 Quoted in Regis College Archives, J. Paquin, 'Modern Jesuit Indian Missions in Ontario' (unpublished manuscript), 58–9

23 Quoted in D. Purich, *Our Land: Native Rights in Canada* (Toronto: Lorimer 1986), 83–4
24 See B.W. Morse, ed., *Aboriginal Peoples and the Law: Indian, Metis and Inuit Rights in Canada* (Ottawa: Carleton University Press 1985), 356–97
25 D. Purich, *The Metis* (Toronto: Lorimer 1988), chap. 6
26 J. Leslie and R. Maguire, eds., *The Historical Development of the Indian Act*, 2nd ed. (Ottawa: Indian Affairs 1978; first published 1975), 132, 133
27 J.L. Tobias, 'Protection, Civilization, Assimilation: An Outline History of Canada's Indian Policy,' in Getty and Lussier, *As Long*, 52
28 H.B. Hawthorn, ed., *A Survey of the Contemporary Indians of Canada: Economic, Political, Educational Needs and Policies*, 2 vols (Ottawa: Indian Affairs 1966–7)
29 Unless otherwise noted, this account is based on the excellent analysis in S.M. Weaver, *Making Canadian Indian Policy: The Hidden Agenda 1968–1970* (Toronto: University of Toronto Press 1981).
30 Quoted in J.R. Ponting and R. Gibbins, *Out of Irrelevance: A Socio-political Introduction to Indian Affairs in Canada* (Toronto: Butterworths 1980), 28
31 Quoted in Purich, *Our Land*, 52
32 Quoted in Weaver, *Making Canadian Indian Policy*, 148
33 Canada, Department of Indian Affairs and Northern Development, *Statement of the Government of Canada on Indian Policy* (Ottawa: Indian Affairs 1969), 5–8
34 Ibid., 11
35 Weaver, *Making Canadian Indian Policy*, 197

CHAPTER 13 Political relations after the white paper

1 Indian Association of Alberta, *Citizens Plus: A Presentation of the Indian Chiefs of Alberta to Right Honourable P.E. Trudeau* (np: Indian Association of Alberta [1970]), 4, 7, 9, 12, 19, 16
2 H. Cardinal, *The Unjust Society: The Tragedy of Canada's Indians* (Edmonton: Hurtig 1969), 1, 11, 17
3 Quoted in S.M. Weaver, *Making Canadian Indian Policy: The Hidden Agenda 1968–1970* (Toronto: University of Toronto Press 1981), 171. For the reaction in general see chap. 7.
4 J.R. Ponting and R. Gibbins, *Out of Irrelevance: A Socio-political Introduction to Indian Affairs in Canada* (Toronto: Butterworths 1980), 203. See G. Manuel and M. Posluns, *The Fourth World: An Indian Reality* (Toronto: Collier Macmillan 1974).
5 This is what happened to the Calgary Urban Treaty Indian Alliance's programs in the early 1970s. See J. Ryan, *Wall of Words: The Betrayal of the Urban Indian* (Toronto: Peter Martin Associates 1978).

6 See D. Purich, *Our Land: Native Rights in Canada* (Toronto: Lorimer 1986),
   218–19. See also Manitoba Métis Federation, 'Position Paper on Child
   Care and Family Services (May 15, 1982),' *Native Studies Review* 2, no. 1
   (1986), 125–39.

7 E.P. Patterson, 'Nishga and Tsimshian Land Protests in the 1880s,' *Journal of
   Canadian Studies* 18, no. 3 (autumn 1983), 51

8 The clearest expression of the Indian viewpoint is in the text edited by D.
   Opekokew, *The First Nations: Indian Government and the Canadian Constitution*
   (Saskatoon: Federation of Saskatchewan Indians 1980).

9 *Globe and Mail*, 22 Nov. 1984 and 29 March 1985; Saskatoon *Star-Phoenix*, 2
   Feb. and 4 Dec. 1985

10 The Métis and nonstatus Indian national organization had to initiate legal
   action before Ottawa would agree to its presence at the 1983 conference.
   See Purich, *Our Land*, 181.

11 House of Commons, Special Committee on Indian Self-Government, *Report*
   (Ottawa: Queen's Printer 1983). There is a useful series of analyses of this
   report by political scientist P. Tennant, anthropologist S.M. Weaver, and the
   team of political scientist R. Gibbins and sociologist J.R. Ponting in *Canadian
   Public Policy* 10, no. 2 (1984), 211–24, under the title 'The Report of the House
   of Commons Special Committee on Indian Self-Government: Three
   Comments.'

12 Quoted in M. Davies, 'Aboriginal Rights in International Law: Human
   Rights,' in B.W. Morse, ed., *Aboriginal Peoples and the Law: Indian, Metis and
   Inuit Rights in Canada* (Ottawa: Carleton University Press 1985), 770–3, espec.
   772; Purich, *Our Land*, 137

13 A useful summary of Indian organizations' views is found in J. Green,
   'Sexual Equality and Indian Government: An Analysis of Bill c-31
   Amendments to the *Indian Act*,' *Native Studies Review* 1, no. 2 (1985), 85–93.
   In the summer of 1988 Ottawa announced that the barrier to reinstatement of
   children born to mothers who lost status before 1985 would be removed.
   At the time of writing it is not clear what the results of this change will be, but
   it seems unlikely that Indian organizations will approve of a change that
   increases further the federal government's assertion of the right to dictate
   who shall have band membership, and thereby augment the number of
   potential returnees.

14 This account is based on the excellent survey by S.M. Weaver, 'Indian Policy
   in the New Conservative Government, Part I: The Nielsen Task Force of
   1985,' *Native Studies Review* 2, no. 1 (1986), 1–43.

15 Ibid., 14–15

16 For comprehensive and specific claims, see next chapter.

17 Weaver, 'Nielsen Task Force of 1985,' 20–1

18 Ibid., 29

19 Purich, *Our Land*, 226

CHAPTER 14 Aboriginal rights, land claims, and the struggle to survive

1 J. Ryan, 'Struggle for Survival: The Lubicon Cree Community Fight the Multinationals' (unpublished paper, ACSANZ '86, biennial conference of the Association for Canadian Studies in Australia and New Zealand, Griffith University, Australia, May 1986). I am indebted to Professor Ryan for providing me with a copy of her paper.
2 D. Purich, *Our Land: Native Rights in Canada* (Toronto: Lorimer 1986), 38
3 R. Knight, *Indians at Work: An Informal History of Native Indian Labour in British Columbia 1858–1930* (Vancouver: New Star Books 1978), epilogue, 201
4 A.M. Shkilnyk, *A Poison Stronger Than Love: The Destruction of an Ojibwa Community* (New Haven: Yale University Press 1985)
5 For example, P. Driben and R.S. Trudeau, *When Freedom Is Lost: The Dark Side of the Relationship between Government and the Fort Hope Band* (Toronto: University of Toronto Press 1983)
6 Quoted in B. Richardson, *Strangers Devour the Land: A Chronicle of the Assault upon the Last Coherent Hunting Culture in North America, the Cree Indians of Quebec, and Their Vast Primeval Homelands* (New York: Knopf 1975), 296
7 Quoted ibid., 319
8 Purich, *Our Land*, 56–7
9 Ibid., 188, 57
10 T.R. Berger, *Northern Frontier / Northern Homeland: The Report of the Mackenzie Valley Pipeline Inquiry*, 2 vols (Ottawa: Minister of Supply and Services 1977), I, xxiv–xxv
11 M. O'Malley, *The Past and Future Land: An Account of the Berger Inquiry into the Mackenzie Valley Pipeline* (Toronto: Peter Martin Associates 1976), 140
12 J.R. Ponting and R. Gibbins, *Out of Irrelevance: A Socio-political Introduction to Indian Affairs in Canada* (Toronto: Butterworths 1980), 101–2
13 C.J. Jaenen, 'French Sovereignty and Native Nationhood during the French Regime,' *Native Studies Review* 2, no. 1 (1986), 83–113
14 Quoted in B.W. Morse, ed., *Aboriginal Peoples and the Law: Indian, Metis and Inuit Rights in Canada* (Ottawa: Carleton University Press 1985), 97
15 The Dene Declaration (1975), reprinted in Ponting and Gibbins, *Out of Irrelevance*, 351–2. See also M. Watkins, 'Dene Nationalism,' *Canadian Review of Studies in Nationalism* 8, no. 1 (spring 1981), 101–13.
16 Purich, *Our Land*, 60; *Globe and Mail* 10 Nov. 1988. In 1973 the Temagami Indians of northeast Ontario got a caution placed on all crown land in 110 townships (an area larger than PEI) using the argument that they had not been included in the Robinson Treaties. The case has not been resolved at the highest level as yet. See B.W. Hodgins, *Aboriginal Rights in Canada:*

Historical Perspectives on Recent Developments and the Implications for Australia,
Macquarrie University Public Lecture (np: Macquarrie University Printery
1985), 10–11. I am indebted to Professor Hodgins for supplying me with a
copy of his lecture. Finally, in 1988 the Cree of Lubicon Lake, after erecting a
blockade of roads during the federal election campaign, reached agreement
in principle for the settlement of their forty-eight-year-old claim to a reserve.
17 D.B. Sealey and A.S. Lussier, *The Métis: Canada's Forgotten People* (Winnipeg:
Pemmican Publications 1975), 1
18 See above, chap. 9.
19 Purich, *Our Land*, 58–9
20 Ibid., 151–2
21 Saskatoon *Star-Phoenix*, 31 Aug. 1988

CHAPTER 15 Do we learn anything from history?

1 *Oxford Dictionary of Quotations*, 3rd ed. (New York: Oxford University Press
1979), 244, 216, 414
2 C.J. Jaenen, *Friend and Foe: Aspects of French-Amerindian Cultural Contact in
the Sixteenth and Seventeenth Centuries* (New York: Columbia University Press
1976), 192
3 A.G. Harper, 'Canada's Indian Administration: Basic Concepts and
Objectives,' *America Indigena* 5, no. 2 (April 1945), 127
4 G. Manuel, 'Manifesto for Survival,' *Macleans*, May 1973, 53. I should like to
thank a student, Michelle Amy, who brought this item to my attention.
5 P. Driben and R.S. Trudeau, *When Freedom Is Lost: The Dark Side of the
Relationship between Government and the Fort Hope Band* (Toronto: University of
Toronto Press 1983), 10
6 Indian and Northern Affairs Communiqué 1-8831, 'Policy for the Provision of
Education Facilities and School Space Accommodation Standards:
Backgrounder,' 1
7 Manuel, 'Manifesto,' 28
8 R. Cook, 'Canadian Centennial Celebrations,' *International Journal* 22, no. 4
(autumn 1967), 663
9 Chief Dan George, *My Heart Soars*, with Helmut Hirnschall (Toronto: Clarke,
Irwin 1974), 39, 40
10 R.M. Rilke, *Letter to a Young Poet* (1934), Letter Seven, Rome, 14 May 1904; in
Colombo's Canadian Quotations (Edmonton: Hurtig 1974), 502

Select bibliography

NOTE ON PRIMARY SOURCES

It is impossible to list all the primary sources that are relevant to the study of the history of Indian-white relations in Canada. What follows is a comment on but a minute portion of the primary materials.

The most accessible primary sources for the New France period are travel accounts and reports of missionaries. H.P. Biggar, *The Voyages of Jacques Cartier* (Ottawa: King's Printer 1924); Gabriel Sagard, *The Long Journey to the Country of the Huron*, ed. G.M. Wrong (Toronto: Champlain Society 1939); and W.F. Ganong, ed., *Description and Natural History of the Coasts of North America (Acadia)* (Toronto: Champlain Society 1908), are but three of the former genre. The records, charts and pictorial renderings of Samuel de Champlain constitute another rich collection that is too voluminous to discuss here. The most renowned of religious records are the annual 'public relations' exercises that the Society of Jesus produced to stimulate piety and generosity among their admirers. A particularly fine edition of these records for the seventeenth century is R.G. Thwaites, ed., *The Jesuit Relations and Allied Documents*, 73 vols (New York: Pageant Books 1959). Other useful collections are cited in the 'Bibliographical Notes' in W.J. Eccles, *The Canadian Frontier 1534–1760* (New York: Holt, Rinehart and Winston 1969), which is useful for New France records of all kinds.

Access to primary material for the period between the Royal Proclamation of 1763 and the middle of the nineteenth century is much more difficult. Until 1830 most of these records were produced by military administrators of the British imperial government, and most of them are unpublished. A useful path of entry to these important documents is the endnotes and bibliography of R.S. Allen, 'The British Indian Department and the Frontier in North America, 1755–1830,' Canadian Historic Sites, *Occasional Papers in Archaeology and History* 14 (Ottawa: Indian and Northern Affairs, nd), 109–25. Most of the religious and civil governmental material remains unpublished.

For the period from Confederation onward, primary materials dealing with Indian-white relations are more voluminous and accessible. In particular the records of the federal government and parliament provide useful insights on what policy was intended to do, and less revealing glimpses of the degree to which policy was effective. The annual reports of the Department of Indian Affairs were published in the *Sessional Papers* of parliament each year. Until the period of the Great War these annual surveys were very detailed and useful, but thereafter they became more abbreviated. The other principal records regarding policy are found in Hansard, the verbatim report of parliament's deliberations. Debates on amendments to the Indian Act or on particular problems such as native destitution provide illuminating comments. There are also extensive published records of treaty-making, the most important of which have been condensed in A. Morris, *The Treaties of Canada with the Indians* (Toronto: Belfords, Clarke 1880), which is available in a Coles facsimile paperback edition.

The views of missionaries, officials, and Indian people themselves can be sampled with relative convenience only by means of published reminiscences. Of this type of work the missionary memoir is the most common. Samples include Canon H.W. Gibbon Stocken, *Among the Blackfoot and Sarcee*, new ed. (Calgary: Glenbow Alberta Institute 1976), and A.J. Brabant, *Mission to Nootka 1874–1900: Reminiscences of the West Coast of Vancouver Island*, ed. C. Lillard (Sydney, BC: Gray's Publishing 1977; first published 1900). Most Indian agents, police, and other officials were more inhibited than the clergy when it came to putting their views on the record, but useful exceptions to this constabulary and bureaucratic modesty are W.H. Halliday, *Potlatch and Totem, and The Recollections of an Indian Agent* (London and Toronto: Dent 1935) and C.E. Denny, *The Law Marches West* (Toronto: Dent 1939). It is worth noting that the prairies, especially southern Alberta, and coastal British Columbia have produced more of this sort of material than the rest of the country.

Until fairly recently Indian accounts of their experiences were rare, but that situation is changing very rapidly now. An early exception was Peter Jones, *Life and Journals of Kah-ke-quo-na-by (Rev. Peter Jones), Wesleyan Missionary* (Toronto: Wesleyan Printing Establishment 1860). In the twentieth century it has largely been western Indians whose recollections have been published. Examples from British Columbia include *Guests Never Leave Hungry: The Autobiography of James Sewid*, ed. J.P. Spradley (New Haven: Yale University Press 1969), and Charles James Nowell's *Smoke from Their Fires: The Life of a Kwakiutl Chief*, ed. C.S.

Ford (New Haven: Yale University Press 1949). Dan Kennedy [Ochankugahe], a prairie Assiniboine, published *Recollections of an Assiniboine Chief*, ed. J.R. Stevens (Toronto, Montreal: McClelland and Stewart 1972), and a former resident of the File Hills Colony in Saskatchewan, Eleanor Brass, brought out *I Walk in Two Worlds* (Calgary: Glenbow 1987). Note should also be taken of Harold Cardinal's *The Unjust Society: The Tragedy of Canada's Indians* (Edmonton: Hurtig 1969), which contains considerable autobiographical detail.

Another heartening sign is the increasing effort that is being made to collect and disseminate native recollections. A good deal of Indian oral history is contained in M. Whitehead, ed., *Now You Are My Brother: Missionaries in British Columbia*, British Columbia Sound Heritage Series (Victoria: Provincial Archives of British Columbia 1981); and Penny Petrone, ed., *First People, First Voices* (Toronto: University of Toronto Press 1983), collects material from a longer period and a more representative body of natives. A variety of archival and museum programs that are designed to recover the voices of historically inarticulate native peoples should lead to more such publications in the coming years.

SECONDARY SOURCES

Secondary works are so numerous that only a representative sample can be given here. The works listed below are selected in most cases with an eye to their accessibility as well as their scholarly merit. Those interested in pursuing individual topics are urged to consult the bibliographies and notes of these historical works.

Allen, R.S. 'Big Bear,' *Saskatchewan History* 25, no. 1, winter 1972
– 'The British Indian Department and the Frontier in North America, 1755–1830,' Canadian Historic Sites, *Occasional Papers in Archaeology and History* 14. Ottawa: Indian and Northern Affairs, nd
Andrews, I. 'Indian Protest Against Starvation: The Yellow Calf Incident of 1884,' *Saskatchewan History* 28, no. 2, spring 1975
Axtell, J. *The Invasion Within: The Contest of Cultures in Colonial North America.* New York: Oxford University Press 1985
Bailey, A.G. *The Conflict of European and Eastern Algonkian Cultures 1504–1700: A Study in Canadian Civilization*, 2nd ed. Toronto: University of Toronto Press 1969; 1st ed. 1937
Barman, J., Y. Hébert, and D. McCaskill, eds. *Indian Education in Canada*, vol 1: *The Legacy.* Vancouver: Nakoda Institute and University of British Columbia Press 1986
Barron, F.L., and J.B. Waldram, eds. *1885 and After: Native Society in Transition.* Regina: Canadian Plains Research Center 1986

Bingaman, S. 'The Trials of Poundmaker and Big Bear, 1885,' *Saskatchewan History* 28, no. 3, autumn 1975
– 'The Trials of the "White Rebels," 1885,' *Saskatchewan History* 25, no. 2, spring 1972
Boswell, M.J. '"Civilizing" the Indian: Government Administration of Indians, 1876–1896,' PHD thesis, University of Ottawa, 1977
Brown, D.H. 'The Meaning of Treason in 1885,' *Saskatchewan History* 28, no. 2, spring 1975
Brown, G., and R. Maguire. *Indian Treaties in Historical Perspective*. Ottawa: Indian and Northern Affairs 1979
Brown, J.S.H. *Strangers in Blood: Fur Trade Company Families in Indian Country*. Vancouver: University of British Columbia Press 1980
Cail, R.E. *Land, Man and Law: The Disposal of Crown Lands in British Columbia, 1871–1913*. Vancouver: University of British Columbia Press 1974
Campbell, M. *Halfbreed*. Toronto: Seal Books 1979; 1st ed. 1973
Carter, S.A. 'Agriculture and Agitation on the Oak River Dakota Reserve, 1875–1895,' *Manitoba History* 6, fall 1983
– 'Controlling Indian Movement: The Pass system,' *NeWest Review*, May 1985
– 'The Genesis and Anatomy of Government Policy and Indian Reserve Agriculture on Four Agencies in Treaty Four, 1874–1897,' PHD thesis, University of Manitoba, 1987
Coates, K. '"Betwixt and Between": The Anglican Church and the Children of the Carcross (Chooutla) Residential School,' *BC Studies*, no. 64, winter 1984–5
Codere, H. *Fighting with Property: A Study of Kwakiutl Potlatching and Warfare, 1792–1930*. Seattle: University of Washington Press 1966
Cole, D. *Captured Heritage: The Scramble for Northwest Coast Artifacts*. Vancouver: Douglas & McIntyre 1985
Cook, R. 'The Social and Economic Frontier in North America,' H. Lamar and L. Thompson, eds., *The Frontier in History: North America and South Africa Compared*. New Haven: Yale University Press 1981
Daniel, R. *A History of Native Claims Processes in Canada, 1867–1979*. Ottawa: Indian Affairs 1980
Dempsey, H.A. *Charcoal's World*. Saskatoon: Western Producer Prairie Books 1978
– *Crowfoot: Chief of the Blackfeet*. Edmonton: Hurtig 1972
– *The Gentle Persuader: James Gladstone, Indian Senator*. Saskatoon: Western Producer Prairie Books 1986
– *Red Crow, Warrior Chief*. Saskatoon: Western Producer Prairie Books 1980
– 'The Fearsome Fire Wagons,' in H.A. Dempsey, ed., *The CPR West: The Iron Road and The Making of a Nation*. Vancouver, Toronto: Douglas & McIntrye 1984
Dosman, E.J. *Indians: The Urban Dilemma*. Toronto: McClelland and Stewart 1972

Driben, P., and R.S. Trudeau. *When Freedom Is Lost: The Dark Side of the Relationship between Government and the Fort Hope Band*. Toronto: University of Toronto Press 1983

Duff, W. *The Indian History of British Columbia*, vol. 1: *The Impact of the White Man*, 2nd ed. Np: Royal British Columbia Museum 1969; 1st ed. 1966

Eccles, W.J. *The Canadian Frontier 1534–1760*. New York: Holt, Rinehart and Winston 1969

– *Canadian Society during the French Regime*. Montreal: Harvest House 1968

– *Essays on New France*. Toronto: Oxford University Press 1987

Ewers, J.G. 'Intertribal Warfare as the Precursor of Indian-White Warfare on the Northern Great Plains,' *Western Historical Quarterly* 6, Oct. 1975

Fingard, J. 'The New England Company and the New Brunswick Indians, 1786–1826: A Comment on the Colonial Perversion of British Benevolence,' *Acadiensis* 1, no. 2, spring 1972

Fisher, R.A. *Contact and Conflict: Indian-European Relations in British Columbia, 1774–1890*. Vancouver: University of British Columbia Press 1977

Fisher, R.A., and K. Coates, eds., *Out of the Background: Readings on Canadian Native History*. Toronto: Copp Clark Pitman 1988

Flanagan, T. *Louis 'David' Riel: Prophet of the New World*. Toronto: University of Toronto Press 1979

– *Riel and the Rebellion: 1885 Reconsidered*. Saskatoon: Western Producer Prairie Books 1983

Foster, J. 'Program for the Red River Mission: The Anglican Clergy 1820–1826,' *Histoire sociale/Social History* 4, Nov. 1969

Francis, D., and T. Morantz. *Partners in Furs: A History of the Fur Trade in Eastern James Bay 1600–1870*. Kingston: McGill-Queen's University Press 1985

Fraser, W.B. 'Big Bear, Indian Patriot,' *Alberta Historical Review* 14, no. 2, spring 1966

Friesen, G. *The Canadian Prairies: A History*. Toronto: University of Toronto Press 1984

Fumoleau, R. *As Long as This Land Shall Last: A History of Treaty 8 and Treaty 11, 1870–1939*. Toronto: McClelland and Stewart, nd

Getty, I.A.L., and A.S. Lussier, eds. *As Long as the Sun Shines and Water Flows: A Reader in Canadian Native Studies*. Vancouver: Nakoda Institute and University of British Columbia Press 1979

Getty, I.A.L., and D.B. Smith, eds. *One Century Later: Western Canadian Reserve Indians since Treaty 7*. Vancouver: University of British Columbia Press 1978

Giraud, M. *The Métis in the Canadian West*, 2 vols, trans. G. Woodcock. Lincoln: University of Nebraska Press 1986; 1st French ed. 1945

Goodwill, J., and N. Sluman, *John Tootoosis*, 2nd ed. Winnipeg: Pemmican Publications 1984; first published 1982

Graham, E. *Medicine Man to Missionary: Missionaries as Agents of Change among the Indians of Southern Ontario, 1784–1867*. Toronto: Peter Martin Associates 1975

Grant, J.W. *Moon of Wintertime: Missionaries and the Indians of Canada in Encounter since 1534*. Toronto: University of Toronto Press 1984

Graymont, B. *The Iroquois in the American Revolution*. Syracuse: Syracuse University Press 1972

Green, J. 'Sexual Equality and Indian Government: An Analysis of Bill C-31 Amendments to the *Indian Act*,' *Native Studies Review* 1, no. 2, 1985

Gresko, J. 'White "Rites" and Indian "Rites": Indian Education and Native Responses in the West, 1870–1910,' in A.W. Rasporich, ed. *Western Canada Past and Present*. Calgary: McClelland and Stewart 1975

Hawthorn, H.B., ed. *A Survey of the Contemporary Indians of Canada: Economic, Political, Educational Needs and Policies*. 2 vols. Ottawa: Indian Affairs 1966–7

Innis, H.A. *The Fur Trade in Canada: An Introduction to Canadian Economic History*, rev. ed. Toronto: University of Toronto Press 1956; 1st ed. 1930

Jaenen, C.J. *Friend and Foe: Aspects of French-Amerindian Cultural Contact in the Sixteenth and Seventeenth Centuries*. New York: Columbia University Press 1976

– 'Amerindian Responses to French Missionary Intrusion, 1611--1760,' in W. Westfall and L. Rousseau, eds., *Religion/Culture: Comparative Canadian Studies / Etudes canadiennes comparées*. Ottawa: Association for Canadian Studies 1985

– 'French Sovereignty and Native Nationhood during the French Regime,' *Native Studies Review* 2, no. 1, 1986

Jenness, D. *The Indians of Canada*, 7th ed. Ottawa: Supply and Services Canada 1977; 1st ed. 1932

Judd, C.M., and A.J. Ray, eds. *Old Trails and New Directions: Papers of the Third North American Fur Trade Conference*. Toronto: University of Toronto Press 1980

Knight, R. *Indians at Work: An Informal History of Native Indian Labour in British Columbia 1858–1930*. Vancouver: New Star Books 1978

Laviolette, F.E. *The Struggle for Survival: Indian Cultures and the Protestant Ethic in British Columbia*. Toronto: University of Toronto Press 1961

Leslie, J. 'The Bagot Commission: Developing a Corporate Memory for the Indian Department,' Canadian Historical Association, *Historical Papers*, 1982

Leslie, J., and R. Maguire, eds. *The Historical Development of the Indian Act*, 2nd ed. Ottawa: Indian Affairs and Northern Development 1983; 1st ed. 1975

Lurie, N.O. 'The World's Oldest On-Going Protest Demonstration: North American Indian Drinking Patterns,' *Pacific Historical Review* 40, no. 3, Aug. 1971

MacInnes, T.R.L. 'History of Indian Administration in Canada,' *Canadian Journal of Economics and Political Science* 12, no. 3, Aug. 1945

Maclean, H. 'The Hidden Agenda: Methodist Attitudes to the Ojibwa and the Development of Indian Schooling in Upper Canada, 1821–1860,' MA thesis, University of Toronto, 1978

Macleod, R.C. *The North-West Mounted Police and Law Enforcement*. Toronto: University of Toronto Press 1976

Manuel, G., and M. Posluns. *The Fourth World: An Indian Reality*. Toronto: Collier-Macmillan 1974

Martel, G. *Le messianisme de Louis Riel*. Waterloo: Wilfrid Laurier University Press 1984

Miller, J.R. 'From Riel to the Métis,' *Canadian Historical Review* 69, no. 1, March 1988

Montgomery, M. 'The Six Nations and the Macdonald Franchise,' *Ontario History* 57, no. 1, March 1965

Morris, A. *The Treaties of Canada with the Indians*. Toronto: Belfords, Clarke, 1880; Coles facsimile edition 1979

Morse, B.W., ed. *Aboriginal Peoples and the Law: Indian, Metis and Inuit Rights in Canada*. Ottawa: Carleton University Press 1985

Muise, D., ed. *Approaches to Native History in Canada*. Ottawa: National Museum of Man 1977

O'Malley, M. *The Past and Future Land: An Account of the Berger Inquiry into the Mackenzie Valley Pipeline*. Toronto: Peter Martin Associates 1976

Pannakoek, F. *The Fur Trade and Western Canadian Society 1670–1870*. Ottawa: Canadian Historical Association 1987

– 'The Anglican Church and the Disintegration of Red River Society, 1818–1870,' in C. Berger and R. Cook, eds., *The West and the Nation: Essays in Honour of W.L. Morton*. Toronto: McClelland and Stewart 1976

– 'The Rev. Griffiths Owen Corbett and the Red River Civil War of 1869–70,' *Canadian Historical Review* 57, no. 2, June 1976

Patterson, E.P. *The Canadian Indian: A History since 1500*. Don Mills: Collier-Macmillan 1972

– 'Nishga and Tsimshian Land Protests in the 1880s,' *Journal of Canadian Studies* 18, no. 3, autumn 1983

Pennanen, G. 'Sitting Bull: Indian without a Country,' *Canadian Historical Review* 51, no. 2, June 1970

Peterson, J., and J.S.H. Brown, eds. *The New Peoples: Being and Becoming Métis in North America*. Np: University of Manitoba Press 1985

Petrone, P., ed. *First People, First Voices*. Toronto: University of Toronto Press 1983

Ponting, J.R., and R. Gibbins. *Out of Irrelevance: A Socio-political Introduction to Indian Affairs in Canada*. Toronto: Butterworths 1980

Price, R., ed. *The Spirit of the Alberta Indian Treaties*, 2nd ed. Edmonton: Pica Pica Press 1987; 1st ed. 1979

Purich, D. *Our Land: Native Rights in Canada*. Toronto: Lorimer 1986

– *The Metis*. Toronto: Lorimer 1988

Raby, S. 'Indian Land Surrenders in Southern Saskatchewan,' *Canadian Geographer* 17, no. 1, spring 1973

Ray, A.J. *Indians in the Fur Trade: Their Role as Hunters, Trappers and Middlemen in the Lands Southwest of Hudson Bay, 1660–1870.* Toronto: University of Toronto Press 1974

Ray, A.J., and D. Freeman. *'Give Us Good Measure': An Economic Analysis of Relations between the Indians and Hudson's Bay Company Before 1763.* Toronto: University of Toronto Press 1978

Richardson, B. *Strangers Devour the Land: A Chronicle of the Assault upon the Last Coherent Hunting Culture in North America, the Cree Indians of Quebec, and Their Vast Primeval Homelands.* New York: Knopf 1975

Rousseau, J., and G.W. Brown. 'The Indians of Northeastern North America,' *Dictionary of Canadian Biography*, vol. 1: *1000 to 1700.* Toronto: University of Toronto Press 1966

Ryan, J. *Wall of Words: The Betrayal of the Urban Indian.* Toronto: Peter Martin Associates 1978

Samek, H. *The Blackfoot Confederacy, 1880–1920: A Comparative Study of Canadian and U.S. Indian Policy.* Albuquerque: University of New Mexico Press 1987

Sealey, D.B., and A.S. Lussier. *The Métis: Canada's Forgotten People.* Winnipeg: Pemmican Publications 1975

Shkilnyk, A.M. *A Poison Stronger Than Love: The Destruction of an Ojibwa Community.* New Haven: Yale University Press 1985

Smith, D.B. *Sacred Feathers: The Reverend Peter Jones (Kahkewaquonaby) and the Mississauga Indians.* Toronto: University of Toronto Press 1987

Snow, J. *These Mountains Are Our Sacred Places: The Story of the Stoney People.* Toronto: Samuel Stevens 1977

Sosin, J.M. 'The Use of Indians in the War of the American Revolution: A Re-Assessment of Responsibility,' *Canadian Historical Review* 46, no. 2, June 1965

Sprague, D.N. 'Government Lawlessness in the Administration of Manitoba Land Claims, 1870–1887,' *Manitoba Law Journal* 10, no. 4, 1980

– 'The Manitoba Land Question, 1870–1882,' *Journal of Canadian Studies* 15, no. 3, autumn 1980

Stanley, G.F.G. *The Birth of Western Canada: A History of the Riel Rebellions*, 2nd ed. Toronto: University of Toronto Press 1960; 1st ed. 1936

– 'The First Indian "Reserves" in Canada,' *Revue d'histoire de l'Amérique française* 4, no. 2, Sept. 1950

– 'The Indians in the War of 1812,' *Canadian Historical Review* 31, no. 2, June 1950

Surtees, R.J. 'The Development of an Indian Reserve Policy in Canada,' *Ontario History* 61, no. 2, June 1969

Tennant, P., et al. 'The Report of the House of Commons Special Committee on Indian Self-Government: Three Comments,' *Canadian Public Policy* 10, no. 2 1984

Thistle, P.C. *Indian-European Trade Relations in the Lower Saskatchewan River Region to 1840.* Winnipeg: University of Manitoba Press 1986

Titley, E.B. *A Narrow Vision: Duncan Campbell Scott and the Administration of Indian Affairs in Canada*. Vancouver: University of British Columbia Press 1986

Tobias, J.L. 'Canada's Subjugation of the Plains Cree, 1879–1885,' *Canadian Historical Review* 64, no. 4, Dec. 1983

– 'Protection, Civilization, Assimilation: An Outline History of Canada's Indian Policy,' *Western Canadian Journal of Anthropology*, 6, no. 2, 1976

Trigger, B.G. *The Huron: Farmers of the North*. New York: Holt, Rinehart and Winston 1969

– *The Indians and the Heroic Age of New France*. Ottawa: Canadian Historical Association 1977

– *Natives and Newcomers: Canada's 'Heroic Age' Reconsidered*. Kingston: McGill-Queen's University Press 1985

Upton, L.F.S. *Micmacs and Colonists: Indian-White Relations in the Maritimes 1713–1867*. Vancouver: University of British Columbia Press 1979

– 'The Extermination of the Beothucks of Newfoundland,' *Canadian Historical Review* 58, no. 2, June 1977

– 'The Origins of Canadian Indian Policy,' *Journal of Canadian Studies* 8, no. 4, Nov. 1973

Usher, J. *Duncan of Metlakatla*. Ottawa: National Museum of Man 1974

– 'The Long-Slumbering Offspring of Adam: The Evangelical Approach to the Tsimshian,' *Anthropologica* 13, nos. 1–2, 1971

Vachon, A. 'L'eau-de-vie dans la société indienne,' Canadian Historical Association, *Annual Report*, 1960

Vallery, H.J. 'A History of Indian Education in Canada,' MA thesis, Queen's University, 1942

Van Kirk, S. *'Many Tender Ties': Women in Fur-Trade Society, 1670–1870*. Winnipeg: Watson & Dwyer, nd

Walker, J. 'The Indian in Canadian Historical Writing,' Canadian Historical Association, *Historical Papers*, 1971

Watkins, M. 'Dene Nationalism,' *Canadian Review of Studies in Nationalism* 8, no. 1, spring 1981

Weaver, S.M. *Making Canadian Indian Policy: The Hidden Agenda 1968–1970*. Toronto: University of Toronto Press 1981

– 'Indian Policy in the New Conservative Government, Part I: The Nielsen Task Force of 1985,' *Native Studies Review* 2, no. 1, 1986

– et al. 'The Report of the House of Commons Special Committee on Indian Self-Government: Three Comments,' *Canadian Public Policy* 10, no. 2, 1984

Wise, S.F. 'The American Revolution and Indian History,' in J.S. Moir, ed., *Character and Circumstance: Essays in Honour of Donald Grant Creighton*. Toronto: Macmillan 1970

– 'The Indian Diplomacy of John Graves Simcoe,' Canadian Historical Association, *Annual Report*, 1953

Woodcock, G. *Gabriel Dumont: The Métis Chief and His Lost World*. Edmonton: Hurtig 1975

Yerbury, J.C. *The Subarctic Indians and the Fur Trade, 1680–1860*. Vancouver: University of British Columbia Press 1986

Index

Picture credits